COACHING
Families AND
Colleagues
IN EARLY CHILDHOOD

COACHING
Families AND
Colleagues
IN EARLY CHILDHOOD

BY

| BARBARA E. HANFT, M.A., OTR, FAOTA | DATHAN D. RUSH, M.A., CCC-SLP | M'LISA L. SHELDEN, PT, PH.D. |

·PAUL·H·
BROOKES
PUBLISHING Co.®

BALTIMORE · LONDON · SYDNEY

·P A U L· H·
BROOKES
PUBLISHING C°®

Paul H. Brookes Publishing Co.
Post Office Box 10624
Baltimore, Maryland 21285-0624

www.brookespublishing.com

Typeset by A.W. Bennett, Inc., Hartland, Vermont.
Manufactured in the United States of America by
Victor Graphics, Inc., Baltimore, Maryland.

The case studies described in this book are composites based on the authors' actual
experiences. Individuals' names have been changed, and identifying details have
been altered to protect confidentiality.

Library of Congress Cataloging-in-Publication Data

Hanft, Barbara E.
    Coaching families and colleagues in early childhood/by Barbara E. Hanft, Dathan D.
Rush and M'Lisa L. Shelden.
        p.   cm.
    Includes bibliograpical references and index.
    ISBN 1-55766-722-5
    1. Child development.   2. Children with disabilities.   3. Parents of children with dis-
abilities.   4. Educational counseling.   5. Developmental psychology.   I. Rush,
Dathan D.   II. Shelden, M'Lisa L.   III. Title.
    RJ131.H2735 2003
    305.231—dc22   2003065150

British Library Cataloguing in Publication data are available from the British Library.

CONTENTS

ABOUT THE AUTHORS

Barbara E. Hanft, M.A., OTR, FAOTA, Developmental Consultant, 1022 Woodside Parkway, Silver Spring, Maryland 20910

Ms. Hanft is a developmental consultant with more than 30 years of experience in the early childhood field. Her professional preparation is in occupational therapy and counseling psychology. Recognized as a Fellow of the American Occupational Therapy Association (AOTA) in 1989 for her leadership and advocacy in pediatrics, she has worked across the country in school, home, and community settings with family members and early childhood practitioners from many disciplines. As a member of the government affairs' staff in the national office of the AOTA, Ms. Hanft lobbied Congress and the U.S. Department of Education to amend special education laws and create the early intervention program in 1986. In 1995, she was awarded a Presidential Citation by the AOTA for her development of Promoting Partnerships, a leadership project focused on bringing education and early intervention administrators and occupational therapists together to enhance services and supports to children and their families. Ms. Hanft is on the editorial board of the journal *Infants and Young Children* and has more than 25 publications on early childhood. Her book *The Consulting Therapist: A Guide for Occupational and Physical Therapists in Schools* (with Patricia A. Place, Therapy Skill Builders, 1996) is a popular resource.

Dathan Rush, M.A., CCC-SLP, Associate Director, Family, Infant and Preschool Program, Western Carolina Center, 300 Enola Road, Morganton, North Carolina 28655

Mr. Rush is the Associate Director of the Family, Infant and Preschool Program (FIPP) at Western Carolina Center and a research associate at the Orelena Hawks Puckett Institute in Morganton, North Carolina. Prior to accepting his position at FIPP, Mr. Rush was a clinical assistant professor and personnel development consultant in the Lee Mitchener Tolbert Center for Developmental Disabilities at the University of Oklahoma Health Sciences Center in Oklahoma City. He served as Assistant Director of the Oklahoma SoonerStart Early Intervention Program at the State Department of Health from 1992 to 1999. He served as an editorial board member of the journal *Infants and Young Children* until 2002 and has published articles in the areas of in-service training, coaching, supporting children and families in natural learning environments, and teaming in early intervention. He is past president and former executive council member of the Oklahoma Speech-Language-Hearing Association. Mr. Rush has presented numerous workshops nationally on topics related to team building, use of a primary coach model of support, training of trainers, coaching, and provision of supports in natural environments.

M'Lisa L. Shelden, PT, Ph.D., Director, Family, Infant and Preschool Program, Western Carolina Center, 300 Enola Road, Morganton, North Carolina 28655

Dr. Shelden is Director of the Family, Infant and Preschool Program (FIPP) at Western Carolina Center and an associate research scientist at the Orelena Hawks Puckett Institute in Morganton, North Carolina. Prior to accepting her appointment at FIPP, Dr. Shelden was an Assistant Professor in the Department of Rehabilitation Science at the University of Oklahoma Health Sciences Center. She is a graduate Fellow of the ZERO TO THREE: National Center for Infants, Toddlers, and Families, and she has also served the Section of Pediatrics of the American Physical Therapy Association. She is a member of the editorial board for the *Journal of Early Intervention.* Dr. Shelden has co-authored several articles related to early intervention teamwork and a chapter related to physical therapy personnel preparation. She presents nationally on topics related to transition, inclusion, coaching, evaluation and assessment, use of a primary coach model, and provision of supports in natural environments.

FOREWORD

Establishing the fact that early childhood intervention or therapeutic practices are effective necessitates one set of skills. Promoting practitioner or parent adoption and utilization of evidence-based practices requires a completely different set of skills. *Coaching Families and Colleagues in Early Childhood* bridges the research-to-practice gap by describing how coaching—a particular type of adult learning strategy—can be used as a *capacity-building strategy* for strengthening a practitioner's knowledge of and capabilities to implement evidence-based practices.

Coaching Families and Colleagues in Early Childhood is written in a clear and concise manner, but at the same time it is chock full of detailed descriptions and examples that bring the coaching process alive as the reader progresses from chapter to chapter. After reading this book, one is likely to conclude (as I did) that "finally, here is a process and set of procedures that we know makes a difference in the lives of young children and their families." Why do I say "finally"? Because nearly 100 years of effort to increase knowledge utilization has been less than effective (National Center for the Dissemination of Disability Research, 1996). Why has this been the case? At least one reason for this state of affairs is that we are not implementing knowledge utilization strategies that work.

The knowledge and skills required of a coach necessitate a new way of thinking about knowledge transfer and capacity building. Although the coaching process described by Hanft, Rush, and Shelden at first may appear to some readers as everyday common sense, the coaching process is no quick fix. Readers aspiring to be coaches will need to read and reread, process and assimilate, acquire a deeper understanding of the coaching process, and internalize new ways of interacting with learners (Bransford, Brown, & Cocking, 2000). Readers committed to improving their abilities to help and support others will find *Coaching Families and Colleagues in Early Childhood* an essential tool and reference they will revisit many, many times.

I caution readers who may not agree with my assessment not to jump to the conclusion that the term *coaching* is nothing more than a substitute for other terms used to describe efforts to strengthen learner knowledge and capacity. The coaching process described by Hanft, Rush, and Shelden is not a variation on a theme; it is a different way of doing business. The coaching process, the qualities of an effective coach, and the ways in which coaching must be done continually and consistently to be effective makes this adult learning strategy uniquely different from other adult learning methods. Those who take the time to learn and master the content of *Coaching Families and Colleagues in Early Childhood* will not only develop a deeper understanding of effective learner strengthening strategies, but will gain an appreciation of how and why *Coaching Families and Colleagues in Early Childhood* is different from other adult learning strategy books.

Coaching Families and Colleagues is a refreshing book written at a time when the research-to-practice gap, at least in different early childhood intervention fields, is wider than ever. Mastering the content of *Coaching Families and Colleagues in Early Childhood* and applying this new learning to improving early childhood practices constitutes a new and improved tool for bettering the lives of young children and their families. What is even more refreshing is the fact that the authors are continuing their work in this area to further an understanding of the characteristics of coaching, the key features of the practice, and how coaching is related to and produces desired learner outcomes. For example, Rush (2003b) is completing a review of the coaching literature with an emphasis on learner outcomes and benefits and has developed a scale for measuring adoption and use of the qualities of an effective coach (Rush, 2003a). This work will no doubt add to our understanding of the most important characteristics of coaching and provide an objective basis for measuring and monitoring progress toward becoming a skilled adult learner change agent.

Coaching Families and Colleagues in Early Childhood should become a standard textbook for strengthening learner capacity to engage in evidence-based early childhood intervention and therapy practices. Hanft, Rush, and Shelden have filled a void in a field in need of new thinking. The authors have done the field a tremendous service by sharing their work with us.

Carl J. Dunst, Ph.D.
Research Scientist and Co-director
Orelena Hawks Puckett Institute
Asheville, North Carolina

REFERENCES

Bransford, J.D., Brown, A.L., & Cocking, R.R. (Eds.). (2000). *How people learn: Brain, mind, experience, and school* (Expanded ed.). Washington, DC: National Academies Press.
National Center for the Dissemination of Disability Research. (1996, July). *A review of the literature on dissemination and knowledge utilization.* Austin: TX: Southwest Educational Development Laboratory.
Rush, D. (2003a). *Coaching practices scale.* Unpublished manuscript, Family, Infant and Preschool Program, Morganton, NC.
Rush, D. (2003b). Effectiveness of coaching on adult learning. *Bridges.* Manuscript in preparation.

PREFACE

Coaching Families and Colleagues in Early Childhood was written because of our commitment to ensuring that young children have opportunities to participate in natural settings and engage in actions and relationships that are interesting and meaningful to them and their families. Coaching is a powerful approach to supporting families with young children because it shifts an early childhood practitioner's focus from a child to the adults in the child's life. Coaching provides a structure to guide the interactions between early childhood practitioners, parents, and other care providers in ways that circumvent the hierarchy too often encountered in parent–professional relationships. By focusing on adult learning, coaching promotes another person's ability to support a child's participation in real-life learning opportunities.

Each of us, during our professional preparation, was trained to provide therapist-directed care. We then tried hard the following years as we worked in community-based early childhood settings to unlearn that portion of our training. Separately, we each came to value working side by side with another adult, whether a parent or a colleague, as the means to our end of making a difference for young children. Barbara's "aha!" came when she saw how much more effectively a parent could encourage her $2\frac{1}{2}$-year-old son to crawl while playing with his brother at home rather than bring him in for therapy once a week. Dathan learned that by asking the right questions in the right way at the right time, he could learn what the family liked to do and was already doing that promoted the child's development, then work with them to build on these ideas. M'Lisa realized that in the past she had used her own ideas and interests to guide her interactions with families and other care providers. Her exploration of coaching has provided her with a framework for identifying and building on the ideas of others to redefine her role as a therapist to being a resource and support.

Thus, we each learned that working side by side with family members in their homes and communities helped them achieve their goals for their children to participate in meaningful life activities. In our early experiences, we did not call our reflective conversations with families "coaching" because that word was used for athletic trainers, not therapists. Over the past several years, however, we have enthusiastically observed the positive outcomes of the coaching process we describe in this book. Moreover, our professional development programs for early childhood practitioners around the country have given us numerous opportunities to observe that they are involved in the same struggle we experienced—learning to let go of traditional provider-directed intervention in order to embrace truly family-centered practices. This book describes the coaching process so that early childhood practitioners, as well as students in training, can easily review the literature supporting coaching in education and early intervention and study how the process works.

Our book reflects the beliefs that guide our professional and personal interactions and our commitment to supporting practitioners to use evidence-based practices. One of the essential beliefs that guide our professional partnerships is that we are all life-long learners. We always have something new to learn about supporting families in ordinary and extraordinary life situations. Just when you think you have it, something changes. Your own, or a family member's, life situation improves or is challenged. A baby starts walking, a spouse starts a new job, a family moves to another town. A law is passed, and research is published that prompts review of a professional practice that you thought was firmly established. You change jobs, or a new colleague comes on board, and your lens for viewing the world changes.

Our belief is that these opportunities for learning are shared by early childhood practitioners and family members. Over time, they form the foundation for a partnership that emphasizes mutual respect. In this book, we use the term "learner" to refer to either family members or early childhood practitioners who choose to engage in coaching to learn new information and skills. In actuality, both a coach and a learner must be open to reflecting on *what is* in order to select strategies to reach *what could be* and achieve their commonly held goals. The coaching partners, a coach and a learner, are really *both* learners who have specialized tasks to accomplish as well as information and observations to share in the coaching process.

As you read the text and accompanying coaching stories, reflect on your current relationships with families and colleagues. We urge you to create opportunities to share your reactions with your colleagues and to encourage them to try the learning activities presented throughout this book. We have discovered that a community of learners quickly forms when coaching guides the interaction among all members of a team.

ACKNOWLEDGMENTS

We appreciate the enthusiastic support from Carl J. Dunst, Ann Turnbull, and Camille Catlett, who recognize the benefits of coaching and encouraged us to write our book. We would also like to thank Nina Baker, Ed Feinberg, Karen Holbert, Bonnie Johnson, and Josie Thomas for reading early drafts of our manuscript and sharing their valuable perspectives with us. Heather Shrestha and Janet Betten deserve special thanks for their dedication in helping us organize our ideas and clarify our words. Jan Thelen, Jeanine Huntoon, and the teams of coaches across the state of Nebraska were instrumental in assisting Dathan and M'Lisa in exploring how coaching can promote systems change in early childhood.

We also would like to acknowledge those colleagues who continue to help us refine our thinking about coaching. Many thanks to our colleagues at the Family, Infant and Preschool Program and Orelena Hawks Puckett Institute in North Carolina and the faculty of the Professional Development Leadership Academy at the National Association of State Directors of Special Education.

To our own families, as well as the many other

coaches—families, friends, and colleagues—in our lives

1

COACHING IN EARLY CHILDHOOD

What's it All About?

Since the mid-1980s, early childhood practitioners and family advocates have re-focused their expectations regarding effective partnering with family members (Turnbull, Turbiville, & Turnbull, 2000). These expectations have evolved from parents bringing a child to therapy or a special class for direct service with homework assignments, to supporting family members and other key adults in their efforts to ensure a child's participation in natural learning environments. When this type of support occurs, the opportunities for children to practice and refine their actions and interactions dramatically expand beyond the limited times the children may see an early childhood practitioner in a special session. Coaching is an approach that embraces this expectation for early childhood practitioners because it provides a structure for developing and nurturing partnerships with both families and colleagues and reconceptualizes the role of an early childhood practitioner as a collaborative partner working alongside family members and other caregivers (Gallacher, 1997; Hanft & Pilkington, 2000; Rush, Shelden, & Hanft, 2003; Shelden & Rush, 2001).

A coach is someone who encourages and guides another person to develop his or her competence in a specific role and situation. Coaching is a voluntary, nonjudgmental, and collaborative partnership between an early childhood practitioner and the important people in a child's life. Coaching can also occur between two early childhood practitioners when one desires to learn new knowledge and skills from the other.

The terms *coach* and *learner* describe the two partners who participate in a coaching relationship, each learning from the other. Coaches are individuals with knowledge of child development and family support who agree to guide other adults in selecting and implementing effective strategies to promote a child's participation in family and community settings. Early childhood coaches come from diverse disciplines including education, family advocacy and support, nursing, occupational therapy, physical therapy, psychology, speech-language pathology, and social work. We have chosen *early childhood practitioner* as an umbrella term to identify all individuals who work with young children, birth through 5 years, and their families. (Please see Chapter 4 for an extended discussion of the qualities of an effective coach.)

Learners are the people who collaborate with coaches to acquire new knowledge and skills pertinent to their role in promoting a child's participation in real-life situations. These people include family members, child care providers, and early childhood practitioners who desire to learn a new skill/behavior or refine one already in use. Learners are most often mothers, fathers, guardians, grandparents, child care providers, and early childhood practitioners who engage in a specialized form of colleague-to-colleague coaching (discussed in Chapter 7). Family friends, brothers, sisters, aunts, and uncles can also participate in coaching as learners.

Where and how to support families and their young children raises complex issues that go beyond merely identifying the location of the support. At the heart of any discussion about what practitioners should do in early childhood are questions related to (Campbell, 1997; Harbour & Miller, 2001; Snowball, 1999; Walsh, Rous, & Lutzer, 2000):

- The nature of an early childhood practitioner's relationship with a child and his or her family
- How to support a family in ways that are truly meaningful
- Ensuring that all young children participate in family and community activities
- Using evidence-based practices to guide support for children and families

Rather than identifying which early childhood intervention services a child needs, a far more meaningful action is to identify how to promote a child's participation in real-life situations and who has the skill and experience to support families and other caregivers in ensuring this participation actually happens. When early childhood practitioners focus on remediating a child's problem areas or building skills unrelated to real life, a disconnect occurs between "teaching" or "therapy" and the demands and opportunities a child faces in daily life. Developmental progress is not ensured by increasing the frequency and intensity of service because a child learns new skills during teachable moments that can happen at any time, not just when an early childhood practitioner is present (Brotherson & Goldstein, 1992; Dunst, Hamby, Trivette, Raab, & Bruder, 2000; Hanft & Feinberg, 1997; McWilliam, 2000; O'Neil & Palisano, 2000; Pollock & Stewart, 1998).

Families, however, often request that specific services be delivered based on their belief that more work with early childhood practitioners will result in better

REFLECT ON THIS...

Why coach family members and other caregivers?

- Calculate the number of hours a 2-year-old child is typically awake per day and multiply by 7 days. This figure (12 hours per day x 7 days = 84 hours) represents the available time for parents and other caregivers to take advantage of opportunities for helping a child practice and refine new and emerging skills within a meaningful context.

- Now compare this figure (84 hours) with the number of hours per week (1–2 hours) available to early childhood practitioners to take advantage of the same opportunities through one-to-one sessions with a child.

- The conclusion? When early childhood practitioners coach family members and other caregivers, they dramatically increase the number of learning opportunities for young children to practice and generalize their skills within meaningful contexts.

---

or faster progress for a child. When families are preoccupied with other life events and stressors, early childhood practitioners themselves may increase the frequency and intensity of hands-on time, believing this will help a child progress (Hanft & Striffler, 1995; Montgomery, 1994). Coaching gives early childhood practitioners an alternative perspective about their role because it focuses on a learner's goals, not an early childhood practitioner's, and builds on a learner's current knowledge and skills relative to what he or she wants to do next within a specific context.

COACHING IS A PARTNERSHIP

Coaching focuses on supporting family members, child care providers, and early childhood practitioners to refine their knowledge and experience so that they can enhance their skills and help a child participate in meaningful situations, such as joining Sunday dinner at Grandma's or looking at books with a sibling before bedtime. A coach explores with a learner how and when to use specific strategies and information appropriate to the learner's role and context. The following vignettes introduce three ways coaching is used in early childhood settings.

For 6 months, Amanda, a speech-language pathologist, coached Brigitte, the mother of a very active and inquisitive son, Willie. Brigitte, a German national married to an American army sergeant, wanted Willie to learn to speak German. Amanda supported Brigitte in her efforts to increase Willie's opportunities to play with friends at their neighborhood playground, eat at restaurants with the family, and read bedtime stories with her to promote his ability to express himself more clearly. Brigitte, in turn, taught Amanda key words in German and shared her cultural norms about play for young boys. Each coaching session started with Brigitte's reflections on how things were going with Willie and ended with agreement of who would do what before the next visit.

Dennis, an early childhood educator, admired how a
co-worker, Jonelle, talked with parents to put them at
ease and listen to their family story. He asked Jonelle
to coach him so that he could use some of her winning
ways when he interacted with family members and
colleagues. They developed a coaching plan for the
next 3 months that included time for Dennis to
observe Jonelle and meet with her afterward to talk
about his observations. Dennis also agreed to make
videotapes of himself interacting with colleagues and
families to reflect on and discuss with Jonelle.

Juanita, a program supervisor of a large county early intervention program, initiated a peer-
coaching program to help her staff learn to support families in their efforts to include their
children in everyday situations. Juanita encouraged five staff members to attend a conference on natural learning opportunities. She helped them find time to observe one another
trying out their new ideas and to talk afterwards about their observations. The five colleagues also looked for informal opportunities to prompt one another to think about how
they could implement their new strategies.

In all three situations, a coach promoted another adult's ability to develop
new strategies that directly or indirectly supported a child's participation in everyday experiences and interactions with family members and peers. In the first
example, Amanda coached a parent to learn how to increase learning opportunities in everyday interactions so that her son could play with peers. In the second
scenario, Jonelle coached a colleague to improve communication skills in his daily
professional interactions. Finally, Juanita supported coaching as a professional
development strategy to assist staff to transfer learning from formal training into
daily practice.

ESSENTIALS OF COACHING

Coaching in early childhood is an interactive process of observation, reflection, and
action in which a coach promotes, directly and/or indirectly, a learner's ability to
support a child's participation in family and community contexts. Five interrelated
terms are key to understanding the essential elements of the coaching process:

- Collaborative
- Performance based

- Context driven

- Reflective

- Reciprocal

As a *collaborative* interaction between a coach and a learner, coaching is a series of conversations focused on assisting a learner to achieve a specific, self-selected outcome (Flaherty, 1999; Kinlaw, 1999). Simply stated, learners are people who want to refine what they know or do. In early childhood, learners are typically family members, child care providers and other caregivers, and early childhood practitioners. Coaches support learners to improve their *performance* in a specific

situation, by guiding them to blend new knowledge and skills with what is already known, then to evaluate their progress toward achieving a specific outcome (Fenichel & Eggbeer, 1992). Each learner's role and situation provides the *context* for coaching, for example, a mother feeding her newborn infant or an early childhood practitioner facilitating an assessment within a specific situation.

Dennis, the early childhood educator introduced previously, wanted to improve his ability to communicate with colleagues and families while performing his varied work responsibilities. Jonelle needed to understand who Dennis worked with, how they interacted, and what he hoped to accomplish before she could be helpful. Their reciprocal learning was a shared process of discovery for each partner, and each contributed his or her knowledge and experience related to Dennis's desired outcome.

After Dennis observed Jonelle, she engaged him in a *reflective* conversation focused on his interactions with family members and colleagues. Reflection is part of the verbal, nondirective analysis a coach uses to prompt a learner to think about his or her actions and interactions. It involves active engagement and discussion between a coach and learner to build a learner's ability to self-assess and generalize effective actions to other situations. A coach prompts further reflection by sharing feedback and information about a specific issue or observation. Reflection and feedback complement one another; coaches prompt learners to reflect on how their behavior and reactions move them closer or further away from their desired objectives. Feedback provides an avenue for sharing information and other resources to guide a learner in reaching those objectives.

Amanda's coaching conversations with Brigitte were performance-based in that they focused on increasing competence and mastery of desired skills for both her and Willie in daily play situations and family interactions at home (Doyle, 1999; Dunst, Herter, & Shields, 2000). Amanda and Brigitte worked collaboratively to

REMEMBER THIS . . .
Key elements of coaching

1. Coaching is based on conversations of personal discovery regarding what is known by an individual (or team) and what new learning is desirable.

2. Coaching focuses on improving an individual's performance within a specific context.

3. Coaching provides a process for improving skills, implementing evidence-based practices, experimenting with new approaches, resolving challenges, and building relationships.

identify and select these outcomes, as well as the individualized coaching strategies to help achieve them. Their reciprocal learning was based on shared information and observation. Brigitte knew she wanted her son to learn to speak German, and, as a new mother, she wanted support in promoting his language development in a fun and productive way. Amanda's expertise in language acquisition and experience working with young, active children gave her a good foundation to coach Brigitte. Their reflective coaching conversations prompted Brigitte's personal discovery about blending what she already knew about speaking German with her new learning about parenting Willie (i.e., how to support Willie's participation in play situations and prompt his language development). Amanda used her observations to prompt Brigitte's reflection about her actions and interactions with Willie and focused on helping Brigitte find interesting and fun ways to promote Willie's language.

Coaching conversations focus on helping a learner reflect on how changes in his or her knowledge and behavior ultimately influence a child's and family's life. Each learner's unique context provides the basis for the self-observation, self-correction, and self-generation that are the essential core of coaching. Both a coach and learner engage in reciprocal learning via shared observation and action (i.e., a coach modeling and a learner practicing new behaviors). The discovery process that unfolds during coaching conversations is grounded in self-examination, reflection, feedback, and refinement of a learner's knowledge and skills (Flaherty, 1999; Gallacher, 1997; Kinlaw, 1999). Table 1.1 summarizes the five key descriptors and indicators of the coaching process.

Reciprocal learning is one of the hallmarks of a coaching relationship, and it emphasizes that coaching is built on shared learning between a learner and a coach. Each brings specialized knowledge and experience to the partnership; neither partner has the entire picture without the other's information. Coaches bring their knowledge and experience about child development, adult learning, and building relationships to the partnership. Learners bring a wealth of knowledge about their family story, including who the key members are, their hopes for a child, a child's strengths and challenges, and family rules and mores. Although coaches have a broad understanding of groups of children of different ages and ability levels, they will never know a specific child in the way that family members do. Likewise, family members often desire information from early childhood practitioners to augment what they already know and to help them apply child development theories

Table 1.1. Descriptors of coaching in early childhood

Descriptor	Indicators of coaching
Collaborative	Voluntary participation by both partners—a learner and a coach
	Mutual respect and trust is established between partners.
Reflective	Objective analysis of actions/interactions of coach and learner
	Active engagement and discussion between learner and coach
	Verbal and nondirective feedback following a learner's reflection
Reciprocal	Shared observation and action by a coach and a learner that leads to two-way learning
	Each partner contributes his or her knowledge and experience.
Performance-based	Coaching goals and strategies are individualized for each learner.
	Nonjudgmental observation by each partner of his or her own and the partner's actions and interactions
Context-driven	Learner's current and anticipated situations guide selection of coaching content and outcomes.
	Learner determines where and how to assess outcomes.

and practice to their individual story (Hanft & Thomas, 1995; McBride, Brotherson, Joaning, Whiddon, & Demmitt, 1993; Rocco, 1994). Within the framework of reciprocal learning, all coaching sessions are focused on ensuring that a learner's goals for acquiring specific knowledge and behaviors are achieved.

WHAT HAPPENS DURING COACHING

A coach and learner work together in a partnership that is focused on helping a learner accomplish specific goals, using a nonjudgmental approach that emphasizes three shared components: observation, action, and reflection. These three interrelated components are the central features of coaching and the basis for the mutual conversations that lead to a learner's self-discovery and personal development. Observation, action, and reflection are bound together by two other critical components of the coaching process—initiation and evaluation.

- *Initiation* is a planning process that identifies the purpose for coaching, describes a learner's outcomes and specifies how and when a coach and learner will interact to reach those outcomes. Expectations, ground rules, and issues related to confidentiality, time, and cultural or professional backgrounds can also be discussed.

- *Observation* is a learning strategy for both a coach and a learner. A coach observes a learner's actions in several ways—by joining a learner in a specific situation to understand his or her social, physical, and cultural environment and interactions; by listening to a learner's reports of what transpired during a

REMEMBER THIS . . .
Early childhood coaching partners

The following are key people in coaching relationships.

- *Coach:* a person with knowledge of child development and family support who agrees to guide another adult to acquire or modify knowledge and skills pertinent to his or her role in promoting a child's participation in home and community settings

- *Learner:* a person who wants to refine what he or she knows and does and who collaborates with a coach to acquire or modify knowledge and skills pertinent to his or her role in promoting a child's participation in home and community settings

- *Early childhood practitioner:* an umbrella term that includes educators, family advocates, nurses, occupational therapists, physical therapists, psychologists, speech-language pathologists, social workers, and vision and hearing specialists who work with children with special needs, birth through age 5 years, and their families.

- *Child care providers:* adults who provide ongoing care for young children in their homes or community-based centers while parents/guardians work and fulfill other ongoing commitments

---

particular event; or by reviewing a video- or audiotape of the learner in a specific setting. In similar ways, a learner observes a coach's actions, such as demonstrating and modeling specific strategies with children and/or adults.

- *Actions* are also learning strategies that both a coach and learner use. A learner may practice a new skill or strategy in between coaching sessions or bring up a past experience or an anticipated one to reflect about and discuss with a coach. A coach's actions include modeling and demonstrating selected strategies for a learner.

- *Reflection* is the unique core of the coaching process and incorporates a coach's questions, feedback, and information to prompt learning and self-discovery. Through a process of questioning and active listening, a coach supports a learner in exploring what he or she knows, is doing, and thinks related to a specific situation as the basis for exploring what to try next. These situations are learner selected and provide the basis for coaching conversations.

- *Evaluation* is a formative analysis that periodically assists the coaching partners as they review their progress toward reaching a learner's goals. It leads to plans for what to do next (continuation) or how to end the process once a learner's outcomes have been achieved (resolution).

Initiation and evaluation function as bookends to provide stability for the interrelated components of observation, action, and reflection. (All five components of the coaching process are discussed in detail in Chapter 3.)

COACHING FORMATS

Coaching can occur either as a planned practice with families, other caregivers, and colleagues or can take place as a spontaneous exchange between colleagues interested in professional development (Robbins, 1991). Planned coaching sessions can be an extremely useful approach for supporting families and other caregivers to learn self-selected strategies to help their children participate in specific activities and settings. The term *planned* refers to the scheduling of coaching sessions and not their flexibility in responding to a learner's issues. For example, Amanda scheduled eight sessions with Brigitte as part of their coaching plan. During these sessions, other issues related to Willie's care came up, and Amanda incorporated them in her coaching conversations with Brigitte.

Planned coaching can also be scheduled among early childhood practitioners who seek out a colleague or consultant to support them in expanding knowledge and skills in a specific area, as Dennis arranged with Jonelle. Their coaching plan focused on how Jonelle could help Dennis refine his communication skills with families and colleagues while facilitating a functional assessment of a child's interests and assets in a specific activity setting. In this kind of planned peer coaching with an expert, a learner schedules a specified number of coaching sessions with an experienced and knowledgeable colleague or consultant. Alternately, reciprocal peer coaching can be planned by a small group of colleagues who observe one another implement a new evidence-based practice or strategy. Afterward, they reflect together on their actions and observations.

Juanita supported the use of both spontaneous and planned peer coaching among the early childhood staff under her supervision. The term *spontaneous* refers to the use of informal opportunities for coaching among colleagues for shorter rounds of reflection and dialogue than planned coaching sessions. Juanita encouraged her staff to use spontaneous peer coaching to engage one another in reflective dialogue about their practices during staff meetings and when interacting informally. She also helped staff members engage in planned peer coaching by encouraging them to schedule time for shared observation and reflection sessions with one another following their in-service training. Their coaching sessions focused on implementing specific strategies to promote natural learning opportunities.

DISTINGUISHING COACHING FROM
OTHER APPROACHES TO PROFESSIONAL DEVELOPMENT

Coaching shares characteristics with counseling, mentoring, teaching, tutoring, and supervising. Counseling and mentoring, like coaching, include a one-to-one relationship with another adult who has a specialized area of expertise. *Counseling* focuses on a therapeutic relationship between a client and a mental health professional who is devoted to helping the client uncover attitudes and values that

REFLECT ON THIS . . .
**Coaching redefines the role of
an early childhood practitioner**

The role of an early childhood
practitioner changes from working in provider-directed sessions
with a child to supporting key
learners (i.e., families and other
caregivers) in their efforts to
promote the child's participation
in a variety of natural learning
environments.

affect the client's behavior. Some counselors who specialize in behavioral counseling may incorporate coaching in their sessions. *Mentoring* involves a relationship between an expert (a mentor) and a less-experienced individual (a protégé) who desires to gain new skills and/or seeks guidance with professional development (Ganser, 1998; Robertson, 1992). Mentors often use coaching to help their protégés learn new skills or refine existing ones.

In classroom *teaching* or training, particularly for groups, an educator facilitates the transfer of knowledge (guided by a curriculum or course syllabus) to all students who demonstrate through testing and course requirements that they have reached specific criteria. A coach individualizes information and resources for each learner. *Tutoring* is a specialized one-to-one teaching relationship focused on helping a student acquire specific knowledge. Unlike coaching, tutoring generally does not involve demonstration of a student's learning in a particular context.

Coaching versus Supervision

The use of coaching in supervision deserves careful consideration. A supervisor can coach a supervisee if both choose to establish a coaching relationship in addition to their other roles and the voluntary, nonjudgmental attributes of coaching are preserved. Unlike coaches, supervisors evaluate the performance of employees and may be empowered to deliver rewards (e.g., pay raise, promotion) or sanctions (e.g., probation, demotion) if a supervisee's job performance does not meet certain specifications (see Table 1.2). Obviously, a supervisor may choose from a variety of strategies to influence an employee or supervisee, ranging from directive to reflective supervision. Reflective supervision, in fact, shares many characteristics with coaching and is based on a mutually respectful, collaborative relationship between two adults who share a work environment or professional activities (Gilkerson & Young-Holt, 1992).

Table 1.2.   Distinguishing between coaching and directive supervision

Elements	Coaching	Supervision (directive)
Process	Interactive; reflective	One sided; reactive
Relationship	Collaborative; nonjudgmental	Hierarchical; power-based
Focus	To enhance the learner's performance in self-selected areas	To ensure that employee performance meets criteria
Outcome	Acquisition of knowledge/skills	Rating; evaluation

The distinction between coaching and reflective supervision centers on the degree of authority between the two adults participating in the learning experience. A coach may not have any authority over the work performance of a learner, whereas a supervisor does have responsibility for the performance of employees. Supervisors can coach employees if they distinguish their coaching and evaluation roles. Showers advocated for "divorcing" coaching from evaluating teacher performance and argued that an individual's ability to learn new skills in a supportive environment will be jeopardized if it is not.

> In divorcing itself from evaluation, coaching provides a safe environment in which to learn and perfect new teaching behaviors, experiment with variations of strategies, teach students new skills and expectations inherent in new strategies, and thoughtfully examine the results. By placing the major responsibility for coaching with peers, status and power differentials are minimized. (Showers, 1985, p. 47)

When job performance is in doubt, the supervisor-as-coach must clearly and directly specify any expected changes separate from coaching suggestions and prompts for reflection. In other words, if a supervisee's performance is questionable, the supervisor should be clear about what the supervisee needs to do to make improvements. Coaching should be reserved for teaching a new skill or enhancing overall professional development with an interested partner.

Hands-On versus Hands-Off Intervention

The issue of hands-on versus hands-off intervention, or direct therapy versus consultation, and whether these approaches are mutually exclusive has long been debated in the literature (Campbell, 1987; Casper & Theilheimer, 2000; Dunn, 1990; Wilcox, 1989). With coaching, these arguments are unnecessary. The role of the coach is to support the learner when, where, and how the support is needed. Just as a football coach leaves carrying the ball to the players on the field, the coach in early childhood supports learners in developing (or refining) their ability to facilitate a child's active involvement in his or her community and family. Coaches use hands-on strategies with children primarily for two critical purposes: assessing a child's reactions and abilities and modeling suggestions for other adults to implement (Rush et al., 2003).

For example, Amanda and Brigitte may agree to address another of Brigitte's desires that Willie learn to go to the bathroom. Amanda could, at different times, use hands-on intervention in the following ways with guidance and input from Brigitte:

- She may assess what Willie does in the family bathroom.

- She may try the effectiveness of several possible strategies to prompt desirable behaviors.

- She may model one strategy until Brigitte is comfortable with it and wants to try it herself.

As a coach, Amanda's role has shifted from directing Willie in therapist-chosen activities to supporting Brigitte as joint problem-solver, encourager, and resource for new ideas and information. Hands-on intervention with Willie is reserved for assessing what works and then modeling specific strategies so that Brigitte can adapt them for herself.

BENEFITS OF COACHING

Coaches can help family members and other caregivers learn methods to interact more meaningfully with children. Neuroscience research in early childhood emphasizes that young children must be engaged in meaningful relationships with primary caregivers in order to grow and develop in *all* areas.

> When young children and their caregivers are tuned in to each other, and when caregivers can read the child's emotional cues and respond appropriately to his or her needs in a timely fashion, their interactions tend to be successful and the relationship is likely to support healthy development in multiple domains, including communication, cognition, social-emotional competence and moral understanding. (Shonkoff & Phillips, 2000, p. 28)

Coaching is an interactive process of observation, action, and reflection in which a coach promotes a learner's ability to support a child in being with the people he or she wants and needs to be with and doing what he or she wants and needs to do (Shelden & Rush, 2001). Coaching also develops a learner's competence and confidence to integrate new information and experiences with current ones. This includes implementing strategies to increase a child's learning opportunities and participation in daily life, knowing when the strategies are successful, and making necessary changes in current situations, as well as generalizing ideas and solutions to different circumstances and settings.

For early childhood practitioners, coaching provides a structure for supporting adult learners who ultimately make a difference in a child's life. A coach facilitates an exchange of observations, ideas, and information with a learner, oriented to enhancing his or her competence in essential roles from family member to caregiver to practitioner. The three coaching stories introduced in this chapter highlight the key descriptors of coaching as a collaborative, reciprocal, context-driven, performance-based, and reflective process.

- Amanda coached a mother, Brigitte, to find ways to identify learning opportunities so that her son could play with peers at the playground in their apartment complex and express his needs to her. Amanda and Brigitte exchanged information about how young children develop and use words and focused on Brigitte's desire that her son learn German, her native language.

- Jonelle coached Dennis, a colleague, to improve communication skills in his daily professional interactions with families and colleagues. She and Dennis used planned coaching and set up times for Dennis to observe her interactions. Then, Jonelle met with Dennis to reflect about what he saw and heard and to relate what he had observed to specific situations in which he was involved.

- Juanita supported coaching as a professional development strategy to assist staff members in transferring learning from formal training at a conference into their daily practice. The staff alternated coach and learner roles to encourage one another to learn how to support families in identifying and using natural learning opportunities.

ORGANIZATION OF THIS BOOK

This book provides guidelines for early childhood practitioners regarding whom, when, and how to coach and describes the key components of the coaching process: initiation, observation, action, reflection, and evaluation. The first four chapters lay the foundation for how to coach effectively by discussing the literature in support of coaching, the qualities of an effective coach, and the key components of the coaching process. This chapter has provided an overview of the "who, what, and why" of coaching and introduces a five-step coaching process of initiation, observation, action, reflection, and evaluation. Chapter 2 reviews literature related to coaching in education and early childhood and describes how reflective thinking, narrative stories, and adult learning support coaching as a process of self-discovery and learning. Chapter 3 explains, with brief coaching stories, how to use a five-step coaching process to begin a coaching relationship and develop a coaching plan (initiation); use observations to define a learner's context and introduce new information and experiences (observation); model, demonstrate, and practice (action); analyze actions and observation; plan and problem-solve (reflection); and assess the coaching relationship and process (evaluation). Chapter 4 illustrates, with brief coaching stories, the essential qualities (competency, objectivity, adaptability, caring, and honesty) and communication skills (observing, listening, responding, and planning) a coach must possess to effectively coach another adult.

Chapters 5–7 use in-depth stories to illustrate how to coach families, child care providers, educators, and early childhood practitioners who work with very young children and their families. Chapter 5 describes the critical issues that influence coaching families in their homes and communities. Chapter 6 describes the critical issues that influence coaching in group settings, such as preschools and child care. Finally, Chapter 7 describes the critical issues that influence coaching colleagues (e.g., approaches, formats, administrative support, setting up the right climate for lifelong learning, matching a coach and learner, changing professional practices).

The content introduced in each chapter is supplemented by the following to help readers integrate the information about coaching in their professional and/or personal roles.

- Coaching stories—Anecdotes and vignettes are interspersed throughout the text to illustrate specific points about the process of coaching. Readers are encouraged to think about how coaching might be useful in their own interactions with families and colleagues.

- Reflect on this—Issues are posed to the reader at key points for reflection, to simulate the experience of working with a coach.

- Remember this—Concise listings of information draw attention to critical points emphasized in the text.

- Try this—Suggestions for action are included for readers to practice coaching in their early childhood practice.

- Resources—Annotated lists of select web references, articles, books, and other print resources are included at the end of Chapters 2–7 for readers interested in learning more about the coaching topics discussed.

CONCLUSION

Coaching is a positive approach for building competence in another adult. Its personal, interactive nature ensures that adult learners can achieve their desired outcomes by helping them package new information and experiences in small increments. Coaching provides opportunities to practice new skills in a safe environment, with follow-up support from a coach who can help assess what works and why. Such an approach encourages learners to stretch what they know and do and to reach for additional knowledge and experiences. Coaching facilitates. It makes the process of learning easy because it is timely and focuses exactly on what each individual or team needs (Kinlaw, 1999).

REFERENCES

Brotherson, J.J., & Goldstein, B.L. (1992). Time as a resource and constraint for parents of young children with disabilities: Implications for early intervention services. *Topics in Early Childhood Special Education, 12*(4), 508–527.

Campbell, P. (1987). The integrated programming team: An approach for coordinating professionals of different disciplines in programs for students with severe and multiple handicaps. *Journal of The Association for Persons with Severe Handicaps, 12,* 107–116.

Campbell, S. (1997). Therapy programs for children that last a lifetime. *Physical and Occupational Therapy in Pediatrics, 7*(1), 1–15.

Casper, V., & Theilheimer, R. (2000). Hands on, hands off, hands out: Choices teachers make in the teaching-learning relationship. *Zero to Three Bulletin, 20*(6), 5–11.

Doyle, J.S. (1999). *The business coach: A game plan for the new work environment.* New York: John Wiley & Sons.

Dunn, W. (1990). A comparison of service provider models in school-based occupational therapy services: A pilot study. *Occupational Therapy Journal of Research, 10*(5), 300–320.

Dunst, C.J., Hamby, D., Trivette, C.M., Raab, M., & Bruder, M.B. (2000). Everyday family and community life and children's naturally occurring learning opportunities. *Journal of Early Intervention, 23*(3), 151–164.

Dunst, C.J., Herter, S., & Shields, H. (2000). Interest-based natural learning opportunities. In S. Sandall & M. Ostrosky (Eds.), *Young Exceptional Children Monograph Series No. 2* (pp. 37–48). Denver, CO: Division for Early Childhood of the Council for Exceptional Children.

Fenichel, E., & Eggbeer, L. (Eds.). (1992). *Preparing practitioners to work with infants, toddlers, and their families: Issues and recommendations for educators and trainers.* Washington, DC: ZERO TO THREE/National Center for Clinical Infant Programs.

Flaherty, J. (1999). *Coaching: Evoking excellence in others.* Boston: Butterworth-Heinemann.

Gallacher, K. (1997). Supervision, mentoring and coaching. In P.J. Winton, J.A. McCollum, & C. Catlett (Eds.), *Reforming personnel preparation in early intervention: Issues, models, and practical strategies* (pp. 191–214). Baltimore: Paul H. Brookes Publishing Co.

Ganser, T. (1998, Winter). Metaphors for mentoring. *The Educational Forum, 62,* 113–119.

Gilkerson, L., & Young-Holt, C. (1992). Supervision and the management of programs serving infants, toddlers and their families. In E. Fenichel & L. Eggbeer (Eds.), *Preparing practitioners to work with infants, toddlers, and their families: Issues and recommendations for educators and trainers.* Washington, DC: ZERO TO THREE/National Center for Clinical Infant Programs.

Hanft, B., & Feinberg, E. (1997). Toward a new paradigm for determining the frequency and intensity of early intervention services. *Infants and Young Children, 9*(1), 27–37.

Hanft, B., & Pilkington, K. (2000). Therapy in natural environments: The means or end goal for early intervention? *Infants and Young Children, 12*(4), 1–13.

Hanft, B., & Striffler, N. (1995). Incorporating developmental therapy in early childhood programs: Challenges and promising practices. *Infants and Young Children, 8*(2), 37–47.

Hanft, B., & Thomas J. (1995). Evolution and revolution: David is growing up. *American Occupational Therapy Developmental Disabilities Special Interest Section Newsletter, 18*(1), 1–4.

Harbour, R., & Miller, J. (2001). A new system for grading recommendations in evidence based guidelines. *British Medical Journal, 323,* 334–336.

Kinlaw, D.C. (1999). *Coaching for commitment: Interpersonal strategies for obtaining superior performance from individuals and teams.* San Francisco: Jossey-Bass.

McBride, S., Brotherson, M., Joaning, H., Whiddon, D., & Demmitt, A. (1993). Implementation of family-centered services: Perceptions of families and professionals. *Journal of Early Intervention, 17*(4), 414–430.

McWilliam, R.A. (2000). It's only natural . . . to have early intervention in the environments where it's needed. In S. Sandall & M. Ostrosky (Eds.), *Young Exceptional Children Monograph Series No. 2* (pp. 17–26). Denver, CO: Division for Early Childhood of the Council for Exceptional Children.

Montgomery, P. (1994, March). Frequency and duration of pediatric physical therapy. *Magazine of Physical Therapy,* 42–91.

O'Neil, M.E., & Palisano, R.J. (2000). Attitudes toward family-centered care and clinical decision making in early intervention among physical therapists. *Pediatric Physical Therapy, 12,* 173–182.

Pollock, N., & Stewart, D. (1998). Occupational performance needs of school-aged children with physical disabilities in the community. *Physical and Occupational Therapy in Pediatrics, 18*(1), 55–68.

Robbins, P. (1991). *How to plan and implement a peer coaching program.* Reston, VA: Association for Supervision and Curriculum Development.

Robertson, S. (1992). *Find a mentor or be one.* Bethesda, MD: American Occupational Therapy Association.

Rocco, S. (1994). New visions for the developmental assessment of infants and young children: A parent's perspective. *Zero to Three Bulletin, 14*(6), 13–15.

Rush, D.D., Shelden, M.L., & Hanft, B.E. (2003). Coaching families and colleagues: A process for collaboration in natural settings. *Infants and Young Children, 16*(1), 33–47.

Shelden, M.L., & Rush, D.D. (2001). The ten myths about providing early intervention services in natural environments. *Infants and Young Children, 14*(1), 1–13.

Shonkoff, J.P., & Phillips, D.A. (Eds.). (2000). *From neurons to neighborhoods: The science of early childhood development.* Washington, DC: National Academy Press.

Showers, B. (1985). Teachers coaching teachers. *Educational Leadership, 42*(7), 43–48.

Snowball, R. (1999). Finding the evidence: An information skills approach. In M. Dawes, P. Davies, A. Gray, J. Mant, K. Sears, & R. Snowball (Eds.), *Evidence-based practice: A primer for health care professionals* (pp. 15–46). New York: Churchill Livingstone.

Turnbull, A., Turbiville, V., & Turnbull, H. (2000). Evolution of family-professional partnerships: Collective empowerment as the model for the early Twenty-First Century. In J. Shonkoff & S. Meisels (Eds.), *Handbook of early childhood intervention* (2nd ed., pp. 630–650). New York: Cambridge University Press.

Walsh, S., Rous, B., & Lutzer, C. (2000). The federal IDEA natural environments provisions. In S. Sandall & M. Ostrosky (Eds.), *Young Exceptional Children Monograph Series No. 2* (pp. 3–15). Denver, CO: Division for Early Childhood of the Council for Exceptional Children.

Wilcox, M. (1989). Delivering communication-based services to infants, toddlers and their families: Approaches and models. *Topics in Language Disorders, 10*(1), 68–79.

2

SUPPORT FOR COACHING

This chapter discusses the support for coaching in education literature as an important tool in professional development for all personnel. In early childhood, coaching assists family members, caregivers, and early childhood practitioners to refine their knowledge and experience so they can help families promote their children's participation in meaningful activities every day, throughout the day. A coach explores with a learner how and when to use specific strategies and information appropriate to a learner's role and the context in which he or she interacts with a child. Coaching in early childhood provides a structure for developing the competence and skills of other adults in an interactive, nonjudgmental manner that guides adult learners to achieve their individualized, context-specific goals. It is a partnership between adults in which a learner is encouraged to integrate new knowledge and experience with what is already known. This partnership is the focal point of coaching and is supported by research in adult learning. Two practices—narrative process and reflective thinking—used by professionals across such diverse fields as psychology, cross-cultural studies, and education help sustain coaching conversations with their emphasis on viewing the world from another's perspective and analyzing one's own actions and interactions.

The following sections review the literature supporting coaching in education and summarize the connections between coaching and adult learning, reflective thinking, and narrative process.

COACHING IN EDUCATION

While coaching has long been part of athletic training (Thompson, 1995) and leadership development for business CEOs and managers (Goldsmith, Lyons, & Freas, 2000; Hudson, 1999), it became an accepted practice in the professional preparation and supervision of educators and administrators in the mid-1980s (Ackland, 1991; Brandt, 1987; Joyce & Showers, 1981; Mid-Continent Regional Educational

Laboratory, 1983). Various coaching models were incorporated in professional development programs that focused on building collegial relationships, resolving specific instructional problems, and learning and refining new skills (Costa & Garmston, 1986; Joyce & Showers, 1982; Mello, 1984). More recently, coaching has been used in education to promote:

- Partnerships between general educators and administrators (Guiney, 2001; Phillips & Glickman, 1991; Roberts, 1991)

- Professional development of special educators (Kohler, Crilley, Shearer, & Good, 1997; Miller, 1994) and educators in rural schools (Decker & Dedrick, 1989)

- Inclusion of students with individualized education programs (IEP) in general classrooms (Gersten, Morvant, & Brengelman, 1995; Hasbrouck & Christen, 1997; Pugach & Johnson, 1995)

- Preservice preparation of special and general educators (Cegelka, Fitch, & Alvarado, 2001; Harlin, 2000; Morgan, Gustafson, Hudson, & Salzberg, 1992)

These coaching programs and studies use a similar process as presented in this book: nonjudgmental interaction between the coaching partners, reflection, and observation paired with feedback to prompt a learner's self-discovery and acquire or refine knowledge and skills. The education literature emphasizes the noneval-uative function of coaching, viewing it as a safe environment for teachers to learn and experiment with new teaching behaviors and strategies and then thoughtfully examine the results (Robbins, 1991; Showers, 1985). In a review of 25 coaching programs for classroom teachers, reflection and feedback between a teacher-coach and teacher-learner was the essential step in helping teachers improve their instructional strategies (Ackland, 1991). These education-coaching programs define a learner's goals in terms of improving daily teaching practices, developing staff relationships, and finding solutions to specific problems. Such coaching outcomes are also highly desirable for early childhood practitioners who engage in peer coaching in their quest to gain knowledge and skills to improve their interactions and practices.

COACHING IN EARLY CHILDHOOD

Coaching has been acknowledged as an important practice supporting professional development in early intervention. Gallacher (1995, 1997) developed a coaching model for early intervention professionals and described how it helped practitioners effectively support families and children by:

- Sustaining efforts to practice unfamiliar skills or apply new knowledge by offering the support, encouragement, and reassurance of other colleagues

- Reducing isolation and facilitating collaboration through the exchange of ideas, methods,
  experiences, and resources among participants
- Promoting the development of trust and collegial family–professional relationships
- Encouraging staff to engage in continued
  learning through examination, discussion, and
  refinement of professional practices

Following initial instruction on specific early
intervention topics, peer coaching was used to
assist learning teams in seven areas of one state
to integrate participants' learning in their inter-

REMEMBER THIS...
Goals of coaching

Coaching in education and early
childhood share similar goals.

- Individualized strategies and
  support for children and families
- Better relations among early
  childhood practitioners
- Options for addressing specific
  issues

actions with families as well as refine individually identified priorities related to
home-based intervention. Instruction regarding how to use coaching was provided
through a "train-the-trainer" approach to develop facilitator coaches for each of
the learning teams.

An increasing recognition exists from leaders in pediatric therapy and education that coaching in early childhood can help practitioners refocus their traditional
direct service role in order to assist others in their efforts to enhance children's participation in everyday environments. Hanft and Pilkington encouraged early childhood specialists to reconceptualize their role "to move to a different position
alongside a parent as a *coach* rather than lead player" because this generates many
more opportunities to facilitate developmentally appropriate interactions and
activities than direct intervention by the specialist (2000, p. 2). Bruder recognized
the need to *coach* adults and peers to facilitate meaningful developmental interactions for children with special needs throughout the day (personal communication, December 1, 2001). Dinnebeil, McInerney, Roth, and Ramaswamy studied
the role of itinerant early childhood special education teachers and concluded that
itinerant teachers "should be prepared to act not simply as consultants to early
childhood teachers but as coaches" (2001, p. 42) because this offers a more structured system for jointly identifying specific teaching behaviors or skills to be learned
through feedback and modeling from a coach. Campbell suggested that contem-
porary practice supports therapists to view themselves:

> As advisors, counselors, and purveyors of information to families . . . than as
> direct care providers, and that they need to maintain a long-term perspective.
> The concept is more akin to being a coach or personal trainer than a hands-on
> provider. (1997, p. 3)

HOW ADULT LEARNING SUPPORTS COACHING

Adult learners are self-directed problem solvers who learn best when they can
relate new information to past experience (Guskey, 1986; Knowles, 1996; Moore,

1988). Knowles (1980), the Father of Andragogy (adult learning), identified in the 1980s that the major difference in learning between adults and children is that adults prefer learning that has a direct application to their jobs and daily responsibilities. This transfer of learning is one of the most complex and important elements in the learning process connected with adult education (Bellanca, 1995). Successful transfer of learning occurs when a learner gathers new information, integrates it with prior knowledge, then reflects on the optimal conditions for when and how to use the learning. This process is an active one, and in early childhood, coaching reinforces how to support a learner to take responsibility for learning and using new knowledge and actions.

A synthesis of a broad body of research on the science of learning highlights three findings that have important implications for adult learners in education and professional development programs as well as K–12 education (Donovan, Bransford, & Pellegrino, 1999). The findings, and their application to coaching, are described next.

Learners have preconceptions about how the world works. Coaches must draw out what learners already know about a particular topic and help shape their understanding to reflect new information in a way that integrates all their concepts and knowledge. If, for example, a grandmother would like her granddaughter to participate in family outings at a restaurant and enjoy her food, a coach would explore with the grandmother what she has already tried and what she thinks would improve mealtimes *before* sharing new information and suggesting strategies (actions) to try.

Learners must have both a deep foundation of factual knowledge and a strong conceptual framework in order to develop competence in an area of learning. Experts draw on a richly structured information base and develop concepts that help them transform their information from a set of facts into usable knowledge. This conceptual framework provides a base for organizing and storing information into meaningful patterns so that it can be retrieved for problem solving in new situations. One of the primary outcomes of coaching is to help learners organize their knowledge and generalize their actions across environments. If, for example, this grandmother learns that her granddaughter can use a certain kind of cup to drink without choking, the coach can help the grandmother understand why this works and how she can use this information to review other environments in which her granddaughter eats and drinks.

Strategies can be taught that enable learners to monitor their understanding and progress in problem solving. Experts monitor their understanding carefully, noting when additional information is required, how consistent new information is with what is already known, and what analogies can be drawn to further their understanding of a topic. When they problem-solve, experts use an internal form of reasoning to consider alternatives and evaluate how helpful any alternative is to reaching their goals. The coaching process incorporates reflection-on-action by both a learner and coach at critical junctures to develop such a "culture of inquiry" (Donovan et al., 1999). A coach prompts a learner to engage in a process of self-reflection and reflect on and draw conclusions from his or her knowledge and experiences.

Early childhood coaches also can consider how motivation, learning environment, experience, self-direction, learning style, critical thinking, and integration of new information influence all adults when they desire to learn new material (Guskey, 1986; Knowles, 1996; Moore, 1988). These seven factors also affect each relationship coaches develop with adult learners (i.e., family members and colleagues).

1. Motivation—adult learners must have (or be coached to develop) the desire to accomplish specific outcomes and engage in a coaching relationship

2. Respectful learning environment—the physical and emotional climate promotes how adult learners acquire new information/skills and engage in self-reflection

3. Past and current experience—what adult learners already know and have experienced provides the critical foundation for merging new knowledge and experience

4. Achieving self-direction and active involvement—adult learners have unique perspectives regarding what they want to learn and how fast they can integrate new information and practices to change their current behavior and thinking

5. Learning styles/coping strategies—adult learners have individualized strategies for processing information, meeting challenges, and accomplishing a task. (Figure 7.4 on page 176 suggests coaching strategies that take advantage of a variety of learning styles.) Coaches can discuss these options with a learner when developing their coaching plan, as well as any other approaches a learner can identify that have helped him or her take in and apply new knowledge to current experiences

6. Critical, reflective thinking—adult learners must be given the opportunity to review their efforts to make changes and learn new practices in order to achieve self-direction

7. Transition time to integrate new ideas—putting new learning into practice on a consistent basis takes time, effort, and support

Adult learners are influenced by their level of motivation to engage in a new experience, their desire for self-direction, the presence of a supportive environment that uses their unique learning styles, their ability to build on prior experiences, and ongoing support to put new knowledge into practice. Self-reflection questions for a coach to consider when initiating a coaching relationship with a

Table 2.1. Self-reflection questions for a coach to consider

Reflective thinking	Self-reflection by a coach
What features do I notice when I observe a child and/or adult?	What is a learner doing, saying, feeling?
	What is the nature of a child's participation in a specific setting?
	How do others in the environment influence a learner and vice versa?
What are the criteria by which I share observations and suggestions?	How will we (learner and coach) know a learner has achieved his or her goal?
	How does my knowledge of evidence-based practices and past experience affect my interaction with and suggestions for this learner?
	What internal criteria do I use to judge how I am doing as a coach?
What procedures do I use when I perform this skill (coaching)?	How developed are my general coaching skills (observing, listening, responding, and planning)?
	How can I improve my skills in any of these areas?
	When do I ask for help from another colleague and/or supervisor?
How do I frame the issue I am facing?	How can I share my professional knowledge/experience, and what information is appropriate to share?
	What prompts and information would help a learner achieve his or her goals?
	How can I use my knowledge/experience to support a learner's attempts to enhance a child's participation in a specific environment?

learner and when evaluating the effectiveness of coaching strategies are suggested in Table 2.1. The following discussion explains how reflective thinking and narrative process influence the effectiveness of a coach's skill in communication and analytic skills (see Chapter 4 for further discussion).

REFLECTIVE THINKING AND COACHING

Reflective thinking refers to the critical and analytical thinking of early childhood practitioners across a broad spectrum of disciplines and includes clinical reasoning and cognitive reflection (Mattingly & Fleming, 1994; Schon, 1983, 1987; Sparks-Langer & Colton, 1991). It is a form of reflection-on-action that describes both the conscious and unconscious knowledge and problem-solving strategies used by human service professionals in their daily practice. Two hallmarks of reflective thinking—adapting a strategy as it unfolds and reassessing progress—provide structure for taking a close look at the learner–coach interaction and assessing whether suggested strategies are helping a learner achieve his or her desired outcomes. Reflective thinking supports each round of observation, action, and reflection in the coaching process and may change the perspectives of either, or both, a learner or coach regarding their subsequent actions and interactions.

Coaching has been described as "not telling people what to do, [but] giving them a chance to examine what they are doing in light of their intentions" (Flaherty, 1999, p. xii). Such examination is also part of how reflective thinking is used by individuals to analyze and describe a problem when they think about what they are doing, even while engaged in specific action. How practitioners think in action has been the focus of researchers and professionals in fields as diverse as nursing, occupational therapy, physical therapy, psychotherapy, social work, urban planning, competitive chess, navigation, and architecture (Benner & Tanner, 1987; Burke & DePoy, 1991; Dreyfus & Dreyfus, 1980, 1986; Lazare, 1973; Schon, 1983, 1987). Reflective thinking, a process of self-discovery, assists a coach to prompt a learner to think about his or her actions and intention. It also guides a coach to use his or her professional knowledge during self-reflection about the coaching process. See Table 2.1 for a list of questions typical of reflective thinking translated as self-reflection questions for a coach to ask during the evaluation phase of coaching (described in Chapter 3).

Because any coaching plan may change and shift as strategies are implemented, a coach must be willing to modify his or her working hypothesis about assisting a learner. The essence of reflective thinking is what to do when unexpected interactions, conversations, or outcomes occur, necessitating immediate consideration about next steps. This process is also crucial for underscoring the partnership between a coach and learner as each set of observations, actions, and reflections may result in a new understanding of a learner's context. A coach then reflects further on new variables to prompt a learner to generate his or her own reflection-on-action.

Fleming (1991) provides a model of the clinical reasoning used by many occupational therapists that is uniquely suited to the complexity of early childhood practice. Her model, described as a *three track mind*, emphasizes the way in which therapists look beyond an individual's physical or cognitive impairments (*procedural track*) to incorporate more complex levels involving the meaning of their experiences (*conditional track*) as well as the unique characteristics of an individual interacting within relationships or contexts (*interactive track*). This way of thinking and problem solving is well suited for supporting families and colleagues to promote a child's participation in meaningful settings (Hanft & Anzalone, 2001). It ensures that a coach will look beyond the procedural track (i.e., a child's delays and problem areas) to consider how family members see a child, their priorities for the child's daily interactions, and the world from the child's perspective (*conditional*

TRY THIS . . .
Using reflective thinking

A coach uses reflective thinking to consider multiple and changing forms of information, impressions, and insight while observing a learner in a specific context. To practice your observation skills, watch a person engaged in a task in a specific environment, such as a friend preparing dinner, a child swinging at the playground, or a receptionist in an office. Consider what you can observe about the person's lifestyle and characteristics, such as

- Family life, routines, values, and needs
- Physical and psychosocial characteristics
- Roles and responsibilities (e.g., friend, parent, worker)
- Personality and preferred style of learning
- Ethnic and cultural background
- Socioeconomic status
- Play, work, and/or school setting
- Special skills and interests

---

track). In addition, a coach must consider how environments and relationships affect a child and a learner and how to support their priorities in coaching (*interactional track*).

Reflective thinking helps a coach collect, analyze, and interpret observations of a learner's actions and interactions, as suggested in the Try This exercise above. Both coaching and reflective thinking emphasize learning to "do *with*" learners instead of "do *to*" them (Mattingly & Fleming, 1994). Collaborating *with* learners to individualize strategies in a way that honors their knowledge, experience, and goals is the basis of effective coaching.

NARRATIVE STORYTELLING AND COACHING

Narratives are stories, either told or held unspoken by the individual experiencing them and, as such, are powerful descriptors of a person's life and expectations for the future. Listening to a learner's story is a strategy that enables an early childhood coach to understand a learner's perspective within the context of the learner's daily life well enough to create a coaching plan *with* him or her, not *for* him or her. The coach builds an understanding of a learner's story through observation of the learner's actions as well as the learner's self-report and reflections. This story becomes the focal point for developing an individualized coaching plan with each learner that includes goals to support a child's participation within specific natural settings (see Chapter 3 for further discussion). An effective coach determines, with a learner, how to enter his or her life story in a positive way to provide prompts for a learner's self-discovery about his or her actions and interactions; share feedback, instruction, and other resources; and suggest strategies to help a learner reach his or her goal.

Many cultures incorporate a tradition of storytelling to share values, mores, and expectations from one generation to another (Campbell & Moyers, 1991). For example, the White River Sioux tell a story about Rabbit Boy to explain how their world began. Rabbit Boy started life as a rabbit and became a little boy with the help of Takuskanskan, the mysterious power of motion (Erdoes & Ortiz, 1985). The story of Rabbit Boy emphasizes the Sioux view of the earth and the whole universe as a never-ending circle in which man is just another animal, and all wildlife and plants are related as brothers and cousins. This myth, like the myths and stories of other cultures, depicts events and people in a way that is easy to remember and cherish.

REMEMBER THIS . . .
Narrative process

Elements of the narrative process, or storytelling:

- Are universal and cross-cultural
- Place events within a temporal, physical, and cultural context
- Shape our lives and our perceptions of one another and of ourselves

Three groups of storytellers—learners, coaches, and children—each bring their special stories to the coaching process. These stories guide and shape the behavior and attitudes of both the storytellers and others around them. These narratives provide details about a learner's life, roles, interests, and what he or she can do or hopes to do in the future. Coaches tell stories that describe and highlight their abilities as a coach to support a learner in acquiring new skills. Once they are old enough, children tell their own stories that describe their interests and achievements. Children of all ages can be dramatically affected by the stories told about them.

Early childhood coaching stories contain several elements (i.e., characters, context, and expectations) that are very helpful for coaches to learn to listen for and elicit from learners because they provide important cues for making coaching meaningful. The *characters* in a learner's story are the people who influence a learner and child in meaningful ways. Family stories most often include other family members, child care providers, neighbors, and people from the community who support them in roles such as friend, parent, grandparent, aunt, and uncle. The stories told by early childhood practitioners as learners also include family members and children, as well as colleagues and administrators when their coaching goals focus on improving their team relationships and actions.

The *context* in coaching stories is the specific setting in which a learner wants to put new skills and knowledge into action. Families usually know the particular activity settings they would most like to see their children participate in and can be prompted by a coach to reflect on and describe the ones they would most like to support their children in (Chapters 5 and 6 describe coaching in home, community, and group settings in detail). Practitioners also have ideas about the knowledge and skills they would like to use in specific situations related to their role in early childhood, from learning to do a functional assessment of a child engaged in a context specific task, to improving their time management skills. In order to understand a learner's story, a coach must listen closely to the learner's *expectations* for gaining new skills and then help the learner translate these desires into specific goals to guide the coaching process. Each of the coaching stories presented in Chapters 5–7 identify the characters (coach, learners, child), context (activity setting, situations), and expectations (expressed as the purpose and expected outcomes).

Narratives also offer coaches an opportunity to help learners think about the future and describe different actions and interactions for themselves and a child. A coach can encourage a learner to describe what "could be" and prompt a learner to explore various strategies and actions to reach his or her goal. Examples of questions a coach can ask to elicit information from family members and early childhood practitioners include (Burke, 2001; Fadiman, 1998):

- What is the child's life like now?
- What are the child's interests?
- Who are the key family members and other caregivers who spend time with the child, and in what settings?
- What are the child's primary roles (e.g., son, granddaughter, friend, brother), and how much can he or she do within these roles?
- What do family members think about the child's interests and roles?
- What are the family's priorities for how, where, and when to support the child in being with others and doing what is meaningful?
- What support from a coach would be helpful in making this happen?

CONCLUSION

Coaching is an interactive, nonlinear approach to supporting another person in his or her attempts to refine knowledge and skills. Coaching in early childhood has been accepted since the 1980s as an evidence-based professional development practice. It provides a structure for developing the competence and skills of family members and early childhood practitioners to support a child's participation in home and community settings in meaningful ways. Coaching helps practitioners reframe the nature of their interaction with families and colleagues by focusing on a learner's perspectives and goals and building on a learner's knowledge and skills. Using observations and reflective listening, prompting, and questioning, a coach guides a learner through a process of self-discovery about what he or she already knows, is doing, has tried, and thinks about in relation to a specific situation.

Table 2.2.   Relating adult learning, reflective thinking, and narrative process to coaching

Adult learning depends on	Reflection questions for coaches
Motivation	What motivates each learner to acquire knowledge and/or try new routines or activities? How is that similar or different from my experiences or other learners' experiences?
Respectful learning environment	What physical and emotional factors are important components of a successful learning environment for myself and each learner I coach?
Past and current experience	Do I understand each learner's "story" about supporting a child in natural settings? Interacting with early childhood practitioners? Finding and adapting community resources?
Achieving self-direction and active involvement	How can I help the families/colleagues I coach feel that they are in charge of their learning?
Learning styles/coping strategies	How can I support each learner in processing and coping with new information and experiences, especially if the information and experiences are different from mine?
Transition time to integrate new ideas	How can I guide each learner to try new ideas or actions and adapt them to use in his or her own routines and interactions?
Critical, reflective thinking	When and how do I reflect with each learner about our interactions and progress?

The interaction and reflection a coach and learner engage in is grounded in two practices, reflective thinking and narrative process, which help a coach view the world from another's perspective and analyze the actions and interactions of others as well as him- or herself. Reflective thinking is a process of self-reflection that guides a coach to think about what to do when engaged with a learner, especially when unexpected interactions, conversations, or outcomes occur. A learner's story helps a coach to understand the learner's perspective and expectations with the context of his or her daily life.

As you conclude this chapter, consider the self-reflection questions posed in Table 2.2. The questions, organized by the key factors influencing adult learning, guide a coach when initiating a relationship with a learner and when evaluating the effectiveness of the coaching process.

RESOURCES

Fadiman, A. (1998). *The spirit catches you and you fall down.* New York: Farrar, Straus & Giroux.

Fadiman, a medical anthropologist, illustrates the narrative process in her true story of Lia Lee, born in San Joaquin Valley in California to Hmong refugees. When she was 3 months old, Lia showed signs of having what the Hmong know as *quag dab peg* (the spirit catches you and you fall down), the condition diagnosed by Western doctors as epilepsy. Fadiman traces the clash of Western treatment by medication with the introduction by Lia's family of folk remedies to coax her wandering soul back to her body. Fadiman expertly identifies the profound cultural differences and linguistic miscommunication that ensues and highlights issues for early childhood practitioners to consider in their interactions with families across cultural groups.

Schon, D. (1983). *The reflective practitioner: How professionals think in action*. New York: Basic Books.

Schon, a social scientist, examines psychology, architecture, engineering, town planning, and management to study how various professionals think in action. Effective professionals engage in a process of reflection that builds on their technical knowledge. They are able to "name and frame" an issue or problem and formulate a tentative plan of action. Then, a process of examination and analysis begins, with the professional appraising results of their implemented actions, which Schon calls a "reflective conversation with the situation." This type of reflective reasoning is also a foundation of effective coaching.

REFERENCES

Ackland, R. (1991). A review of peer coaching literature. *Journal of Staff Development, 12*(1), 22–27.

Bellanca, J. (1995). *Designing professional development for change*. Arlington Heights, IL: Skylight Press

Benner, P., & Tanner, C. (1987). *Clinical judgment: How expert nurses use intuition*. Menlo Park, CA: Addison-Wesley.

Brandt, R. (1987). On teachers coaching teachers: A conversation with Bruce Joyce. *Educational Leadership, 44*(5), 12–17.

Burke, J. (2001). Clinical reasoning and the use of narrative in sensory integration assessment and intervention. In S. Roley, E. Blanche, & R. Schaaf (Eds.), *Sensory integration with diverse populations* (pp. 203–214). San Antonio: Therapy Skill Builders.

Burke, J., & DePoy, E. (1991). An emerging view of mastery, excellence and leadership in occupational therapy. *American Journal of Occupational Therapy, 45*, 1027–1032.

Campbell, J., & Moyers, B. (1991). *The power of myth*. New York: Anchor Books.

Campbell, S. (1997). Therapy programs for children that last a lifetime. *Physical and Occupational Therapy in Pediatrics, 7*(1) 1–15.

Cegelka, P., Fitch, S., & Alvarado, J. (2001). The coach-of-coaches model for preparing rural special education teachers. In *Growing partnerships for rural special education*. Conference proceedings, San Diego, March 29–31, 2001. (ERIC Document Reproduction Service No. ED453031)

Costa, A., & Garmston, R. (1986). Some distinctions between supervision and evaluation. In K. Tye & A. Costa (Eds.), *Better teaching through instructional supervision: Policy and practice*. Sacramento: California School Boards Association.

Decker, R., & Dedrick, C. (1989). *Peer mentoring exchange program: Opportunities for professional improvement*. Arlington, VA: Council for Exceptional Children. (ERIC Document Reproduction Service No. ED317347)

Dinnebeil, L., McInerney, W., Roth, J., & Ramaswamy, V. (2001). Itinerant early childhood special education services: Service delivery in one state. *Journal of Early Intervention, 24*(1), 35–44.

Donovan, S., Bransford, J., & Pellegrino, J. (Eds.). (1999). *How people learn: Bridging research and practice.* Washington, DC: National Academy Press, Committee on Learning Research and Educational Practice.

Dreyfus, H., & Dreyfus, S. (1980). *A five stage model of the mental activities involved in directed skill acquisition.* Unpublished report supported by the Air Force Office of Scientific Research (AFSC), USAF (contract F49620-79-C-0063), University of California at Berkeley.

Dreyfus, H., & Dreyfus, S. (1986). *Mind over machine.* New York: The Free Press.

Erdoes, R., & Ortiz, A. (Eds.). (1985). *American Indian myths and legends.* New York: Pantheon Books.

Fadiman, A. (1998). *The spirit catches you and you fall down.* New York: Farrar, Straus & Giroux.

Flaherty, J. (1999). *Coaching: Evoking excellence in others.* Boston: Butterworth-Heinemann.

Fleming, M. (1991). The therapist with the three track mind. *American Journal of Occupational Therapy, 45,* 1007–1014.

Gallacher, K. (1995). *Coaching partnerships: Refining early intervention practices.* Missoula: Montana University Affiliated Rural Institute on Disabilities.

Gallacher, K. (1997). Supervision, mentoring and coaching. In P.J. Winton, J.A. McCollum, & C. Catlett (Eds.), *Reforming personnel preparation in early intervention: Issues, models, and practical strategies* (pp. 191–214). Baltimore: Paul H. Brookes Publishing Co.

Gersten, R., Morvant, M., & Brengelman, S. (1995). Close to the classroom is close to the bone: Coaching as a means to translate research into classroom practice. *Exceptional Children, 62*(1), 52–66.

Goldsmith, M., Lyons, L., & Freas, A. (2000). *Coaching for leadership: How the world's greatest coaches help leaders learn.* San Francisco: Jossey-Bass

Guiney, E. (2001). Coaching isn't just for athletes: The role of teacher leaders. *Phi Delta Kappan, 82*(10), 740–743.

Guskey, T. (1986). Staff development and the process of teacher change. *Educational Researcher, 15*(5), 5–12.

Hanft, B., & Anzalone, M. (2001). Issues in professional development: Preparing and supporting occupational therapists in early childhood. *Infants and Young Children, 13*(4), 67–78.

Hanft, B., & Pilkington, K. (2000). Therapy in natural environments: The means or end goal for early intervention? *Infants and Young Children, 12*(4), 1–13.

Harlin, R. (2000). Developing reflection and teaching through peer coaching. *Focus on Teacher Education, 1*(1), 22–32.

Hasbrouck, J., & Christen, M. (1997). Providing peer coaching in inclusive classrooms: A tool for consulting teachers. *Intervention in School and Clinic, 32*(3), 72–77.

Hudson, F. (1999). *The handbook of coaching: A comprehensive resource guide for managers, executives, consultants and human resource professionals.* San Francisco: Jossey-Bass.

Joyce, B., & Showers, J. (1981). Transfer of training: The contribution of coaching. *Boston University Journal of Education, 16*(3), 163–172.

Joyce, B., & Showers, J. (1982). The coaching of teaching. *Educational Leadership, 40,* 4–10.

Knowles, M. (1980). *The modern practice of adult education: From pedagogy to andragony.* Chicago: Associated Press/Follett.

Knowles, M. (1996). Adult learning. In R. Craig (Ed.), *Training and development: A guide to human resource development.* New York: McGraw Hill.

Kohler, F., Crilley, K., Shearer, D., & Good, G. (1997). Effects of peer coaching on teacher and student outcomes. *Journal of Educational Research, 90,* 240–250.

Lazare, A. (1973). Hidden conceptual models in clinical psychiatry. *The New England Journal of Medicine, 288*(7), 345–351.

Mattingly, C., & Fleming, M. (1994). *Clinical reasoning: Forms of inquiry in a therapeutic practice.* Philadelphia: F.A. Davis.

Mello, L. (1984). *Peer-centered coaching: Teachers helping teachers to improve classroom performance.* Indian Springs, CO: Associates for Human Development. (ERIC Document Reproduction Service No. ED274648)

Mid-Continent Regional Educational Laboratory. (1983). *Coaching: A powerful strategy in improving staff development and inservice education.* Kansas City: Author.

Miller, S. (1994). Peer coaching within an early childhood interdisciplinary setting. *Intervention in School and Clinic, 30,* 109–113.

Moore, J.R. (1988). Guidelines concerning adult learning. *Journal of Staff Development, 9*(3), 1–4.

Morgan, R., Gustafson, K., Hudson, P., & Salzberg, C. (1992). Peer coaching in a preservice special education program. *Teacher Education and Special Education, 12,* 249–258.

Phillips, M., & Glickman, C. (1991). Peer coaching: Developmental approach to enhancing teacher thinking. *Journal of Staff Development, 12*(2), 20–25.

Pugach, M., & Johnson, L. (1995). Unlocking expertise among classroom teachers through structured dialogue: Extending research on peer collaboration. *Exceptional Children, 62*(2), 101–110.

Robbins, P. (1991). *How to plan and implement a peer coaching program.* Alexandria, VA: Association for Supervision and Curriculum Development.

Roberts, J. (1991). Improving principals' instructional leadership through peer coaching. *Journal of Staff Development, 12*(4), 30–33.

Schon, D. (1983). *The reflective practitioner: How professionals think in action.* New York: Basic Books.

Schon, D. (1987). *Educating the reflective practitioner.* San Francisco: Jossey-Bass.

Showers, B. (1985). Teachers coaching teachers. *Educational Leadership, 42,* 43–48.

Sparks-Langer, G., & Colton, A. (1991). Synthesis of research on teachers' reflective thinking. *Educational Leadership, 48*(6), 37–44.

Thompson, J. (1995). *Positive coaching: Building character and self esteem through sports.* Portola Valley, CA: Warde Publishers.

3

THE COACHING PROCESS

Coaching is a *mutual conversation* between two individuals who each have information to share and skills to gain from interacting with each other (Kinlaw, 1999). The coach has knowledge and skills to share about child growth and development, specific intervention strategies, and enhancing the performance of young children with disabilities. The family or other caregivers have intimate knowledge of a child's abilities, challenges, and typical performance in a given situation. In addition, parents have knowledge of their child's and family's daily routines and environments, lifestyle, family culture, and ideas about desirable goals for themselves and their child. A colleague assumes the role of learner in peer coaching and has knowledge and skills from his or her experience in supporting families of young children.

Through coaching, the learner, whether family or colleague, may gain insight regarding child behavior and adult–child interaction as well as new or expanded skills in promoting child performance and behavior. One size does not fit all, however. A strategy that may work for one family member, child care provider, or early childhood practitioner may need to be completely revised for the next.

GOALS OF COACHING IN EARLY INTERVENTION

Two primary goals guide all coaching sessions in early childhood intervention: 1) to support learners in recognizing what they are already doing that promotes learning for a child and 2) to assist learners in creating ongoing learning opportunities for the child when the coach is not present. The goals of the coaching process should be finite; achievable; and, obviously, desired by the learner rather than imposed by the coach. Not only must the skills that are to be mastered by the learner be specified, but the strategies for achieving them must also be clearly understood. The coach and learner mutually agree on criteria during the first component (initiation) of the coaching process that can be used for measuring the

TRY THIS . . .

Opportunities for coaching other team members

The next time one of the following situations comes up, think about how you could use coaching strategies when a friend, family member, or colleague

• Requests assistance

• Wants to learn a new skill

• Desires help in solving a problem

• Asks for encouragement

• Desires a new challenge

learner's mastery of new skills leading to a change in a child's performance.

WHEN DO YOU COACH?

Every conversation with parents, other caregivers, or colleagues is a potential opportunity for coaching. Parents whose children participate in an early childhood program may themselves have coaching conversations with early childhood practitioners about supports to assist them in caring for their young child (McWilliam & Scott, 2001). All coaching interactions with family members should acknowledge existing interests and strengths of the child and offer supports to key caregivers. As trust, respect, and good communication develop between the practitioner and caregiver, individual coaching conversations will include more specific requests and recommendations for information and support. Examples of topics include, but are not limited to, strategies for helping a child move from tube to oral feedings, developing a plan for a family to take their child to a family reunion, helping a child care provider include a child with physical disabilities in circle time, or linking families whose children are the same age.

Opportunities for coaching colleagues include requesting assistance, wanting to learn a new skill, desiring help in solving a problem, needing encouragement, or desiring new challenges. Coaching may occur during co-visits, team meetings, or one-to-one conversations. Coaching is a useful strategy for building the capacity of all team members and promoting effective teaming.

Coaching may be planned or occur spontaneously. Planned coaching sessions with the family or child caregivers generally occur during a scheduled visit. During this time, the coach and learner use coaching to discuss actions that occurred since the last visit, reflect, and try new ideas and activities to support the child's participation and development in family, community, and early childhood activity settings.

Planned coaching sessions may also take place with colleagues, commonly known as peer coaching (discussed in detail in Chapter 7). In peer coaching, the coach and learner schedule regular conversations for reflection and discussion. The coach and colleague-as-learner may also schedule visits with families and caregivers, during which time the coach may observe the learner, then provide an opportunity for reflection and feedback at a later time.

Spontaneous coaching most often occurs with colleagues. A person experiences a challenging situation or wants to learn a new skill and approaches another colleague who could serve as a coach, or a colleague with expertise in an area invites another colleague to participate in a coaching conversation. Some examples of opportunities for spontaneous coaching conversations include hearing a colleague express frustration regarding failure in achieving the intended outcome of a home visit or receiving a particular question or request for support in learning a new skill. Chapter 7 explores this topic in greater depth and provides specialized case examples of spontaneous coaching with colleagues.

COACHING PROCESS

Coaching requires a "specialized set of learned skills" to assist in "developing people on purpose" (Doyle, 1999, p. 4). Whereas Chapter 4 describes the general skills necessary for coaches to be effective, this discussion outlines coaching skills as they relate to the specific components of the coaching process. The five components of the coaching process include 1) initiation, 2) observation, 3) action, 4) reflection, and 5) evaluation.

As seen in Figure 3.1, coaching is a not a linear process. Each situation determines the order in which the coaching components unfold; however, during the coaching relationship, the coach and learner will move through each of the components. Observation, action, and reflection—shown as the three interlocking rings of the coaching diagram—are the critical links to self-discovery and personal development of the learner. They are bounded like bookends by the components of initiation and evaluation. Throughout the coaching relationship and even specific coaching conversations, the coach and learner are likely to move in and out of these components a number of times. Figure 3.2 outlines the coaching process and provides key considerations in order for coaches to meet the jointly developed goals of the coaching relationship. This figure also provides sample questions and activities that may be used by the coach at each component in the coaching process.

Initiation

During the initiation component of the coaching process, either the coach identifies an opportunity for coaching and invites the learner into a coaching relationship, or the learner seeks the experience of the coach and opens the door for a coaching conversation. Initiation can either be planned or spontaneous.

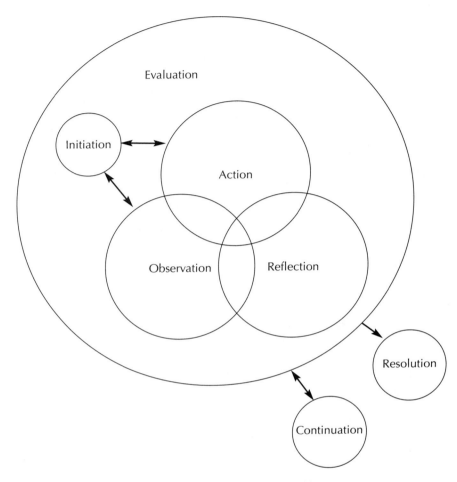

Figure 3.1.   The coaching process. (From Rush, D.D., Shelden, M.L., & Hanft, B.E. [2003]. Coaching families and colleagues: A process for collaboration in natural settings. *Infants and Young Children, 16*[1], 40; adapted by permission.)

Planned Initiation

In a planned coaching relationship, the coach and learner jointly develop a plan that includes the purpose and specific learner outcomes of the coaching process. For example, the purpose of most coaching with families and caregivers is to support the child's participation and development in ordinary family and community life. The short-term outcomes of coaching families are typically the goals on the individualized family service plan (IFSP) or IEP, whereas the intended long-term outcome is an

Initiation	
Coach focuses on learner's goals by helping	*Examples of questions to ask*
• Specify relationship between coach and learner, especially focusing on the learner's priorities • Clarify child's and/or coaching partner's abilities and desired outcomes • Pair developmental outcomes to particular intervention strategies • Determine evidence for child's and/or learner's progress	• What would help you (in your role as parent, teacher, physical therapist, etc.)? • What supports would be helpful for you/your child? • What have you thought about doing (or tried)? • What will indicate to you that your child is learning this?

Observation and action	
Coach gathers data by soliciting information about	*Coach may use*
• Child development and behavior • Learner's interactions, strategies, and decisions	• First-hand observation, audiotapes, video-tapes, and progress reports • Storytelling, dialogue, and interviews • Demonstration, guided practice, modeling

Reflection	
Coach enhances learner's perception and actions by helping	*Questions to ask*
• Summarize impressions of actions/events • Compare planned-for and obtained results • Analyze relationships between child behavior and learner decisions/behavior • Apply new information and reflect on coaching process	• What happened when you...? • What did you do to influence what happened? How is this different? • What changes would you make, if any, the next time? • What have you learned from this process?

Evaluation	
Coach reviews the effectiveness of the coaching sessions, either alone or with the learner to	*Questions to ask*
• Review the strengths and weaknesses of the coaching session • Analyze the effectiveness of the coaching relationship • Determine whether progress is being made to achieve intended outcomes, resulting in continuation or resolution of the coaching process	• Do I need to make any changes in the coaching process? • Am I assisting the learner to achieve the intended outcomes? • Should I continue as the coach, or will another teammate have the specialized experience/skills needed at this time?

Figure 3.2. Coaching tasks and questions to support learners and ensure positive outcomes for children. (From Rush, D.D., Shelden, M.L., & Hanft, B.E. [2003]. Coaching families and colleagues: A process for collaboration in natural settings. *Infants and Young Children, 16*[1], 41; reprinted by permission.)

ongoing ability on the part of the child's family members and other caregivers to support the child across activity settings and natural learning environments.

Consider a sample script for a coach to initiate a planned coaching relationship with a family member

"You've requested early intervention services from our local program. I'm looking forward to getting to know you and your family better. My role is similar to a coach. I'll be here to support you, your family, and other important people in your child's life. Together, we will focus on your priorities and your child's interests to come up with ways for supporting and increasing your child's participation in family and community life. My goal is to assist *you* in helping your child learn and grow. I need to spend some time getting to know you and your family so I know what is important to you, what you like and need to do, and how you prefer to spend your time. You know more than I could ever hope to know about your child and family. Also, you and the other important people in your child's life spend more time with him than I ever could. So, my intent is for us to pinpoint what you're already doing that promotes learning and work together to find ways to do this even more. We'll also work to overcome any challenges you may be experiencing."

Spontaneous Initiation

Some coaching may occur spontaneously. An effective coach recognizes serendipitous opportunities for initiating a coaching conversation. A coach could say, "When [describe situation], I noticed [state observation]. Is that accurate? [If so] I'd like to take a few minutes to talk about [situation]. Is now a good time?"

Following is a sample script for initiating a spontaneous coaching conversation with a colleague.

Coach:	When we were at the Do's home yesterday for Phu's evaluation, I noticed that you seemed to be uncomfortable with the interpreter sharing the evaluation results. Is that an accurate assessment?
Colleague:	You're right. I always worry that the interpreter may not share everything I'm trying to say to the parents.
Coach:	I'd be happy to take a few minutes for us to share our experiences in using interpreters. Is now a good time?

After the coach assists the learner in selecting goals as part of their planned coaching relationship, the coach and learner clarify ground rules, such as confidentiality or time constraints. During the initiation component, the coach also may obtain information about current child and family activities, existing supports, and intervention strategies used by caregivers. To conclude the initiation component, the coach and learner identify and resolve any barriers that may impede the coach-

REMEMBER THIS . . .
Coach's key considerations prior to the initiation component

Begin to reflect on and gather this information prior to initiating a formal coaching relationship. Answers to some of the questions may become clearer during the initiation component. (Doyle, 1999; Schon, 1987)

- Who is the learner?
- What do I know about this person?
- How does this person's behavior, knowledge, or practice compare to the research in this area (i.e., what we know about child learning and development) and our program's guiding principles, values, and beliefs?
- What is the learner's current level of competence and confidence?
- What are the desired outcomes of the coaching process?

---

ing process (Kinlaw, 1999). Barriers may include a lack of communication, commitment, time, trust, and respect between the coach and learner, as well as cultural considerations, such as the need for an interpreter, that must be addressed.

In preparation for a planned coaching relationship or opportunity, the coach should consider a few key questions prior to the initiation component. If, however, the coach is seizing an unexpected moment as an opportunity for learning and self-discovery for the learner, he or she may already know the answers to these key questions based on an ongoing relationship or previous conversations.

The following coaching story illustrates a spontaneously initiated coaching conversation between two colleagues, Jack and Doris, after Doris overheard Jack's phone conversation with a family while working at her desk in the office they share.

"Jack, I couldn't help but hear your end of the telephone conversation with Sienna's family. You sounded frustrated," stated Doris. *(Observation)*

"You're right. The last three times I've been scheduled to go on a home visit, no one has answered the door. I don't know why I bother. They never follow through on any of the homework I give them anyway," Jack responded.

Doris sensed the frustration building in Jack's voice. "You know, this has happened to me, too. Would you be interested in talking more about what to do when scheduled visits don't occur?" *(Initiation)*

"Sure. I guess it couldn't hurt."

"Is now a good time? Or would you like to schedule another time that would be more convenient?"

"Now is fine."

"Okay then, let me start by saying that what we talk about is confidential. I won't share what we discuss with other team members. Let's take about 20 minutes to think through this situation and, if we both feel we need more time, we can schedule it for later in the week." *(Initiation)*

"Sounds good."

"First, have you shared your concerns with the family or thought about reasons why they might not be home when you are scheduled to visit?" Doris asked.

Note how after spontaneously initiating a coaching conversation with Jack, Doris clarified the ground rules of confidentiality and time parameters, then moved the conversation to the reflection component of the coaching process. Doris used the *observation* phase when she noticed Jack's frustration, precipitating invitation for coaching. She employed the *initiation* phase when she invited Jack into a coaching conversation. She also used the *initiation* phase to establish ground rules for the coaching relationship.

Observation

Depending on the situation, the coach may facilitate the use of any of four different types of observations within this component of the coaching process:

1. Coach observes the learner in some type of action or practice

2. Learner observes the coach modeling some type of action or activity

3. Learner observes him- or herself (self-observation)

4. Coach and/or learner observe aspects of the environment (ecological assessment)

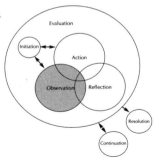

Coach Observes the Learner in Some Type of Action or Practice

The coach may observe the learner using an existing skill or practicing a new skill that was just discussed or that the learner had been trying between coaching visits. On occasion, the coach may observe the learner demonstrate knowledge and understanding of a skill as part of a coaching conversation rather than direct observation of the learner's use of the skill in the context of a real-life activity. For example, the coach and a parent may practice how to coach the child care provider on ways to support the child during mealtime. The coach may also observe the learner during an unplanned activity and use this as an opening to then initiate a spontaneous coaching conversation. The observation component may be used as well when the learner wants to share a particular challenge with the coach; therefore, the coach observes the particular difficulty prior to further discussion.

As an example, a father wanted his coach to observe how he followed his child's lead while they read a book together and how he encouraged the child's attempts to use words during this activity. The coach also observed the father naming pictures and asking the child specific questions such as, "What color is the leaf?" The coach used these observations to reinforce what the father was already doing well. In addition, the coach can make other unintended observations that can be informative for the learner, such as allowing the child to turn the pages of the book. The purpose of these observations is to assist in building the learner's competence and confidence in using a skill or information when the coach is not present.

Learner Observes the Coach Modeling Some Type of Action or Activity

The observation component may also be used as an opportunity for the learner to observe the coach demonstrate or model a particular skill, technique, or strategy prior to using it him- or herself. This action by the coach and observation by the learner, depicted in Figure 3.1 in the overlap between observation and action, allows the learner to see the skill or strategy as modeled by the coach, then reflect on how the task might need to be adjusted for him- or herself, another adult, or the child. For instance, consider a family who has just received a new wheelchair for their daughter. With family members observing, the coach might demonstrate how to position the 2-year-old in the chair and adjust the straps. Then, the coach could observe the family positioning their child in the new chair.

Learner Observes Him- or Herself

One of the goals of the coaching process is for the learner to use self-assessment in order to revise and refine his or her skills. Through self-observation, the learner consciously observes him- or herself during an activity or situation by thinking about personal behaviors that could promote his or her learning or another adult's or child's learning. The learner then uses these observations and the self-assessment to initiate new ways of doing things or revise previously used strategies. Consider an occasion when a coach is working with another colleague on using a family-centered process for gathering information from families during an initial conversation. The coach may ask the learner to observe the families' reactions to the questions and gauge the usefulness of each question. In the coaching diagram in Figure 3.1, self-observation is the overlap between observation and reflection.

Coach and/or Learner
Observe Aspects of the Environment

Because the learner may want or need to make modifications to an environment and/or the behavior of people within the environment in order to enhance child learning, observation of the environment by the coach and learner may be a useful activity. Think about a situation in which a child care director is considering asking a family to find alternative child care for their daughter, Maya. The child care director wants to know how to include Maya in routines and activities at the center because Maya moves quickly from one activity to another, strikes out at the other children, and tries to run out the door if it is left open. The coach and child care director decide to spend some time observing Maya's classroom to consider how Maya's interests and assets are being matched to activities available within the classroom. As a result of their observations and discussion with the teacher, the director realizes Maya's interests, such as her love for animals, have not been considered as a way to engage her in classroom activities and interaction with the other children.

Action

Actions are events or experiences that are planned or spontaneous; occur in the context of a real-life activity or are practiced first in a simulated situation; and may take place when the coach is or is not present. At least four different types of actions could occur during this component of the coaching process. The coach may *model* a skill or strategy for the learner as part of a coaching opportunity, or the learner may *practice* a new skill or strategy that was discussed during a previous coaching conversation, *experience* a situation to discuss with the coach during an upcoming conversation, or *anticipate* how to handle a future event.

Modeling

Modeling is an action depicted in Figure 3.1 as the area of overlap between the observation and action components of the coaching process. Modeling may occur as part of the observation and/or action components. The coach and learner may decide that an effective method for learning is for the coach to demonstrate or model a particular technique, skill, or strategy while the learner observes the coach in action (Joyce & Showers, 1995). In this way, the coach and learner may find it beneficial for the coach to use hands-on strategies with the child or another adult in the context of a real-life activity as a frame of reference for the learner. Following demonstration by the coach, the learner and coach discuss the actions that were demonstrated. The coach then invites the learner to practice the strategy while the coach is present. If the learner believes that the strategy is less than effective, the coach and learner work together to generate alternative ideas. Once the coach and learner are comfortable with the actions to be taken, the learner practices the strategy as part of daily activities when the coach is not present.

Evaluation
Initiation
Action
Observation
Reflection
Resolution
Continuation

For example, a grandmother wants to prevent her grandson, Malachi, from sliding out of his highchair during mealtimes. The coach and grandmother have explored what she has already tried for keeping Malachi in the highchair (i.e., towel rolls, Grandpa's belt as a restraint, duct tape on the seat of his pants). The grandmother shared that Grandpa's belt actually worked fairly well, but seemed to ride up too high on Malachi's chest, which caused him to fuss and not want to eat. With the grandmother's consent, the coach sat Malachi in the highchair and placed Grandpa's belt around his waist. The coach pointed out to the grandmother that when Malachi kicked his legs, his bottom would slide forward in the chair and the belt would ride up under his arms.

The coach removed Grandpa's belt from around Malachi's waist, scooted his bottom to the back of the highchair seat, and wrapped the belt under the seat of the highchair across Malachi's lap similar to a seat belt in a car. The grandmother and coach decided that Malachi seemed comfortable and happy with this new arrangement. The coach drew the grandmother's attention to how Malachi was positioned in the highchair and explained the importance of having his bottom against the back of the seat to promote better sitting posture and balance and make it easier for him to remain upright in the highchair. The grandmother noted how well he looked, then took Malachi out of the chair so he could play on the floor. Before the coach left, the grandmother demonstrated sitting Malachi in the highchair with his bottom to the back of the seat and the strap across his lap. The grandmother agreed to try using the "seat belt" for the next week and also told the coach that she would try a similar strategy in the grocery store with the shopping cart with his bottom scooted all the way to the back of the seat.

Practice

Practice may occur during a coaching conversation when the coach is present (as noted with Malachi's grandmother) or between conversations when the coach is absent. During a coaching conversation, the learner may use an existing strategy or practice a new technique or behavior followed by reflection by the learner and feedback from the coach. As part of the coaching conversation with the caregiver, the coach and learner plan how any new strategies can be used to increase and support the child's participation in family, community, or early childhood activity settings (Bruder & Dunst, 1999/2000).

During the coaching visit, whenever possible, practice by the learner should occur as part of a typical activity or event. For example, if the caregiver wants to promote positive behavior of his or her child in the grocery store, the coach and caregiver may discuss options and ideas before going to the store, and the coach may arrange to join the caregiver at the grocery store as he or she practices this new skill. In another example, if a parent wants the child to join the family during mealtime, the coach would make an effort to be present with the family at lunch while the parent practices supporting the child's use of words to request desired food at the table.

In some instances, practice between the coach and adult learner may occur in simulated situations. For example, the coach may role-play with a colleague how to introduce the concept of coaching to a family that has just entered the early intervention program prior to the colleague actually practicing this with the family. This simulated situation may then be followed by an occasion that would allow for direct observation of the learner's practice of the targeted skill by the coach. In this way, the coach can better promote reflection and provide feedback on the learner's use of the skills. Actions that occur *between* coaching conversations when the coach is not directly observing the action of the learner are shared by the learner during follow-up conversations.

Practice opportunities may also be planned or spontaneous. Typically, practice within the coaching visit or conversation is planned as the coach and learner identify opportunities during the visit in which the learner can practice the targeted skills. Practice between coaching visits when the coach is not present may include planned opportunities discussed between the coach and learner as well as spontaneous opportunities in which the learner recognizes a chance to use the new skill.

For example, a parent expresses interest in her child actively participating in washing the dishes after mealtime. During the coaching session, the mother demonstrates how they currently wash dishes. The coach explores with her what previous strategies she has used to engage the child in using the sponge to clean the dirty dishes. The coach and the mother decide that over the next week, the mother will practice the strategies they discussed by verbally prompting her daughter to use the sponge to wash plates and cups and gently remind her as necessary to try to keep the water in the sink. The mother will also label each dish as her daughter washes it, and they will take turns naming the next dish she will wash. During the follow-up coaching session, the parent describes the results of practicing these actions.

Experience

Coaching may be initiated after a learner experiences a situation that prompts a desire for coaching. As a part of the coaching conversation, the learner shares an experience that occurred prior to seeing the coach. Based on this situation, the coach and learner move directly to the reflection component of the coaching process. An example of an experience that leads to the coaching conversation might be when a father becomes frustrated during a shopping trip at the grocery store. When his daughter is not allowed to have candy while waiting in the checkout line, she falls on the floor crying, kicking, and screaming. In an attempt to control his daughter's behavior, and out of desperation, the father gives her the candy. Recognizing this is not a behavior that he wants to encourage in his child, the father brings this action to the coaching session for joint problem solving.

> **REFLECT ON THIS . . .**
> **Open-ended questions**
>
> "Telling or asking closed questions saves people from having to think. Asking open questions causes them to think for themselves" (Whitmore, 1996, p. 39). Observe yourself or another person for a day, and note the use of closed and open-ended questions and whether they expand or limit the conversation.

Anticipation

If the learner anticipates an event or situation that causes him or her to question his or her judgment, confidence, and/or competence in a specific area, the learner may request support related to this potential action either within the context of an ongoing or a new coaching conversation. Once the learner brings this situation or question to the coach, they begin to reflect on the anticipated action. To illustrate this situation, consider a mother preparing for the arrival of her mother-in-law for a 2-week stay in the family home. Based on her previous experiences, the mother anticipates that her mother-in-law will insist that her grandchild is not receiving enough therapy. Although the mother believes that the role of the early intervention program is to support her and her husband in improving their son's participation in family life, she's worried that she will have difficulty explaining this to her mother-in-law (anticipated action). During the next visit with her coach, the mother will ask the coach for support.

An example of discussing an anticipated action with a colleague during a coaching conversation is a situation illustrated by June, an audiologist, who anticipates talking with a mother about the results from a recent audiological evaluation that indicated her child has a significant hearing loss. When June approaches Allen, her colleague, about the situation, Allen asks June if they can set up a coaching conversation. June immediately agrees, and they decide to talk during lunch.

Reflection

Reflection, one of the most important components of the coaching process, differentiates coaching from typical problem solving and information sharing among practitioners, caregivers, and other team members (Fenichel, 1991; Gallacher, 1997). The reflection component consists of the following steps:

1. The coach asking the learner questions to cause him or her to think about his or her current and/or desired knowledge, experience, or practice

2. Feedback by the coach on the learner's use of a targeted skill or practice

3. New information to the learner

4. Acknowledgment and affirmation of what the learner is doing, learning, or already knows

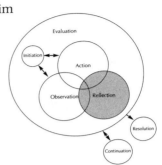

The goal of this component is to promote continuous improvement by assisting the learner to analyze his or her practices and behavior through the use of a reflective discussion between the coach and learner (Gallacher, 1997). As illustrated in Figure 3.1 and depicted by the overlaps between the three circles, during this component of the process, the learner reflects on observations and actions. The intent of this reflective discussion is for the learner to discover what he or she may already know or be doing, to identify what he or she may need to know or do, then to make any necessary or desired changes. Ultimately, the outcome of the coaching process and more specifically, reflection, should be to build the capacity of the learner to self-assess, self-correct, and generalize to other situations.

As discussed in Chapter 2, Schon (1987) described this reasoning process as reflection-on-action. During the discussion, the coach explores what the learner already knows, is doing, has tried, and thinks about a specific situation or need. Through a process of questioning and active listening, the coach supports the learner in comparing his or her actions and observations to characteristics of effective practice, research findings, program models, or core values and beliefs. As part of this process, the learner discovers existing strategies and potential ideas to build on current strengths to address identified questions, priorities, and interests.

During the reflection component, the coach must ask the right questions, at the right time, and in the right way (Kinlaw, 1999). Questions should be open, rather than closed.

Questions may be objective, comparative, or interpretive. *Objective* questions begin with "what," "when," "where," "who," or "how." *Comparative* questions help clarify the learner's past experiences and current experience, such as "How does what happened compare to what you would have liked to see happen?" *Interpretive* questions seek the learner's impression of a given situation and ask the coaching partner to make a decision about what to do next. The coach should avoid the use of "why" questions as they tend to lay blame or make the learner feel as if he or she did something incorrectly.

Another way of thinking about the types of questions that can be asked during the reflection component of the coaching process is described by Whitmore (1996), who suggests a sequence of questions that can be grouped into four cate-

REMEMBER THIS...
Asking reflective questions

The following are examples of objective questions:

- What did you want to have happen?
- What are you doing now?
- What's happening now?
- What have you tried?
- When does this behavior occur?
- Who is involved?
- What evidence do you have from research to support your ideas about how you are going to change or modify your practices?

The following are examples of comparative questions:

- How does this compare to what we know about _____ ?
- Tell me about a time when...
- Based on what you know now, what would you do differently next time?
- How does this relate to our program principles?

The following are examples of interpretive questions:

- What does it mean when he...?
- What would you do if...?
- When are you going to...?

---

gories using the acronym GROW. *Goal-oriented questions* focus on identifying what happened during the observation component and what was intended or anticipated during the action component. *Reality questions* seek to identify objective statements that define the current situation and thinking of the learner. These questions assist in exploring how the learner thinks and feels about a situation. *Option questions* promote creative exploration of many possible alternatives. They should challenge the learner to think beyond standard solutions or realize new and different possibilities. The question *"Who is going to do what by when?"* assists the learner in considering a plan of action and prioritizing possible solutions.

The following coaching story on reflecting with family members illustrates how Jennifer, an occupational therapist with the local early intervention program, uses reflection as part of a coaching conversation with Lani's parents, Brian and Laura. Brian and Laura were interested in helping their 2-year-old, Lani, learn to walk. Lani did not want to use her walker and preferred to scoot around on the floor. The action planned between coaching visits was for Brian and Laura not to place Lani's toys on the floor.

Jennifer began by inviting Brian and Laura to reflect with her on what was discussed during the last coaching visit. Then, she asked them to reflect on the success of the practice and actions between coaching visits.

"Last time, we discussed a plan to place Lani's toys up off the floor so she might use her walker more frequently to stand and reach for them," Jennifer said. "Tell me how that worked."

"Oh, it worked great here at home," replied Brian. "Once Lani realized she needed to stand to reach her toys, she grabbed the walker and has used it ever since."

Laura interjected, "It didn't work at my mom's house. She said she thought it was a cruel thing to do and that she shouldn't have to work so hard just to get to play with her toys."

"What did you say to your mom?" Jennifer asked. *(probing for further explanation)*

"I tried to explain that Lani needed a reason to use her walker and, since she really likes her toys, she was motivated to stand and get them," shared Laura.

"What did your mom say then?"

"She said that she understood that but that at Grandma's house she was going to have fun."

"So, tell me how much time she spends at your mother's house," asked Jennifer. *(asking open-ended questions)*

"Well, beginning Monday, she'll be staying with her 3 days each week because I'm starting a part-time job."

Lani had been playing quietly on the floor during the conversation. Brian watched Lani as she crawled to her walker and prepared to use it to pull herself up. Brian positioned himself near Lani so that he could steady the walker if needed. Brian looked toward Laura and Jennifer. "I think Lani's been making quite a bit of progress in this area, and I want to see her challenged to continue to use the walker."

Laura smiled as she watched Brian helping Lani. "We have to help Mom see that using this walker can help Lani have more fun."

"Right," nodded Brian.

"What ideas do you have about how she could still have fun and use her walker while at your mom's house?" Jennifer asked. *(exploring learner's ideas)*

"What if we asked again about putting toys up high but we kept some on the floor? That way, she would have access to some toys without the walker but would need it to get to some of the very special toys?" Laura suggested.

"We're going over to your mom's for lunch on Sunday," Brian said. "Let's take some of her favorite toys with us and show your mom what we mean. That way, we can be there to support her if it doesn't go well." Brian initiated a planned action to occur between coaching visits as part of his reflection on this issue.

"We could even make it like a game and maybe give Mom some new ideas for playing with Lani!" Laura exclaimed as she added to their plan.

Jennifer nodded in agreement. She was delighted in Brian and Laura's self-discoveries of ideas to try with Laura's mom. "This sounds like a great plan. Let me know how it goes next week."

In this scenario, Jennifer used reflection to assist Brian and Laura in developing a plan for getting Laura's mother to promote Lani's independence through use of the walker by building on what they already know motivates Lani and gets her to use the walker. Notice how first Jennifer probed to encourage Brian and Laura to explain further about what happened at Laura's mother's house. Then, she asked open-ended questions to learn about the amount of time Lani spends with her grandmother. The information she learned was useful as Brian and Laura discussed their options for involving the grandmother. Jennifer sought to have Laura and Brian identify possible strategies to ensure their outcomes for Lani could be achieved at Laura's mother's home because Laura's mother would soon become a primary caregiver. Finally, Jennifer explored with Brian and Laura their ideas about what to do.

The next coaching story shows how Harriet, an occupational therapist on the team, uses reflection with her colleague, Sabrina, a physical therapist, during a spontaneous coaching opportunity.

Sabrina visited Shaundra's family once every other week as part of the early intervention program. Sabrina wanted to ask Harriet if she could see Shaundra on the weeks Sabrina isn't there to give Shaundra more practice on feeding skills.

Grabbing a cup of coffee before the weekly staff meeting, Sabrina turned to Harriet and said, "Harriet, I think Shaundra needs more practice on her self-feeding skills. I'm only seeing her two times each month. If you could go on my off weeks, she will be seen at least once each week. I try to make time for working on feeding, but just don't think I'm doing it justice."

"I appreciate your awareness of Shaundra's feeding skills," Harriet replied. "I know that Shaundra's family included her participation in mealtime as one of the IFSP goals. What ideas have you shared with them about how to support Shaundra in learning to feed herself?" (*acknowledging concerns, encouraging reflection*)

"Oh, I've been so focused on other things that I've not really talked with them much about it until they mentioned that their family mealtime was a big part of their day and they really wanted Shaundra to participate," Sabrina answered.

"What's happening now during mealtime?" (*asking open-ended questions*)

"As a matter of fact, I don't really know," Sabrina said with a look of dismay.

"What are some strategies you could use to find out more information?" (*encouraging reflection and planning*)

"I guess I could ask the family the same question you asked me about what's currently happening during mealtime," responded Sabrina.

"What else?"

"I could offer to observe a mealtime so I could be more helpful," Sabrina said. "Then, why don't I come back and share my observations, what the family has been doing, and the new ideas that I talk about with the family with you? After that, if I need more support, I'll have you join me for a co-visit, and you can help us with some ideas. Would you be willing to continue this conversation?"

"Sure. In fact, let's go ahead and schedule another time to talk," Harriet replied as she headed to get her calendar.

In this situation, Harriet could easily have agreed to go visit Shaundra and her family to explore mealtime activities; however, Harriet supported Sabrina in thinking through this situation by reflecting on what she could do to gather more information. Notice how Harriet responded by first acknowledging Sabrina's concern; then, she shifted the focus to supporting the family rather than doing some type of feeding therapy with Shaundra. At the same time, Harriet asked Sabrina to reflect on what she may have already done in this regard. Then, Harriet probed again with an open-ended question. Finally, she pushed for further reflection and planning by Sabrina.

Feedback

Once the coach has supported the learner in exploring his or her knowledge, skills, and experience regarding the topic of the coaching conversation, the coach may facilitate additional reflection and discussion by providing feedback on the observation or practice. Feedback can be useful to provide new insights to the learner regarding use of a targeted skill or practice. Feedback should always follow reflection by the learner as the coach's intent is to learn what the coaching partner's insights, ideas, and reflections are before the coach provides his or her own. In the ideal coaching conversation, self-discovery on the part of the learner would address any and all points a coach might have intended to make as part of his or her feedback. If, however, feedback from the coach would be useful for the learner, the feedback should be specific and focus on only one observation, issue, or challenge at a time. The coach shares the feedback concretely rather than in general terms.

Feedback should be clear and provided in such a way that the learner knows exactly what the coach means. The coach leaves no room for confusion with other issues. Feedback must also be concise, with the coach using as few words as possible and only sharing necessary information. Also, feedback should be shared in a timely manner or as soon after the observation as possible. Finally, feedback should be sincere. Sincerity promotes trust, respect, and open communication. Feedback is not criticism. Whereas criticism tends to lay blame and focus on the negative, feedback is used to provide support in a positive and constructive manner.

The following coaching story explores providing feedback to a colleague. Bonita and Andy, colleagues from the early intervention program, are driving back to the office following their visit with Paulette and her nephew, Paschal, who they met for a scheduled visit at the neighborhood park. Andy had asked Bonita to coach him regarding ways to promote a parent's or caregiver's involvement in activities that were initiated and found interesting by the child rather than those that the caregiver initiated and tried to engage the child in doing. As a result of this request, Bonita joined Andy to observe him during this visit.

"When we were at the park with Paschal and his aunt," Bonita began. "I noticed that when you saw Paschal struggling to reach the bucket and shovel, you told Paulette to label what Paschal wanted by saying 'bucket,' then to wait for him to respond. You didn't just jump into Paulette's and Paschal's activity; rather, you provided a suggestion for Paulette. That's one strategy. Is there anything else you could have done in that situation?" (*encouraging reflection*)

Andy thought for a moment, then responded, "I could have waited longer to see what Paschal's aunt would do."

"That sounds like a good idea. What else?"

"I guess I could have observed to get additional information," Andy said, "or I could have done what I did, which was to tell Paulette what to do instead of just doing it myself. I don't really know what else."

"What about if next time you try asking Paulette what she could do to encourage Paschal to make a sound or use a word?" Bonita suggested. "That way, you could provide Paulette with an opportunity to demonstrate what she already knows or allow her to try a new strategy. Afterwards, you could provide feedback and additional information."

Andy frowned. "But, what if she doesn't have any good ideas or just sits there with a blank look on her face?"

"What would make you think an idea isn't good?" Bonita asked.

"Well, if I know it won't work," Andy replied.

"Hmm," Bonita said, thinking to herself. "Our program principles are based on the use of family-centered practices. How do you think those principles could be applied to this situation?" (*asking open-ended questions*)

"I don't know," Andy said. "What do you think?"

"Well," Bonita said. "In this situation, our practices would focus on supporting the caregiver in generating ideas. Our role would be to assist her in using or developing the skills to come up with ideas on her own. She could use these ideas when we aren't around. We would continue to ask her about her ideas or we would expand on the ideas she suggests."

"I guess," Andy said, "but like I said, what if she doesn't have any good ideas?"

Bonita frowned and said, "I'm a little concerned about what sounds like an assumption on your part that her ideas are not 'good' ones. Is it possible you're letting your personal beliefs or preferences interfere with your ability to support this parent? In our program, we believe that families are capable and competent participants in this process."

"Oh wow, I certainly would never want to give that impression!" Andy said. "I guess my comment does reflect my views about this parent. You're right, these views aren't consistent with our program principles." He paused for a moment and reflected. "I need to take some time to rethink this. I want to be sure that my choice of words and actions is consistent with this organization."

"Okay," Bonita said. "Let's follow up next week." (*scheduling follow-up*)

"I'd like that," Andy responded. "And thanks for your feedback."

In this coaching story, Bonita provided feedback based on her observations of Andy's practices. She sought his reflection on what occurred during the visit and shared additional information as appropriate. Bonita also provided immediate feedback on Andy's comments about the caregiver to cause him to reflect on how closely his words were aligned with the program's guiding principles. Bonita and Andy scheduled a follow-up meeting to continue discussing the feedback.

Sharing Information

Flaherty wrote that the coach's role is to "offer new ways of seeing the situation that can lead to more effective action" (1999, p. 110). After reflecting with the learner about his or her observations or actions and providing any necessary feedback, the coach may also share information. For a family member or child care provider, sharing information could include knowledge, skills, or resources that he or she may use to support the child in the context of family or community life or participation in an early childhood program. For a colleague, information shared could include knowledge, skills, or resources (human or material) to promote the colleague's ability to support child development. By sharing additional information, the coach must never devalue the learner's ideas or inhibit the learner's ability to self-assess, self-reflect, and generate new ideas on his or her own.

In the coaching story with Malachi, his grandmother, and the highchair, the coach engaged the grandmother in sharing information about strategies she had used to help Malachi sit in the highchair. The coach used the information shared by the grandmother as the foundation for an idea to modify placement of Grandpa's belt. The coach demonstrated how to scoot Malachi back in the highchair for more effective placement of the belt across his lap. In this coaching story, information sharing was reciprocal as the coach and grandmother both shared ideas to keep Malachi from sliding out of the highchair. Rather than creating a new seating system, the coach built on the grandmother's original idea. The grandmother even took an additional step of generalizing how she could use this strategy in other settings (i.e., the shopping cart at the grocery store).

Confirmation and Affirmation

Once the learner and coach have reflected on the observation or action and generated strategies for addressing the situation, the coach confirms the learner's accomplishments or perspectives by reviewing the discussion, observations, or actions. This review serves as a mechanism for assessing the understanding of the learner and checking for commitment to ongoing action. The coach affirms the learner throughout the coaching process by acknowledging his or her strengths, competence, and mastery of the skills practiced and information discussed. Through the use of confirmation and affirmation, the coach promotes ongoing competent performance of existing skills, as well as newly learned behaviors (Flaherty, 1999; Kinlaw, 1999).

In the coaching story of Brian and Laura, Jennifer provided affirmation to the couple by acknowledging that they had developed a good plan for supporting Laura's mother. Laura's mother, who was getting ready to become Lani's child care provider 3 days per week, indicated that her house was for Lani to have fun, not a place where she had to use the walker to try and reach her toys. Brian and Laura decided that they would support her mother's desire for Lani to have fun but still encourage Lani to use her walker to get around. Jennifer confirmed their thinking and planned to follow-up with them at their next visit.

Within a single coaching conversation, the learner and coach typically move from observation and/or action to reflection a number of times, as shown in Table 3.1. The coach, for example, may model a new technique, or the learner may practice an agreed-on method that the learner and coach reflected on and may reflect on again during a follow-up conversation. During another coaching conversation, the coach and learner may focus the reflection conversation on a situation that occurred between coaching sessions. Then, the learner could observe the coach model some strategies with the child followed by another reflection conversation.

> **REMEMBER THIS...**
> **Conclusion of reflection component**
>
> When concluding the reflection component of the coaching process:
> • Summarize the discussion
> • Review observations made during the coaching visit
> • Discuss observations that the learner could make between coaching conversations
> • Plan actions and/or practice opportunities to occur between coaching conversations
> • Affirm the learner's participation and skill development

EVALUATION OF THE COACHING PROCESS

The purpose of the evaluation component is to review the effectiveness of the coaching process, rather than evaluating the learner. For this reason, Figure 3.1 depicts the observation, action, and reflection components within the larger circle of the evaluation component. The coach should self-reflect as part of the coaching process evaluation after every coaching conversation regarding changes needed in the coaching process, continuing as the coach, and helping the learner progress toward the intended outcomes.

When the learner is present during evaluation of the coaching process, the coach should ask questions to obtain feedback from the learner regarding the strengths and weaknesses of the coaching process, effectiveness of the coaching relationship, and whether the process should continue or the intended outcomes

Table 3.1.   Examples of how coaching is not a linear process

Example 1

Observation	You hear a telephone conversation between a colleague and family. The family hasn't been home the last three times the colleague went for the home visit. The colleague is clearly frustrated when he finishes the call.
Initiation	You mention to the colleague that you heard the call and sense his frustration. When he agrees, you invite him into a coaching conversation.
Reflection	(*Probing*) You ask the colleague about his thoughts as to why the family may not be home for the visits and what he's done to ensure that the time is good for the family and that they really want him as a support. He shares his thoughts and what he's tried. You ask additional questions that lead to three new ideas that he would like to try.
Action	You role-play the conversation that he will have with the family.
Evaluation	(*Resolution—Plan*) Your colleague leaves with a plan. Although no further coaching conversations are anticipated, the colleague will share the outcomes of his conversation with the family with you.

Example 2

Initiation	A colleague comes to you and shares his frustration that a family hasn't been home the last three times he has tried to make a home visit.
Reflection	(*Probing*) You ask the colleague about his thoughts as to why the family may not be home for the visits and what he's done to ensure that the time is good for the family and that they really want him as a support. He shares his thoughts and what he's tried. You ask additional questions that lead to three new ideas that he would like to try.
Action	You role-play the conversation that he will have with the family.
Evaluation	(*Resolution—Plan*) Your colleague leaves with a plan. Although no further coaching conversations are anticipated, the colleague will share the outcomes of his conversation with the family with you.

Example 3

Initiation	You are going to serve as the primary coach for a family. You discuss any barriers to the coaching process and ground rules. Based on the individualized family service plan, the family identified some ways you could support them in promoting their child's development.
Reflection	The family tells you how they would like for their child to sit in the cart at the department store so that they can do their shopping and so that he can see what's going on around him. You ask what they've been doing and how well it's worked. You and the family brainstorm some ideas to try.
Action	You go with the father and child to the department store. The father practices putting the child in the seat of the cart and strapping him in as the two of you had discussed.
Observation	You observe how the father positions the child and notice that the child's bottom is not scooted all the way to the back of the seat.
Reflection	You ask the father how the child's position matches what the two of you had discussed. He shares his thoughts. You provide feedback on the position and suggest that he scoot the child's bottom to the back of the seat.
Observation	You observe how well the child sits in the seat and his ability to be actively engaged with his father and participate in the shopping trip.
Reflection	You ask the father how well he thought the shopping trip went and what caused him to think that. You ask him what, if anything, he might do differently next time. You ask the father how the cart seats at the grocery store are different and what he might need to do differently to position the child in the cart.
Evaluation	(*Continuation—Plan*) You and the father develop a plan that includes actions and practice that will occur during shopping trips until your next coaching conversation.

Example 4

Initiation	You are going to serve as the primary coach for a family. You discuss any barriers to the coaching process and ground rules. Based on the individualized family service plan, the family identified some ways you could support them in promoting their child's development.
Reflection	The family tells you how they would like for their child to sit in the cart at the department store so they can do their shopping and so he can see what's going on around him. You ask what they've been doing and how well it's worked. You and the family brainstorm some ideas to try.
Evaluation	(*Continuation—Plan*) The father will try the ideas discussed during the next trip to the department store.
Action	The father and child go to the department store. The father practices putting the child in the seat of the cart and strapping him in as the two of you had discussed.
Reflection	During your next coaching conversation, you ask the father how the strategies worked. What went well? What did he have to do differently than discussed? What was the result? What would he do differently next time? How would he generalize this experience to the cart at the grocery store?
Evaluation	(*Continuation—Plan*) You and the father develop a plan that includes actions and practice that will occur during shopping trips until your next coaching conversation.

have been achieved (Gallacher, 1997). Also, as part of the evaluation of the coaching process, the coach and learner must decide whether to continue with coaching conversations (continuation) or not if the intended outcomes of the coaching relationship have been achieved (resolution).

Continuation

The continuation component occurs after the coach and learner have evaluated the coaching process and determined additional coaching conversations are needed to achieve the desired outcomes. The purpose of the continuation component is to summarize the results of the coaching session and develop a plan for what observations or actions need to occur before and during the next coaching conversation. Some actions include planning for learning opportunities, practicing new skills, and accessing needed resources and supports. The Coaching Follow-Up Planning Tool in the chapter appendix can be used to assist in this process by delineating specific actions to take place related to observations, practice, and resources including the person responsible and timeline for completion.

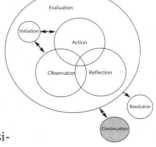

The bidirectional line in Figure 3.1 connecting continuation to evaluation demonstrates that the decision to continue coaching is made during the evaluation process. Once the coach and learner develop a plan, they return to the other components in the process as part of or following implementation of the plan.

REFLECT ON THIS . . .
Self-reflection questions

Self-reflection questions guide the evaluation of the coaching process.

- Is the learner accomplishing the agreed-on outcomes of the coaching process?
- If not, why?
- Do I need to make any changes to the coaching process?
- If yes, what changes need to be made?
- Am I the best person to continue as this learner's coach?
- If not, who might be more effective in the coaching role?

Resolution

Resolution occurs when the coach and learner mutually agree that the outcomes of the coaching process have been met. As a result of the coaching process, the learner has developed the competence and confidence to self-assess, self-correct, and generate new ideas and strategies across activity settings without the coach being present. In doing so, the learner knows when the strategies are successful, makes necessary changes in current situations, and generalizes knowledge and skills to new and different circumstances, people, and settings (Flaherty, 1999; Kinlaw, 1999). Upon resolution of the coaching relationship, the coach and learner create a plan for ongoing improvement of desired skill(s) or behavior(s), as 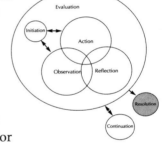 well as a strategy for reinstituting the coaching relationship if necessary. The unidirectional line in Figure 3.1 leading from evaluation to resolution indicates that the outcomes of the coaching relationship have been achieved and the coaching process is concluded.

The coaching stories presented in this chapter illustrate continuation or resolution. In the coaching story about June and Allen, resolution was reached at the conclusion of the initial conversation. June left with a plan for talking with the parents. As part of coming to resolution, June planned to contact Allen to share the outcome of the conversation with the parents; however, they agreed that she would not require further coaching on the topic.

The coaching story about using a walker for Lani illustrates continuation. In this coaching story, Jennifer, along with Brian and Laura, decided to continue their coaching conversation after the Sunday visit with Laura's mother. During that visit, the parents planned to propose how Lani could have fun at Grandma's house while using her walker to reach some of her favorite toys. Brian and Laura will share the results of this plan with Jennifer, as well as how they may have modified the plan while visiting with Laura's mother.

The coaching story with Harriet, the occupational therapist, and Sabrina, the physical therapist, also shows continuation. After Sabrina's next visit with the family, the two planned for Sabrina to contact Harriet to perhaps participate in a co-visit, but minimally for them to have a follow-up conversation about the visit. If, at that time, Sabrina has the information she needs to support the family in promoting the child's involvement in mealtime, then they may decide to move to resolution. In doing so, Sabrina and Harriet would develop a plan for how both of them will be responsible for reinitiating a coaching conversation when necessary.

Initial Coaching Conversations versus Follow-Up Conversations

The structure of a coaching conversation may differ based on whether it is an initial or a follow-up conversation. During an initial conversation, the coach and learner work through the initiation component of the coaching process, which could then be followed by reflection and lead to observation and/or action. In some instances (e.g., a spontaneous coaching opportunity with a colleague regarding a very specific issue), an initial coaching conversation may be the only conversation necessary if the learner's outcomes can be met during this time. In most situations, however, even spontaneous and brief coaching conversations result in a follow-up in which the learner shares the result of a jointly planned observation or action following reflection during the initial conversation (see Tables 3.2 and 3.3).

Follow-up coaching conversations typically begin with reflection on the observation and/or actions that occurred between coaching visits or conversations. In addition, the follow-up conversation may include observations, practice opportunities, and further reflection. Prior to the conclusion of the conversation, the coach and learner plan for the observations and actions that will take place between coaching sessions as well as the next coaching visit.

The Coaching Worksheet (in the chapter appendix) provides an outline of each component within the coaching process and elements that may occur within each component. This tool may be used prior to and during the initial coaching conversation, as well as follow-up conversations. The worksheet may be completed by the coach and/or learner to document observations, actions, and reflections that occur during or between coaching conversations and joint planning between the coach and learner at the conclusion of the coaching visit. A separate worksheet may be used for each coaching conversation, or a single worksheet may be used across coaching conversations.

CONCLUSION

As you begin to use coaching in your own work with families and colleagues, remember these key points about the coaching process:

- Coaching is a mutual conversation based on specific, mutually agreed-on outcomes.

- Coaching is a reciprocal process in which both the coach and learner share and receive information, ideas, and feedback.

- Coaching relationships can be developed with families, child caregivers, and early childhood practitioners.

- Every conversation is a potential opportunity for coaching.

- Coaching may be planned or occur spontaneously.

- The coaching process involves five nonlinear components: initiation, observation, action, reflection, and evaluation.

- Reflection is the most important component in the coaching process as it emphasizes self-discovery and promotes self-correction and generation of new ideas.

This chapter has described each of the five components of the coaching process—initiation, observation, action, reflection, evaluation—and presented brief illustrations of each component. Chapter 4 presents the qualities of an effective coach and general coaching skills that may be used within each of the five

Table 3.2.   Outline of an initial coaching conversation

1.   Initiation
       Identify coaching opportunities
       Clarify the purpose and outcomes of coaching
       Identify and address any barriers to making the coaching process effective
       Clarify the ground rules

2.   Reflection
       Assist the learner in discovering what he or she already knows or needs to discover about the topic through the use of probing questions and active listening

3.   Observation or action (Select one or more)
       Observe the learner engaged in an activity related to use of targeted skill
       Provide opportunity for learner to observe coach use targeted skill
       Allow the learner to practice the targeted skill with the coach present

4.   Reflection
       Ask the learner about the skill or activity observed or practiced
           What went well?
           What would you do to improve on the practice?
           How will you do this under different conditions, circumstances, or in different settings?
       Provide feedback on observation and/or action
       Share information, resources, and supports (as necessary)
       Confirm understanding of the learner
       Review what has been accomplished
       Plan new actions or strategies to observe and/or implement between coaching conversations

Table 3.3. Outline of a follow-up coaching conversation

1. Reflection

   Ask the learner about the skill or activity observed or practiced between coaching conversations

   What was your intent? What did you want to accomplish?

   What actually happened?

   What went well?

   How did you adapt the activity in process?

   What would you do differently next time?

   How will you do this under different conditions, circumstances, or settings?

   Provide feedback on observation and/or action

2. Observation or action (Pick one or more)

   Observe the learner engaged in an activity related to use of targeted skill

   Provide opportunity for the learner to observe coach use targeted skill

   Allow the learner to practice the targeted skill with the coach present

3. Reflection

   Ask the learner about the skill or activity observed or practiced

   What went well?

   What would you do to improve upon the practice?

   How will you do this under different conditions, circumstances, or in different settings?

   Provide feedback on observation and/or action

   Share information, resources, and supports (as necessary)

   Confirm understanding of the learner

   Review what has been accomplished

   Plan new actions or strategies to observe and/or implement between coaching conversations

components of the coaching process. Chapters 5, 6, and 7 provide more detailed information and examples of how the coaching process can be used effectively when coaching within the contexts of the family, group settings, and colleagues.

As you conclude this chapter, reflect on these questions:

- What opportunities exist for you to initiate a coaching conversation with a family member or colleague?

- How might you resist your urge to immediately tell a family member or colleague what to do rather than first supporting them in reflecting on what they are already doing?

- What three questions might you use to begin the process of reflection with a family member or colleague?

RESOURCES

Costa, A.L., & Garmston, R.J. (1994). *Cognitive coaching: A foundation for renaissance schools.* Norwood, MA: Christopher-Gordon Publishers.

   The authors provide a four-phase model for cognitive coaching. The text includes examples of coaching dialogue and questions to use during the reflection process.

Flaherty, J. (1999). *Coaching: Evoking excellence in others.* Boston: Butterworth-Heinemann.
Flaherty outlines a five-stage coaching process and two types of coaching encounters (i.e., single conversation coaching sessions and multiple conversation coaching sessions). Flaherty also provides examples of coaching interactions using his five-stage process.

Hanft, B., & Place, P. (1996). Assessing the school environment. In B. Hanft & P. Place, *The consulting therapist: A guide for occupational and physical therapists in the schools* (pp. 61–72). San Antonio, TX: Therapy Skill Builders.
Observation is an important part of coaching as a way to gather information and review progress. This chapter includes a three-page checklist to observe children in a school setting that coaches can also use for observation in preschool settings.

Joyce, B., & Showers, B. (1995). *Student achievement through staff development.* White Plains, NY: Longman Publishers USA.
Joyce and Showers provide research studies that document the effectiveness of the coaching process as a strategy to promote adult learning. In addition, the authors outline a brief history of the process of coaching and the critical components necessary to make coaching effective.

Kinlaw, D.C. (1999). *Coaching for commitment: Interpersonal strategies for obtaining superior performance from individuals and teams.* San Francisco: Jossey-Bass/Pfeiffer.
This text provides a similar three-stage process for coaching that includes both specific and general coaching skills necessary at each stage. In addition, Kinlaw provides detailed examples of coaching conversations.

REFERENCES

Bruder, M.B., & Dunst, C.J. (December 1999/January 2000). Expanding learning opportunities for infants and toddlers in natural environments: A chance to reconceptualize early intervention. *Zero to Three Bulletin,* 34–36.

Doyle, J.S. (1999). *The business coach: A game plan for the new work environment.* New York: John Wiley & Sons.

Fenichel, E. (1991). Learning through supervision and mentorship to support the development of infants, toddlers, and their families. *Zero to Three Bulletin, 12*(2), 1–6.

Flaherty, J. (1999). *Coaching: Evoking excellence in others.* Boston: Butterworth-Heinemann.

Gallacher, K. (1997). Supervision, mentoring and coaching. In P.J. Winton, J.A. McCollum, & C. Catlett (Eds.), *Reforming personnel preparation in early intervention: Issues, models, and practical strategies* (pp. 191–214). Baltimore: Paul H. Brookes Publishing Co.

Joyce, B., & Showers, B. (1995). *Student achievement through staff development.* White Plains, NY: Longman Publishers USA.

Kinlaw, D.C. (1999). *Coaching for commitment: Interpersonal strategies for obtaining superior performance from individuals and teams.* San Francisco: Jossey-Bass/Pfeiffer.

McWilliam, R.A., & Scott, S. (2001). A support approach to early intervention: A three-part framework. *Infants and Young Children, 13*(4), 55–66.

Rush, D.D., Shelden, M.L., & Hanft, B.E. (2003). Coaching families and colleagues: A process for collaboration in natural settings. *Infants and Young Children, 16*(1), 33–47.

Schon, D. (1987). *Educating the reflective practitioner.* San Francisco: Jossey-Bass.

Whitmore, J. (1996). *Coaching for performance.* London: Nicholas Brealey.

Appendix

1. Components of the Coaching Process
2. Coaching Follow-Up Planning Tool
3. Coaching Worksheet

Components of the Coaching Process

Initiation

Identify coaching opportunities
Clarify the purpose and outcomes of coaching
Identify and address any barriers to making the coaching process effective
Clarify the ground rules

Observation

Coach observes the learner in some type of action or practice
Learner observes the coach modeling some type of action or activity
Learner observes him- or herself (self-observation)
Coach and/or learner observe aspects of the environment

Action

Coach models a skill for the learner
Learner practices using an existing or new skill discussed with the coach
Learner experiences a behavior, issue, or situation that precipitates a discussion with the coach
Learner anticipates a behavior, issue, or experience to discuss with the coach prior to the event

Reflection

Assist the learner in discovering what he or she already knows or needs to discover by asking the right questions in the right way

- What's happening now? What happened?
- What do you want to accomplish?
- How did you decide where to focus?
- What have you tried? What did you do?
- How could you do it differently?
- How will you know when you are successful?

Provide feedback on observation and/or action
Share information, resources, and supports (as necessary)
Confirm understanding of the learner
Review what has been accomplished
Plan new observations and/or actions or strategies to implement between coaching conversations

Evaluation

Review the coaching process
- Continuation
- Resolution

Coaching Families and Colleagues in Early Childhood by Barbara E. Hanft, Dathan D. Rush, & M'Lisa L. Shelden

Coaching Follow-Up Planning Tool

Date: _____

Learner: _____

Coach: _____

Coaching topic: _____

_____

Coach/learner plan next steps Observations	Who	What	When
Practice			
Resources			

Coaching Worksheet

Learner: _____ Coach: _____ Date: _____

INITIATION

Coaching opportunities observed or presented

The purpose of the coaching relationship is

Intended learner outcomes resulting from the coaching relationship

Barriers to the coaching process	Strategies to address barriers

Ground rules

OBSERVATION

	What/where	When
Coach observes learner's actions and interactions		
Learner observes coach model actions		
Learner observes self		
Coach/learner observe environment		

ACTION

	What/where	When
Coach models for learner (coach present)		
Learner practices an action (coach present/absent)		
Learner describes experience (coach absent)		
Coach/learner observe environment		

REFLECTION

	Description		
Learner reflects on action or observation			
Coach gives feedback about observation or action following reflection			
Learner uses resources (e.g., print, video, peer)			
Coach confirms learner's understanding and summarizes			
Coach/learner plan next steps Observations Practice Resources	Who	What	When

EVALUATION

Coach Self-Reflection

1. Is the learner accomplishing his or her goals?

2. What changes, if any, do I need to make in the coaching process?

3. Should I continue as this learner's coach? (If not, who would be more effective?)

Coach Asks Learner

1. Shall we continue coaching or have your goals been accomplished (continuation)?

   If continuing coaching:

   • What changes need to be made in the coaching plan?

   • What observations and/or actions should take place between coaching sessions?

   • How will we communicate in between sessions?

   • Do we have a plan for the next session?

2. If goals have been reached (resolution):

   • Is the learner committed to and capable of self-assessment, self-correction, and self-generation?

   • Has a plan for reinstituting coaching been discussed?

4

QUALITIES OF
AN EFFECTIVE COACH

While every coaching encounter is unique, success depends on qualities and skills demonstrated by the coach that form the basis of this unique relationship. This chapter provides an overview of the qualities and skills necessary for establishing and maintaining a positive coaching relationship. The intent of this chapter is to promote self-reflection in order for readers to assess whether they have the qualities and skills necessary to be recognized by others as an effective coach.

The coaching relationship is a joint partnership in which two people engage in ongoing sharing and learning from one another. The coach must have skills to engage the learner in a reflective conversation following an observation or action by either the learner or coach. The coach must also know when and how to share new information and ideas in a way that supports the learner in achieving mutually agreed-on outcomes.

A learner must recognize five key qualities in the coach: competency, objectivity, adaptability, caring, and honesty.

COMPETENCY

Before a learner will be motivated to enter into a coaching relationship, the coach must demonstrate that he or she has information, ideas, and skills that may be useful to the learner and that he or she knows when and how to build on the learner's current knowledge and skills. In a coaching relationship, the role of the coach is not to simply tell the learner what he or she should or could be doing, but rather to build on the learner's existing knowledge. The learner may be aware of the coach's skill in asking the right questions to help him or her discover new ways to solve a difficult problem, gather information, or develop a new skill. A learner's self-discovery is the key to seeing what the learner may already know or do to

REMEMBER THIS . . .
Five key qualities
of an effective coach

- Competency
- Objectivity
- Adaptability
- Caring
- Honesty

achieve the desired outcomes. In this way, the coach builds the learner's capacity to identify strategies and/or solutions to address current and future situations. A competent coach knows how to promote self-discovery by the learner and share his or her own knowledge and skills as needed.

Lucy, a speech-language pathologist, has been providing consultation to Frieda, a preschool teacher, and Estelle, a paraprofessional, since the beginning of the school year to support them in promoting the language development of Ramon, who was diagnosed as having autism. Typically, Frieda and Estelle anxiously wait for Lucy to arrive so they can ask her questions and have her tell them what to do. They believe that she has knowledge and skills they need to support Ramon in their classroom.

After attending a workshop on the coaching process, Lucy invites Frieda and Estelle into a coaching relationship. Lucy realizes that the expert-driven model she has been using is causing dependence and does not require involvement on Frieda and Estelle's part. On her next visit, rather than launching into telling them what to do based on their inquiries, Lucy begins asking them questions about what they have tried, what has been successful, and what adaptations they have made to these strategies. *(Reflection—encouraging learners to reflect)* Although they are a bit surprised at first, Frieda and Estelle quickly realize that they have evidence-based knowledge and good ideas for application that enable them to be very effective in supporting Ramon in their classroom.

On a follow-up visit a few weeks later, Frieda asks Lucy a difficult question. She wants to know how to support Ramon so that recess will be a positive experience for him. Lucy knows that she does not know the answer, but she does know the questions to ask to help Frieda resolve the issue and identify a successful strategy. Later, as Lucy reflects on her interaction, she realizes that in her expert-driven model of how to work with a teacher, she would not have been perceived as competent by either herself or the teachers in this situation if she did not have the specific answer. *(Reflection—self-realization)* Her self-discovery that day is that she is an effective coach even though she does not have all the answers.

Did Frieda recognize competence in Lucy as her coach? She absolutely did. Did Lucy have to answer all questions to be considered competent? No, she demonstrated her competence in the coaching process by helping Frieda discover an answer using her own knowledge and expertise. Lucy used the reflection phase of the coaching process to probe Frieda to reflect on her own ideas.

OBJECTIVITY

A person seeking a coach typically looks for a coach who will be objective and fair (Doyle, 1999). People often listen to others through filters that block or distort the ability to hear what the other person is saying (Burley-Allen, 1995). Our filters contain our biases, prejudices, strong personal feelings, past experiences, assumptions about the other person or situation, and expectations of performance. Examples of filters include our beliefs about what good parenting looks like, our expectations of family life, or assumptions about people based on how they present themselves.

An effective coach learns to recognize and set aside these filters in order to focus on the learner's perspective, interests, and intent. This leads to consideration of the other person's idea or input regardless of how similar or different it might be from his or her own. The coach's responsibility is to support the person in examining the idea for its own merit rather than immediately judging the idea or speculating why the idea will not work or may be inappropriate. Next, the coach determines what unbiased, evidence-based standard could be used to guide the learner to self-discovery and compare his or her own ideas and practices to the established standards.

TRY THIS . . .
Decrease your use of filters

During the next opportunity you have to meet a person for the first time, make no assumptions about the individual based on how the person is dressed, the person's accent or dialect, or your past experiences with people of this culture, socio-economic status, racial group, or education level. Rather, seek to know this person based on your conversation and interactions with him or her.

Mary Ann, an early childhood special educator, is influenced by her understanding of current research and her expanding role as an itinerant teacher. She supports the participation of all children in inclusive environments. At one point in her career, she taught children in segregated preschool classrooms, but she helped her school district move to an inclusive model and now consults with general educators. Mary Ann understands the challenges associated with changing a school system and realizes that not all school personnel are at the same place regarding their knowledge and support of inclusive practices.

During an initial consultation visit at Riverview Elementary School, Mary Ann meets Jerry, a kindergarten student with disabilities. After school, Ginger, his teacher, comments to Mary Ann that she doesn't understand why Jerry's parents even bring him to school because "he just sits all day and stares into space. He should be in a special classroom."

Mary Ann responds, "Wow. It sounds like teaching Jerry is a challenge for you. What could I do to support you in developing some ideas and strategies to provide more opportunities for him to participate in your class?" (Reflection—encouraging learner to reflect, objectivity)

If Mary Ann were the type of person to make assumptions about Ginger's willingness to include Jerry in her classroom, she would have judged her as insensitive or intolerant of children with disabilities and would have argued with her about Jerry's right to be in her classroom. Instead, Mary Ann remained objective and used the reflection phase of the coaching process to explore Ginger's feelings and encourage her to reflect. Mary Ann's question resulted in opening a dialogue and creating the potential for coaching.

ADAPTABILITY

Someone once said, "Blessed are the flexible for they will never be bent out of shape." Although the coach and learner develop a coaching plan (see Chapter 3) to help them achieve a learner's outcomes, the flow of each coaching conversation is based on observations that occur either prior to or during a coaching visit or the learner's actions that have taken place between conversations. The coach may anticipate what might be discussed, thus preparing resources and information to share. Depending on the situation, however, the conversation may need to switch from the planned course to meet the unique needs and interests of the learner at that time. Such reasoning is often employed during coaching to take advantage of spontaneous learning situations that address the learner's goals, as in the following coaching story.

During a recent coaching conversation, Walt and his coach, Natasha, an early childhood teacher, had discussed strategies for increasing his use of open-ended questions with his son, Danny, and waiting for Danny to respond during "tickle time" before bed. For the next visit, Natasha was prepared to discuss how this strategy had worked and then planned to explore the use of increasing open-ended questions during other play activities. Upon arrival for the visit, Natasha and Walt began talking about the successful use of the strategies for increasing his open-ended questions. While they talked, Danny snatched a toy from his brother and ran to the bedroom. A chase ensued, and the situation quickly escalated to running and screaming throughout the house.

"Danny's behavior is becoming increasingly challenging," Walt told Natasha. "I think it's due in part to his frustration in not being able to communicate his desires."

Seizing the moment as an opportunity for coaching on a related topic, Natasha modified the discussion to ask Walt what he would typically do in this situation. "What do you generally do when this happens?" Natasha asked. *(Reflection—determining usual response)*

"Well," Walt paused as he watched Danny and his brother dash past Natasha, then run down the hall toward the bedrooms dodging furniture with arms flailing and barely missing a glass lamp on the end table. As his face reddened, Walt responded, "I guess I usually yell for them to stop or I'll take the toy away from Danny, but that usually results in a terrible temper tantrum." *(Reflection—considering usual response)*

Natasha looked at the toys lying on the living room floor, "Didn't you tell me that Danny likes playing with his toy cars? Maybe you could redirect him." (*coaching on related topic*)

"What do you mean?" Walt asked.

"I mean you could get Danny interested in playing with his toy cars or something else that you know he really likes."

"Danny," Walt stood and headed down the hall as the screaming in the bedroom reached its peak. "Let's go find your cars. I'm gonna find your red car to play with. Which one are you going to get?" (*Action—trying new idea*) The screaming quieted, then Danny's brother emerged from the bedroom and headed toward the living room area followed closely by Danny and Walt.

"Redirection. I'll remember that," Walt said as he smiled and knelt on the floor to find the red car.

"We can also think of some other ideas you could try when this happens," Natasha added.

"Sounds good to me!"

Natasha had a plan for how she thought the coaching meeting would go, but she seized the moment as an opportunity for coaching on a related topic. She modified the discussion to encourage Walt to reflect on what he would typically do in that situation. Using previously identified child interests, Walt and Natasha used the reflection phase of the coaching process to brainstorm a short list of other strategies that Walt could use in the future to diffuse similar situations. If Natasha had just stuck to her original plan, she would have missed this wonderful opportunity to support Walt in learning how to use Danny's interests to redirect challenging behavior.

CARING

In a coaching relationship, the learner needs to know that the coach genuinely cares about his or her development in order for him or her to be open to the coaching process and be willing to work together to achieve the desired outcomes. The coach demonstrates caring through encouragement, patience, and creating a supportive environment. The learner must feel safe enough to ask for assistance without feeling judged or criticized. Reflect on the principles of adult learning discussed in Chapter 2. A caring coach creates an environment in which the learner generates and implements new strategies and accepts that mistakes may occur in the process. As part of this process, the coach assists the learner to reflect on less than effective actions and improve performance. The coach helps guide the learning to promote ongoing assessment leading to self-discovery and continuous improvement. The coach empathizes with challenges and seeks opportunities to celebrate the learner's achievements.

For the past 3 months, an occupational therapist, Carol, has been coaching Vickie, an in-home child care provider, to support 2½-year-old Trey, who is blind. Upon her arrival, Vickie tells Carol that her assistant quit yesterday and that she is completely overwhelmed with just the day-to-day activities and care for the children. She tells Carol that she decided that morning that it would be safest for now to keep Trey in a playpen because she didn't feel as if she could supervise him adequately.

"You must be very overwhelmed by the responsibility to keep all of the children in your care safe," Carol said. "Keeping Trey in a playpen is one strategy. What other options did you consider?" *(Reflection—acknowledging strategy, encouraging learner to reflect)*

"It's all I could think of at the time, so I just did it," responded Vickie.

"While the children nap, let's talk about some ways that we could keep him safe and also support his participation in learning and interaction with the other children throughout the day. After that, let's talk about how you can find another assistant." *(Reflection— exploring options)*

In this coaching story, Carol demonstrated that she cares about Vickie's development by acknowledging the strategy that she used based on current circumstances. Then, she used the reflection phase of the coaching process to explore other options for supporting Trey as well as Vickie.

HONESTY

A coach's honest feedback is an essential part of helping a learner continually improve. Without honest feedback, the coach cannot expect the learner to continue to use or modify existing activities and skills or develop new abilities. The coach must provide straightforward feedback after observing the learner practice new skills and whenever answering the learner's questions. A coach should provide complete and unbiased information to the learner. This information includes both complimentary and constructive feedback to assist the learner in achieving success. Complimentary feedback acknowledges and reinforces what the learner is doing well. In the coaching relationship, constructive feedback builds on the strengths, assets, and knowledge of the learner as he or she works to improve current skills and develop new abilities. Evidence-based suggestions and ideas provided by the coach are individualized to the learner's situation.

Although being honest and providing constructive feedback is sometimes difficult for the coach, this quality strengthens the coaching relationship by building trust and demonstrating respect for one another.

On a visit in a family's home, Catherine asked her coach, Matt, a physical therapist, if her 2-year-old son, Alex, would ever walk. Catherine said, "I just don't see how Alex is going to walk. Because of the cerebral palsy he has such a hard time just holding up his head. Alex won't ever walk, will he?"

Matt, keeping in mind Catherine's strong emotions, responded, "What we know about predicting walking is that the type of cerebral palsy and at what age sitting is achieved are very important. We know that when a child sits alone by the age of 2 years, the likelihood of walking is increased. We also know that if a child has cerebral palsy with spastic quadriplegia,

> **REMEMBER THIS . . .**
> **General skill areas**
> **for effective coaching**
> • Observing
> • Listening
> • Responding
> • Planning

the likelihood of walking is drastically decreased [see Montgomery, 1998]. As we've discussed and observed, Alex likes watching his older sister, Tricia, and seems to be interested in doing whatever she is doing. We'll continue to think of ideas to help Alex do things with Tricia. This may include helping him learn to walk, but certainly includes helping him to get around on his own."

Catherine said, "I appreciate you sharing all of this information. No one has ever been quite this candid with me before. The information is hard to hear, but I'm not giving up hope that Alex will walk. For now, will you help us figure out how to help Alex pester Tricia like a little brother should?"

Catherine and Matt laughed as Matt said, "Sure."

When Catherine asked Matt if Alex would ever walk, Matt shared complete and unbiased information with Catherine based on the most current research available. Matt did so in a concise, straightforward, yet sensitive manner. He then let Catherine decide how she was going to use these data or if she wanted additional information from him.

To see if you have learned the five qualities of an effective coach, take the quiz in Figure 4.1.

GENERAL COACHING SKILLS

In order for a learner to agree to participate in the coaching process, he or she must recognize that the potential coach has some degree of competence in the content area and the skills necessary to promote the learner's ability to apply new information. Not everyone who has content knowledge maintains the skills necessary to promote another person's development; therefore, to be an effective coach, one must become aware of and develop additional skills in order to effectively support the learner. These skills include observing, listening, responding, and planning. Reflect on your current level of coaching skills by completing the General Coaching Skills Rating Scale in the chapter appendix. Then, use the information contained in the remainder of this chapter to improve your current skill level.

Qualities of an Effective Coach

Have you learned the qualities of an effective coach? Assess your coaching expertise by completing the following quiz.

1. When parents and colleagues ask me questions that require me to draw on my area of expertise
   a. I almost always have the answers.
   b. I freak out if I don't have the answers.
   c. I evade the question if I don't have the answers.
   d. I use what I know, add that to what the learner knows, and encourage the learner to build on what he or she knows.

2. When a caregiver shares an idea with me
   a. I immediately compare it to my own values, beliefs, and preferences.
   b. I evaluate how realistic it actually is.
   c. I consider it in light of the caregiver's intended outcome.
   d. I immediately agree or disagree and let the caregiver know what I think.

3. When working with a caregiver or colleague
   a. I focus on my agenda or plan so I can be efficient.
   b. I follow the other person's lead during a conversation to determine how I can be helpful.
   c. I focus on the other person's issue at that moment, then bring the conversation back to my plan for the visit.
   d. I get frustrated when he or she cannot stay on task.

4. When people describe me, they tend to use words such as
   a. Supportive, encouraging, and caring
   b. Busy, rushed, and hardworking
   c. Opinionated, directive, and to the point
   d. Sympathetic, soft-hearted, and forgiving

5. When working with caregivers and colleagues
   a. I tend to tell people what I think they want to hear.
   b. I share complete and unbiased information.
   c. I give only positive feedback.
   d. I wait to avoid sharing difficult information as long as I possibly can.

Figure 4.1.   Self-assessment quiz. Read pages 65–71 to review the answers to the quiz. (1d–Competency, 2c–Objectivity, 3b–Adaptability, 4a–Caring, 5b–Honesty.)

Observing

"If the purpose of coaching is to change behavior, then the coach's mission is to find what affects behavior in a way that will bring about the desired changes," (Flaherty, 1999, p. 31). What the coach observes is contingent on the mutually agreed-on outcomes for the coaching session identified during the initiation component of the coaching process. Observations may include, but are not limited to, 1) the learner's behavior including actions and interactions, 2) reactions of others to the learner, and 3) the physical and social environment. Observations of the learner and others in the environment help the coach understand the learner's perspective and are generally the focus and starting point for reflection. Figure 4.2 is an observation checklist for coaches to fill out.

TRY THIS . . .
Improve your observation skills

The next time you stand in line at the movies or the store or you wait for someone, pick out a parent and child to observe. Notice how the environment (e.g., layout of furniture and equipment, traffic patterns and use of space) influences the actions and responses of both the child and parent.

Listening

Good listening communicates respect and a desire to understand the point of view of the learner. When the learner believes that the coach is listening and understanding the message that he or she is trying to convey, the learner is encouraged to share more information. Listening is an opportunity to gather more information about the perceptions, values and beliefs, interests, knowledge, and understanding of the learner. The coach shares this information with the learner to prompt reflections that clarify information or to assist the learner in acknowledging and analyzing what he or she already knows or is doing. This information may also be used when the coach joins with the learner in developing new ideas and strategies. Three key components of good listening are attending, acknowledging, and associating.

Attending

To attend means to show that you are listening with your whole body and are fully interested in what the person has to say. Whole body listening includes direct eye contact, positive facial expressions, an open body posture, and close proximity to the speaker. An effective listener eliminates any barriers between the speaker and listener, such as desks and auditory and visual distractions that might include ringing telephones, cellular telephones, pagers, open doors with people walking by, and computer monitors with incoming e-mail.

When attending to a learner, a coach must focus on the present moment and listen to the words, meaning, and feelings the learner is trying to convey without passing judgment (Kinlaw, 1999). The coach should demonstrate openness to the

Observation Skills Checklist

Use this checklist as a mental or physical reminder of the types of observations to make of the learner and the environment. The checklist is meant as a guide to improve your own observation skills. The information obtained from the observations may be used to, but is not limited to: assess your communication partner's level of understanding of your communications, improve your communication skills, determine if or when to modify your message, and determine how you may be a resource or support to your communication partner.

During coaching conversations, I make the following observations of the learner:

☐ Nonverbal communication including:
Eye contact
Facial expressions
Vocal inflections
Body posture

☐ Physical reactions indicating level of understanding or openness to the information shared during the coaching conversation

☐ Ability to explain or demonstrate a particular idea, event, or point

☐ Comfort in asking questions or asking for clarification

☐ Response to specific activities or strategies used by the coach

☐ Interaction with others (colleagues, caregivers, or the child)

☐ Continuity between the learner's current behavior and what we know from research related to effective practices for adult and child learning

☐ Nonverbal communication of others in the environment that would indicate their reactions to the information provided or need for more information

☐ Level of understanding of information or supports shared by the coach

☐ Ability to use information or supports shared by the coach

I make the following observations of the environment:

☐ Physical arrangement of the environment (e.g., layout of furniture and play equipment, traffic patterns within a home or classroom, available space for quiet and active times)

☐ Factors in the environment that may affect the learner's intended outcomes (e.g., influence of other children or adults, use of space, architectural barriers)

☐ Availability, access, and use of family and community resources (e.g., library, playgrounds, shopping, friend's home)

Figure 4.2. Observation skills checklist.

other person's thoughts, ideas, concerns, feelings, and rationale while avoiding the need to take sides on the issue or topic. Another effective strategy is being quiet to allow the other person time to reflect and organize his or her thoughts. An effective coach learns to be comfortable with periods of silence and suppresses the need to fill every moment with conversation.

REMEMBER THIS . . .
The 3 A's of effective listening

• Attending
• Acknowledging
• Associating

John asks Ellen if she has a moment to talk with him about additional ways he can support a parent's involvement of her child in meal preparation. As Ellen nods, she invites John to sit down. Ellen moves to a chair next to John. She also turns her cellular phone off. *(removing barriers)* Ellen makes eye contact with John and asks him to share more of the situation with her. When John pauses, Ellen maintains eye contact and waits for John to continue. *(making eye contact, using silence effectively)*

Acknowledging

Acknowledging the message of another person means the listener responds verbally and nonverbally to indicate that he or she has heard what was said. The listener does not immediately agree or disagree with what the other person is saying. Acknowledging the information and/or message indicates that you not only hear but that you also understand or are seeking to understand what the other person is communicating. The goal at this point is to keep the conversation going by encouraging the learner to share additional information and insight into his or her thoughts and feelings. Examples of acknowledgment include head nodding, eye contact, or verbalizations, such as "I see," "I understand," or "Tell me more." In this way, the coach recognizes what has been said and promotes continued sharing by the learner.

Associating

Associating means linking what the learner is communicating with what the coach knows to be true based on research-based practices, the program's mission, philosophy, core values and beliefs, and/or guiding principles, as well as the mutually agreed-on outcomes of coaching identified during the initiation component of the process. This is important to ensure that the coach does not link what the learner says only to the coach's experiences, beliefs, values, or biases. For example, if a colleague in the coaching relationship is describing a parent as "resistant to new ideas, uncooperative during visits, and a bad influence on the child," the coach would associate this statement by the colleague to the program's principle related to family-centered practices. In doing so, this would demonstrate inconsistency between the

TRY THIS . . .
Improve your listening skills

- The next time you watch a movie or television program, observe how well the main character demonstrates good listening skills through nonverbal communication. Note direct eye contact, positive facial expressions, open body posture, and close proximity to the speaker.

- When you are involved in a conversation with a colleague, acknowledge his or her message and encourage him or her to continue by using head nodding, eye contact, or verbalizations, such as "I see," "I understand," or "Tell me more." Note how much longer the conversation is extended.

- Listen to a parent tell her story about caring for her child and identify cues to answer the question "What does the learner believe will support her in promoting her child's development?"

- During your next opportunity to visit with a parent or colleague, observe how many distractions (e.g., telephone, environmental noise, pager) could impede your ability to listen to the other person. Eliminate as many distractions as possible and/or position your body in such a way as to prevent yourself from being distracted.

---

colleague's statements and the program's principles. This inconsistency provides a basis for reflection. When associating the learner's perspective to program guiding principles and evidence-based practices, consider the following questions:

- What are the areas of agreement and/or inconsistency (i.e., what the learner is doing versus results the learner wants to achieve)?

- What research or other evidence did the learner use as a foundation for his or her views, beliefs, position, and actions?

- How can the coach assist the learner in the process of self-discovery related to his or her intent, the learner's desired outcomes, the program's guiding principles, and available evidence related to evidence-based practices?

- How can the coach assist the learner to implement evidence-based practices aligned with the program's guiding principles?

Responding

Responding refers to sharing information in a way that is supportive of the learner in order to build on the learner's knowledge base. Rather than immediately giving the learner suggestions about what to do or what to consider, as occurs in traditional professional–parent interactions or colleague-to-colleague consultations, the coach's responses should promote learning and self-discovery related to a specific topic or intended outcome. Instead of telling a colleague who describes a parent as "resistant and noncompliant" that his or her view is inconsistent with his or her program's guiding principles, within a coaching conversation the coach might ask the colleague to share what he or she means by "resistant and noncompliant." The coach would follow up by asking whether the learner thinks describing parents in such terms is consistent with the program's guiding principles.

As the colleague reflects about how the use of these terms is inconsistent with the principles, the coach could engage the colleague in a discussion about how to talk about families in ways consistent with program principles. The coach's

skill in responding to the learner is critical in the process of reflection, one of the components of coaching described in Chapter 3. Responses initially involve probing the learner's intent and current knowledge, summarizing key discussion and actions, followed with sharing feedback, information, resources, and supports. Depending on the circumstances, the coach and learner may also engage in a problem-solving discussion or the coach may provide feedback to the learner based on a previous observation. Specific examples are provided with each of the following strategies.

Probing

Probing is a technique used to either clarify information provided by the learner or to acquire additional information throughout a coaching conversation. Primarily, the coach clarifies vague information or information that he or she does not understand. For example, when a learner uses phrases like "everyone is concerned," the coach asks who *everyone* includes. Does this mean all of the practitioners and all of the family members or one group but not the other or perhaps even subsets of these groups? The coach may also clarify the meaning of *concerned*. For instance, *concerned* could mean upset, angry, or questioning.

A concrete example of the use of vague words is to describe a child as having "poor behavior." To one individual, an example of poor behavior could be a boy throwing himself on the floor, kicking his feet, beating on himself with his hands, and screaming from the top of his lungs. To another person, an example of poor behavior may be a boy not immediately doing what he was asked to do. Both the coach and learner need a clear understanding of the words used to describe people, contexts, feelings, and events.

The coach may also use probe questions to gather additional information. These types of probe questions may begin with grand types of open-ended statements, such as "Tell me about" or "Tell me more." More specific information may then be gathered through the use of questions beginning with "what," "when,"

TRY THIS . . .
Probing questions

Improve your skill in asking a probing question to help a learner recall, clarify, and contrast.

- The next time a friend makes a vague statement, follow up with a *wh-* question—who, what, when, or where. Avoid placing blame by not asking *why* questions.

- When a colleague asks for help in developing strategies for supporting parents and other care providers in promoting a child's development, ask "What have you tried?" "What would you do differently?" or "What would happen if . . . ?" before providing feedback or sharing additional information.

"where," "who," and "how." The description of the reflection component in Chapter 3 also provides examples of other types of questions that may be used as probes.

Summarizing

Once the coach has supported the learner in exploring his or her knowledge, skills, and experience regarding the topic of the coaching conversation, the coach responds by summarizing what he or she has heard. Summarizing involves recounting the content and feelings shared by the other person in a way that demonstrates that the coach is hearing what the learner is trying to communicate. Summarizing allows the learner to confirm the information or clarify any miscommunication and provides the coach with the opportunity to gather additional information. An example of a summary statement with a parent would be, "So, both you and your child are frustrated when you can't understand what she is trying to say." A coach may summarize information received from a colleague by saying, "What I heard you say was that the reason you use that technique with families is because it is most comfortable for you. Is that correct?" Summarizing may be used to either draw the communication process to a close or recap the important points of the conversation prior to going to the next level or phase in the coaching process.

Sharing Feedback, Information, Resources, and Supports

Once the coach and learner have reflected to the learner's satisfaction about his or her knowledge, skills, and experience regarding the topic of the coaching conversation, the coach then provides the learner with additional information, resources, and supports related to working toward the desired outcomes. The skill required of the coach in responding with such concrete data and support is knowing 1) how to provide enough information without overwhelming the learner and 2) when to provide other human or material resources to the learner and how to make them accessible.

If the coach responds to the learner based on an observation, a specific type of response called feedback will follow the reflection process. Feedback must always be constructive and supportive. Feedback should occur as soon after the observation as possible while the event is still fresh in the minds of the coach and learner. The information shared should be specific, clear, concise, and individualized to the learner. Avoid using directive words with the learner such as *should, must,* and *need to,* as well as absolutes, including *everybody, all the time,* and *never.*

Eva had been coaching her colleague, Betty, about how to use toys and materials that already exist within a child's home or a child care environment rather than taking her own toy bag to each visit. After a few weeks, Betty admitted to Eva, "I'm still struggling with not taking my toys to home visits. A lot of families just don't have developmentally appropriate toys. I know that I should use what the family has, but I want to elicit some new words from the child by introducing novel toys."

Eva agreed, "Introducing novel toys might be one way of eliciting new words from a child. Let's think about other possible ways we can support children's families in getting the child to use new words. *(Reflection—encouraging learner to reflect)* In this way, we can see what other options you might have that can achieve the same outcome. This will also allow you to build on what the family has available in their home that they can use with their child when you aren't around."

"I guess I could talk to the family about ways to elicit words during mealtime by encouraging the child to ask for foods, utensils, and dishes by name. I could talk with them about using getting dressed in the morning and ready for bed at night as an opportunity to introduce body parts and items of clothing." *(Reflection—generating ideas)*

"Right!" Eva said. "And when the child is taking a bath, they could play a game to label body parts then, too."

"Okay, okay! I'm getting it—slowly, but surely!" Betty said with a laugh as she pushed her toy bag under her desk with her foot.

In this coaching story, Eva provided constructive feedback about taking a toy bag on home visits by comparing Betty's desired practice to one of their program's evidence-based principles. Rather than tell Betty what to do, Eva encouraged Betty to reflect on all of the possible ways to achieve the desired outcome rather than taking her own toys to the visit.

Problem Solving

Coaching may be used to help a learner solve a problem. The coach, therefore, must be skilled in using problem-solving methods and showing others how to apply these methods to their current, as well as future, issues. The steps in the problem-solving process are as follows:

1. Identify the problem—Clarify and analyze the problem by determining what is happening currently versus what the learner would like to see happen in the future. Determine when, where, why, how, and with whom this problem is happening.

2. Generate options—Jointly brainstorm possible options to solve the problem.

3. Decide on a possible solution or combination of solutions—Establish criteria for selecting the solutions (e.g., Is this solution within the learner's control? Does the learner have the resources to implement this solution? How long will it take to implement the solution?). Evaluate each of the possible solutions using the criteria established, then select the best solution or combination.

4. Implement the best solution or combination of solutions—Develop an implementation plan that spells out who is going to do what by when, then implement the plan.

5. Evaluate the solution to see if it is effective—Evaluate the solution by measuring its effectiveness in reaching the desired future state identified in the first step of the process.

Planning

Planning is important because it promotes action and accountability on the part of the learner. The coach and learner develop a plan for what is to occur between coaching conversations or visits when the coach is not present. During the planning process, the coach and learner:

- Clarify the purpose and mutually agreed-on outcomes for the coaching relationship. The coach explores the learner's intents and desires. Then, both coach and learner plan the steps they will take.

- Determine what both the learner and coach need to do before and during the next coaching conversation. For example, the learner could agree to introduce her child to a new situation or environment, try out a modification, or talk to another parent about her experiences in promoting her child's participation in family activities. The coach might look for additional data in a professional journal or publication, bring the parent's questions to a colleague for additional input, or observe the child in another environment.

- Identify strategies at the end of a coaching conversation for how the learner will use and generalize the information gained from the coaching relationship as well as next steps or follow-up actions. For example, Betty and Eva identified strategies for how Betty could use naturally occurring activities in the life of a family as opportunities to use words rather than toys from her therapy toy bag. Betty will continue to identify ways she can use the child's own toys and typical family activities as opportunities to promote language development. During her next coaching conversation with Eva, Betty will be prepared to share what new ideas she has tried, how successful these ideas were, and ways she can modify the ideas to make them even more effective.

CONCLUSION

The effectiveness of the coach is dependent on the qualities and skills that the coach uses to engage and support the learner. Coaches and learners are influenced by specific factors, including level of motivation to engage in a new experience, desire for self-direction, presence of a supportive environment that uses their unique learning styles, ability to build on prior experiences, and ongoing support to put new knowledge into practice. This transfer of learning results when conscious plans are made to use new knowledge or skills. Coaching is one vehicle that can ensure that application of new learning occurs in meaningful ways.

This chapter has explained the five qualities necessary for an effective coach and how a learner can recognize the coach as someone who may benefit him or her through the use of the coaching process. Effective coaches demonstrate competency, objectivity, adaptability, caring, and honesty through their interactions with others. The chapter also has outlined four general coaching skills: observing, listening, responding, and planning. By demonstrating the qualities of an effective coach and using the general coaching skills while moving through the coaching components presented in Chapter 3 with a learner, the coach fully implements the process of coaching to promote a learner's use of existing skills and development of new abilities. Whereas the previous chapters have provided foundational information and skills necessary for effectively implementing a coaching approach, the remaining chapters illustrate how to use the process of coaching with families, child care providers, and colleagues.

As you conclude this chapter, reflect on these questions:

- Why would someone want to enter into a coaching relationship with you?

- If someone who knows you was asked to describe you, would they use words similar to the five qualities of an effective coach? If not, what can you do to strengthen those qualities in yourself?

- How can you work to strengthen your abilities in the four coaching skills—observing, listening, responding, and planning?

RESOURCES

Burley-Allen, M. (1995). *Listening: The forgotten skill.* New York: John Wiley & Sons.
    Burley-Allen provides in-depth information on how to become an effective listener and

includes a discussion of listening filters that often impede one's ability to hear a speaker's message.

Whitmore, J. (1996). *Coaching for performance*. London: Nicholas Brealey.
Coaching for Performance contains Whitmore's GROW model for asking effective questions and includes examples of the types and sequence of questions that may be used during the reflection component of the coaching process.

REFERENCES

Burley-Allen, M. (1995). *Listening: The forgotten skill*. New York: John Wiley & Sons.

Doyle, J.S. (1999). *The business coach: A game plan for the new work environment*. New York: John Wiley & Sons.

Flaherty, J. (1999). *Coaching: Evoking excellence in others*. Boston: Butterworth-Heinemann.

Kinlaw, D.C. (1999). *Coaching for commitment: Interpersonal strategies for obtaining superior performance from individuals and teams*. San Francisco: Jossey-Bass/Pfeiffer.

Montgomery, P.C. (1998). Predicting potential for ambulation in children with cerebral palsy. *Pediatric Physical Therapy, 10,* 148–155.

Appendix

1. General Coaching Skills Rating Scale

General Coaching Skills Rating Scale

How would you rate your ability to make the following observations?	Never		Sometimes		Always
• Learner's nonverbal communications	1	2	3	4	5
• Learner's ability to demonstrate a particular skill	1	2	3	4	5
• Learner's comfort in asking questions	1	2	3	4	5
• Learner's interactions with others in the environment	1	2	3	4	5
• Reactions of others in the environment to what you are saying or doing	1	2	3	4	5
• Physical arrangement of the environment	1	2	3	4	5
• Factors in the environment that may affect the learner's intended outcomes	1	2	3	4	5
• Availability, access, and use of family and community resources	1	2	3	4	5

How would you rate your ability to listen to the learner?					
• Use direct eye contact	1	2	3	4	5
• Maintain positive facial expressions	1	2	3	4	5
• Demonstrate an open body posture	1	2	3	4	5
• Maintain close proximity to the learner	1	2	3	4	5
• Focus on the present moment	1	2	3	4	5
• Listen to words, meanings, and feelings of what the learner is trying to convey	1	2	3	4	5
• Listen without passing judgment	1	2	3	4	5
• Avoid listening through filters of personal values and beliefs, prejudices, and past experiences	1	2	3	4	5
• Comfortable with periods of silence	1	2	3	4	5
• Respond verbally and nonverbally without agreeing or disagreeing	1	2	3	4	5
• Encourage the listener to share additional information through the use of noncommittal acknowledgment	1	2	3	4	5
• Associate the learner's perspective to the program's philosophy, guiding principles, and evidence-based practices	1	2	3	4	5

How would you rate your ability to respond to the learner?					
• Respond in a way that will promote learning by asking questions	1	2	3	4	5
• Ask learner for clarification of vague information or information that appears inconsistent with program guiding principles or evidence-based practices	1	2	3	4	5
• Use what, where, when, who, and how questions	1	2	3	4	5
• Assist the learner to compare new information and experiences with previous ones	1	2	3	4	5
• Assist the learner to apply or create new information	1	2	3	4	5
• Reflect back on the content and feelings expressed by the learner	1	2	3	4	5
• Periodically summarize information shared by the learner	1	2	3	4	5
• Share feedback, information, and resources after the learner has shared his or her thoughts and ideas	1	2	3	4	5
• Provide feedback in a concise, specific, immediate, constructive, and supportive way	1	2	3	4	5
• Avoid using directive words such as "should," "must," and "need to"	1	2	3	4	5
• Use a problem-solving strategy with the learner when necessary	1	2	3	4	5

How would you rate your planning abilities?					
• Clarify the purpose and outcomes for the coaching relationship	1	2	3	4	5
• Determine who needs to do what between coaching conversations	1	2	3	4	5
• Identify strategies and opportunities for practice between coaching conversations	1	2	3	4	5

5

COACHING FAMILIES IN
HOME AND COMMUNITY SETTINGS

Coaching can be used to support families in promoting child participation in family and community contexts in accordance with Part C of the Individuals with Disabilities Education Act (IDEA) Amendments of 1997 (PL 105-17). This chapter, along with Chapters 6 and 7, demonstrates how to apply the information presented in the earlier chapters by illustrating the use of coaching in family and community contexts, group settings, and between colleagues. Each chapter provides in-depth coaching stories in which the components of the coaching process are explained. The coaching component and a brief explanation are italicized throughout the coaching stories. Fuller explanations are found in the paragraphs following the coaching stories. In addition, the coaching stories are accompanied by Coaching Worksheets (found in the chapter appendix) that document the major components as they occur as well as the coach and learner's joint action plan. The Coaching Worksheet may be used as a tool for documenting your own coaching conversations (see the Chapter 3 appendix for a blank copy to use).

NATURAL ENVIRONMENTS

The 1997 reauthorization of the Individuals with Disabilities Education Act (IDEA) of 1990 reemphasized the requirement that states ensure that support for infants and toddlers eligible for Part C is provided in natural environments. *Natural environments* according to Part C of the IDEA means "settings that are natural or normal for the child's same age peers who have no disabilities." These activity settings are not necessarily places, but rather activities, experiences, and contexts in which children and their families participate that provide the backdrop for learning opportunities (Bronfenbrenner, 1992, 1993, 1999; Dunst, Hamby, Trivette, Raab, & Bruder, 2000; Gallimore, & Goldenberg, 1993; Gallimore, Goldenberg, & Wesiner, 1993; Goncu, 1999).

REMEMBER THIS...
Activity settings

Activity settings are "experiences and opportunities afforded developing children as part of daily living, child and family routines, family rituals, and family and community celebrations and traditions." (Dunst, Hamby, Trivette, Raab, & Bruder, 2000, p. 151)

The following coaching story (summarized in Figure 5.1) provides an example of how current and desired activity settings based on child and family interests may be used as learning opportunities for a child and family. Examples of child interests, family interests, and activity settings are noted within the story, and as the story unfolds, the text shows how these interests and activity settings are used by the practitioner as opportunities for child learning and development. In addition, this story illustrates how the coaching process may be used within the home and community context. It may be helpful to follow the coaching process outlined in the Coaching Worksheet in the chapter appendix while reading the coaching story. The Coaching Worksheet includes completed sections based on the coaching conversations.

Purpose of coaching:		
To support Tyler's participation in family outdoor activity settings		
Outcomes of coaching:		
1. Tyler's family will identify alternative interest-based activity settings.		
2. James, Felicia, and Tyler will resume outdoor activities as a family.		

Key partners	Child and family interests	Activity settings
Tyler—child *James*—father *Felicia*—mother *Loretta*—speech-language pathologist *Ron*—physical therapist	*Family*—hiking in the mountains, caring for injured owls, gardening, reading books to Tyler, attending medieval fairs, spending time together as a family *Child*—being outdoors, playing in water, helping his mother in the garden	Gardening Hiking in the mountains Caring for Hoot, the owl Face painting at the medieval festivals Reading books before bedtime

Figure 5.1.   A new ride for Tyler.

A New Ride for Tyler

Felicia, James, and their son, Tyler, lived in a large western North Carolina town. Tyler was 2 years old and liked being outdoors, playing in water, and helping his mother take care of their garden. *(child interests)* The family had been participating in the local early intervention program for 8 months. The primary focus of the support was coaching Felicia and James about ways to involve Tyler in family and community activities. Loretta, a speech-language pathologist from the local early intervention program, and Tyler's parents discovered multiple learning opportunities for Tyler. For instance, James and Felicia liked to attend medieval festivals. *(family interest)* Loretta, James, and Felicia identified strategies for preparing Tyler for the festivals that included reading books that introduced him to words, customs, and activities from medieval times.

James and Felicia also participated in an injured owl rehabilitation program. *(family interest)* Through this program they had recently adopted an owl named Hoot that could no longer fly and could not be reintroduced to the wild. Tyler was intrigued by the owl, and Loretta suggested that James and Felicia think about ways to help Tyler care for and use some of his new words to communicate with Hoot.

During a recent visit, James had mentioned to Loretta that they loved taking family hikes in the mountains. *(family interest, activity setting)* Because Tyler was born prematurely, they had stopped hiking altogether for a while. As Tyler became stronger, they went on a few short hikes. When they discovered that Tyler really enjoyed being outdoors, they gradually increased the length of their hikes. Because Tyler wasn't walking yet, James put Tyler in a carrier on his back. Now, Tyler was getting too heavy for James to carry so they were thinking about discontinuing their family hiking activities. *(Action—situation preceding discussion)*

Loretta asked James and Felicia, "Before you give up your family hiking activities, tell me what alternatives you have considered." *(Reflection—determining what has been considered or tried)*

"Well," replied Felicia, "you know James was carrying him on his back, which worked really well until he's gotten so heavy. We're also concerned about Tyler's comfort now that he's gotten taller. Even though he's starting to talk more, we're afraid that he can't or won't tell us when he gets uncomfortable since he loves being out on the trail so much. It's just not feasible for us to go anymore. We considered some type of stroller, but that limits us to flat, smooth trails. We also thought about not taking him with us, but exercising in the mountains has always been an activity that we enjoy doing together." *(Reflection—recalling past ideas)*

"So, you'd like to use the hiking as exercise as well as an opportunity for your family to have a fun activity to do together?" Loretta asked for clarification. *(Reflection—clarifying learners' perceptions)*

"Yes," Felicia said. "We really enjoy being outdoors, we need the exercise, and the mountains are practically right outside our back door."

"Surely there are other forms of exercise that you could do in the mountains that would allow the three of you to still enjoy time together," Loretta said. "What are some similar types of activities that you might be interested in?" (*Reflection—probing learners to generate options*)

James interjected, "Well, we like to ski, rock climb, and snowboard. Tyler's godfather has tried to get us into mountain biking, but we've never taken the time to give it a try." (*Reflection—generating alternatives*)

"Maybe mountain biking would be the solution," Felicia said. "Loretta, remember how your friend from the program, Ron, helped us adapt Tyler's highchair? Do you think he could help us select and adapt a seat for Tyler that would go on the back of a mountain bike?" (*Reflection—self-discovery of option*)

"I'll call to see if we can borrow a couple of our friend's mountain bikes to give it a try," James said. (*Reflection—planning for action*)

"Do you think you will try this fairly soon?" Loretta asked.

"I'd like to give it a try this weekend," James replied, "if you and Ron can come by Friday afternoon to adapt the seat for Tyler." (*Action—using new idea this weekend*)

"I'll give Ron a call. He can either adapt the seat or make a seat insert. I'll also be there, so he can coach me on any follow-up. Ron can coach all of us on how to watch for any signs of problems with the seat and when we'll need to adapt the seat as Tyler grows. Let's plan on Friday afternoon unless you hear from me otherwise. Then, next week we can talk about your biking excursion and see if we need to brainstorm any modifications." (*Reflection—planning what to do, planning for next session*)

Tyler's natural learning environments include his home, the family's garden, medieval fairs, and the mountains near his home. His involvement in these family and community contexts provides opportunities for interaction with other people, physical activity, and communication about what the family is seeing and doing. Loretta's role is not to transplant her therapy activities from the clinic into James' and Felicia's living room or backyard or even a mountain path. Nor is her role to use the natural activities in which Tyler participates as times when therapy activities, such as drilling articulation or stretching his muscles, can occur. Rather, Loretta's goal is to use and promote what the family is already doing or would like to do as a natural part of their family and community life as moments for using Tyler's existing skills and developing new abilities.

Notice how the coaching process began when Felicia and James experienced a situation that prompted them to use the action phase. Tyler was getting too heavy for James to carry, so they were considering discontinuing their family hikes. Loretta used the reflection phase when she probed James and Felicia to determine what ideas they had considered. Felicia in turn used the reflection phase to recall the ideas she had considered to address the situation. In order to clarify Felicia's perceptions, Loretta used the reflection phase to tell Felicia in her own words what she thought Felicia and James wanted. Then, instead of providing suggestions for alternative activities in which the family could participate, Loretta invited the parents to generate options themselves. Felicia subsequently experienced self-discovery of a possible option. Loretta, Felicia, and James planned for an action—adapting the mountain bike. James used the action phase when he decided to put the adapted bike to use the following weekend. Finally, Loretta used the reflection phase to plan what she needed to do following the conversation. She also suggested a plan for the next session.

REMEMBER THIS . . .
Learning opportunities

A learning opportunity is an opportunity that occurs within the context of an activity setting that promotes the child's growth and development.

In supporting young children and their families, the role of the coach should be to:

1. Consider the natural learning environments where the child is or would be if he or she did not have a disability.

2. Join with the family in identifying activity settings within these environments in which the child could, should, or would like to participate.

3. Identify both planned and spontaneous interest-based learning opportunities that do or could occur within these activity settings.

4. Assist the family and other caregivers to use these learning opportunities to lead to desired skills and behaviors.

Coaches should avoid moving their clinic-based, adult-directed therapy activities with associated equipment and materials into the family's natural environments with the exception of adaptive equipment, such as Tyler's adapted bicycle seat, that may be used by the family to support their child's participation in typical activities. The practitioner should also avoid assigning parents the responsibility of completing homework activities, exercises, and drills. Instead, coaches should support the parents in doing what they want to, need to, and have to do as part of real life. In this way, the coach promotes the child's development in virtually all life activities rather than separating therapy for young children from the reality of family life.

The next section in this chapter provides additional information on child and family contexts and types of activities in which young children and their families typically participate. These contexts and activities are prime opportunities for child learning.

FAMILY AND COMMUNITY CONTEXTS

Three primary contexts exist in the life of each child for learning: family, community, and early childhood programs (Bruder & Dunst, 1999/2000). The family and community contexts are discussed in this chapter. (See Chapter 6 for discussion of early childhood programs.) The family context includes a variety of people and activities that provide opportunities to promote the child's development. The family context contains 11 categories of activities that are part of the child's and family's typical routine and daily experiences that serve as sources for children's learning opportunities: family routines, child routines, parenting routines, family rituals, play activities, physical play, entertainment activities, socialization activities, gardening activities, family celebrations, and literacy activities (Dunst, Bruder, Trivette, Raab, & McLean, 2001). Specific settings that typically occur within these categories may include eating breakfast, preparing dinner, doing the dishes, reading a book, going for a walk, throwing a ball in the backyard, celebrating a birthday, and getting ready for bed. These activity settings are opportunities for promoting current skills and developing new ones. The role of the coach is to join a parent in identifying and trying strategies to support the child's participation within these activities using their combined knowledge, experience, and expertise.

The community context also includes 11 categories of activities that can serve as sources of children's learning opportunities: family activities, family outings, play activities, community events, outdoor activities, recreation activities, children's attractions, art/entertainment activities, church/religious activities, organizations and groups, and sporting events (Dunst, Bruder, et al., 2001). Tyler's community activity settings include recreation activities related to the mountains (e.g., skiing, rock climbing, snowboarding, hiking). The family also participates in medieval fairs that occur several times a year in their community as well as surrounding towns. One weekend per month, James and Felicia volunteer at the local nature center with the owl, talking to children about wildlife conservation. Within these family activities are a number of activity settings, such as having a picnic lunch along a mountain trail followed by splashing in a nearby creek, getting Tyler's face painted at the medieval fair, and visiting the animals and meeting other families at the nature center.

By asking the family about their interests, the types of activities in which they participate in a given day or week, and other less frequent activities, such as birthdays, family celebrations, or trips out in the community, the coach can assist the family in beginning to think about learning opportunities. Through Tyler's activity settings, he is exposed to a large number of learning opportunities that include letting his parents know when he wants something to drink, telling his parents what foods he'd like to eat, throwing stones into the creek, pointing to birds he sees along the trail while sitting in his dad's backpack, selecting which character he wants painted on his face, and petting the animals at the nature center. Within these learning opportunities, some examples of skills Tyler is either practicing or acquiring include using words to communicate with his parents and other children, sitting in the backpack so he can see the trail ahead, and picking up stones and raising his arm over his head to throw the stones in the water.

Through the combination of child and family interest-based activities that occur as part of a family's typical day or week, parents and early childhood practitioners can ensure high-frequency practice of existing or newly developing skills (Chen, Krechevsky, Viens, & Isberg, 1998; Wolery & Bailey, 1989). Interest, opportunity, and frequency are key factors for the early childhood practitioner to identify with the parent when discussing activity settings and learning opportunities and for practitioners to promote with parents as they support child learning when the coach is not present. Some questions the coach may use in early discussions with families to elicit this information include:

REMEMBER THIS . . .
Early intervention

"Child participation in activity settings that have development-enhancing qualities and consequences is early intervention in the broadest sense of the term, even when it does not involve specially trained...professionals providing children learning opportunities." (Dunst, Hamby, Trivette, Raab, & Bruder, 2000, p. 161)

- What types of things do you like to do as a family (e.g., playing board games, watching sports games on television, going for walks)?

- What types of things do you have to do (e.g., go to the store, give the children a bath every night, prepare meals)?

- What does your child enjoy doing or what holds your child's attention? How often do the types of activities we've discussed happen?

OPERATIONALIZING NATURAL LEARNING OPPORTUNITIES

Dunst, Trivette, Humphries, Raab, and Roper (2001) presented a three-dimensional framework for operationalizing natural learning environment interventions. This review of research and practice indicates that intervention practices differ across three dimensions—the setting, the type of activity, and the role of the practitioner—each represented by a continuum on the framework. The setting continuum reflects learning opportunities that are either contextualized and meaningful or decontextualized (Goncu, 1999; Lave, 1996). For example, Tyler's communication about Hoot while Tyler and his dad care for the owl is contextualized and functional. Loretta asking Tyler to sit down with her and name pictures of animals that include owls would be decontextualized and would lack meaning and purpose for Tyler. Riding in his dad's backpack or in the seat on the back of the bicycle is contextualized, whereas practicing sitting on the living room floor is decontextualized for Tyler. Throwing rocks while on the trail with his parents is another example of a contextualized activity; however, having Tyler stack or drop blocks in a can to practice his grasp is decontextualized.

REMEMBER THIS ...
Coach's goal, strategy, role, and focus

Goal: To promote the child's ability to "be and do" by facilitating the family's or caregiver's ability to enhance the child's development using what the family and caregiver consider important

Strategy: To consider the activity settings that the family and caregivers value to generate learning opportunities, then let the learning opportunities lead to desired skills and behaviors

Role: A coach or collaborative partner working alongside the family members or other caregivers

Focus: The child's and family's interests and assets

Activities on the continuum vary from those that are child initiated and based on the child's interests to those that are directed by adults. Tyler's interests in the owl, water play, and gardening are opportunities for Tyler to refine his existing skills and develop new ones because these interests prompt activities that are motivating for him and hold his attention for long periods of time.

The role of the coach is measured on the continuum by the amount of involvement in the child's learning. For example, is the coach providing opportunities for learning that are dependent on his or her presence or can they be implemented in his or her absence? By coaching James and Felicia, Loretta is ensuring that Tyler's learning and skill development are ongoing and not limited by her physical presence. Research indicates that the most effective learning opportunities are those that occur within the context of meaningful and functional activities, include a balance of child-initiated and adult-directed practices, and are not dependent on an early childhood practitioner being present (Dunst, Trivette, et al., 2001).

Early intervention's goal should be to promote the child's ability to "be and do" by facilitating the family's or caregivers' ability to enhance the child's development using what they consider important (Shelden & Rush, 2001). For the child, this means being with the people who the child wants and needs to be with and doing what he or she wants and needs to do. The coach's strategy should be to consider the activity settings that the family and caregivers value to generate learning opportunities, then let the learning opportunities lead to desired skills and behaviors (Bruder & Dunst, 1999/2000). The coach's role as a practitioner in the field of early intervention is that of collaborative partner working alongside the family members or other caregivers (Campbell, 1997; Dinnebeil, McInerney, Roth, & Ramaswamy, 2001; Hanft & Pilkington, 2000; Rush, 2000; Shelden & Rush, 2001). The coach's focus should be on the child's and family's interests and assets (Dunst, Bruder, et al., 2001).

During conversations with families early in the coaching relationship, the coach talks with the family to identify existing activity settings, learning opporttunities, and people who are a part of the family context. The conversation also captures current and desired family and child interests, routines, activities, and rituals. In addition, the coach inquires about child and family interests as potential sources for learning opportunities. Questions to initiate this portion of the conversation might include:

- What does your child like to do?

- What makes him or her happy, laugh, and smile?

- What activities does your family like to do together?

- Are there activities that you used to do before your child was born that you would like to be able to do again?

Discussion of these conversation topics should take place initially and then again at any point when family circumstances change as in the addition of a new baby. The coach's responsibility is to remain up-to-date and knowledgeable in the evidence-based practices of his or her own discipline as well as child development, child learning, family support, and coaching and to adjust the supports provided accordingly (Dunst, Bruder, et al., 2001). These conversations about typical family routines, activities, and the frequency of occurrence, in addition to discussion of child and family interests and strengths, provide a framework within which the coach can build and support the capacity of the parents and other caregivers to identify and use natural learning environments that have multiple high-frequency planned and spontaneous learning opportunities.

The challenges coaches often report about these types of conversations include few obvious activity settings, no child interests reported by the family, parents who are quiet and share minimal information, parents who want therapy provided directly by the coach, and parents who want coaches to tell them what they need to do. Minimally, most families participate in some type of eating, bathing, and dressing activity settings. When coaches believe families have limited activity settings and/or interact with a parent who shares minimal information, it is important to begin by jointly identifying at least one activity setting. Virtually all children have some type of interest, whether it be the way a parent moves close to the child's face and talks to him or her or a particularly engaging toy or activity. If, however, the parent is unable to identify a child interest, the coach may look for child interests during the assessment process and/or talk with the parent about his or her own interests as a starting point for identifying interest-based activities.

Often, the most challenging conversations are those in which parents either want the coach to tell them what to do or to work directly with the child. In these scenarios, the coach may need to return to the sample script on page 36 used to initiate the coaching relationship. The coach should again emphasize how child learning occurs in almost all activities and interactions both planned and spontaneous. The reason the coach wants to know more about the family and their activity settings is to identify possible child learning opportunities to support the family in promoting their child's development during all aspects of their life.

Early in their relationship, Loretta learned that Tyler liked being outdoors, playing in water, and helping his mother in the garden. She also discovered that James' and Felicia's interests included hiking in the mountains, caring for injured owls, gardening, reading books to Tyler, attending medieval fairs, and just spending time together as a family. When she found out that James and Felicia were considering giving up their interest of hiking in the mountains because Tyler could no longer participate, Loretta assisted James and Felicia in reflecting on how they could either adapt the activity or develop an equally enjoyable activity to replace hiking. In doing so, Loretta and James and Felicia created new activity settings in which Tyler could participate, thus increasing the number of opportunities for Tyler to practice existing skills and learn new ones.

CRITICAL ISSUES FOR THE FAMILY

Supporting families in their homes and communities enables the coach to observe children with family members engaged in real-life activity settings as opposed to contrived or simulated activities within a clinic-based environment. Being in a real-life environment brings opportunities that would not have otherwise been available, such as supporting child participation at mealtime, bath time, playing with his or her own toys in the backyard, or interacting with older siblings when they arrive home from school. Rather than missing the structure of a clinic or classroom environment, the coach can embrace the complexity of family life situations and seize the moment as unplanned opportunities for promoting learning.

When providing supports in family and community settings, the coach must be aware of at least three critical issues:

1. Supporting family time, lifestyle, and choices
2. Honoring diversity to avoid comparing family activity settings to his or her own values, beliefs, and past experiences
3. Preparing for circumstances when confidentiality of the family's involvement in early childhood intervention could be compromised

Supporting the Family's Time, Lifestyle, and Choices

Time is a critical factor for most families. The role of the early childhood practitioner as coach is to schedule coaching conversations at times that are convenient for family members. Then, during the conversation, the coach works closely with the family to identify opportunities for learning that are a part of the family's planned or spur-of-the-moment activities rather than having the family embed therapy activities or exercises at the beginning of, within, or at the end of the day. The coach promotes the family's ability to identify and use just-in-time learning opportunities with the child. In this way, supporting child development is a part of their parenting rather than separated from their parenting and lifestyle.

Because both James and Felicia worked, Loretta had to be flexible with them to find times when she could plan to visit them, in addition to her visits with Tyler's primary caregiver, his aunt, who took care of Tyler when James and Felicia were at work. This sometimes meant going to James' and Felicia's home after work or on Felicia's day off during the week. When Loretta visited James, Felicia, and Tyler after work, they were often getting ready for dinner, caring for animals, or packing for a day trip in the mountains. Rather than becoming frustrated, Loretta engaged James and Felicia in conversations related to the activity of the moment. While Loretta asked questions related to their joint goal of promoting Tyler's participation in these types of activities, James and/or Felicia reflected on how they could achieve that goal by modifying the activity; adapting a toy, piece of furniture, or other equipment for the activity; or modifying their own behavior to assist Tyler in the use of a developing skill.

Loretta supported the family's time, lifestyle, and choices by 1) being flexible to find times that were convenient for them to meet, 2) engaging the family in conversations relative to what was happening at that time in their life, and 3) linking the conversation to the jointly established goals of the coaching process and working together to identify strategies to promote and support the child's participation.

Honoring Diversity

Families' real-life activity settings are as unique as the families themselves. Coaches must be cautious and avoid making observations through their own filters of values and beliefs. Issues related to cleanliness, family composition, routines, or other factors that may differ from that of the coach must be seen as different instead of right or wrong. The coach must be able to recognize extreme situations in which the coach's or a family member's personal safety may be at risk, then identify alternatives or options for objectively addressing the issue.

When Loretta first came to know Tyler's family, she was concerned that they were putting a 16-month-old child in a backpack and climbing mountains. Loretta was raised in a large Midwestern city where the nearest mountains were hundreds of miles away. She would never consider doing anything like this with her own child. After getting to know James, Felicia, and Tyler over the next few months and learning about the types of hikes and mountain climbing they did with Tyler, she learned that they were very cautious. Loretta quickly realized that she had been viewing their activities through the filter of her own upbringing and values about parenting and what she believed to be appropriate parent–child activities. Not only did she learn about mountain hiking, but she even tried it with her own family. The more she talked with Felicia and James, the more learning opportunities she discovered that could be part of these types of activities. Loretta honored the family's values and beliefs by 1) setting aside her personal values and beliefs about appropriate parent–child activities, and 2) building on their values and experiences to identify current and future activity settings and learning opportunities.

Protecting Confidentiality

Coaches should prepare for circumstances where confidentiality of the family's involvement in early childhood intervention could be compromised. When the coach participates with the family in home and community settings, the family is placed in a position in which others may learn or ask about their involvement with the coach. The coach should discuss this with the family prior to the possibility of such an occurrence and develop a plan for how the family would like to address the situation. The plan should include how families can respond when encountering friends while out in the community with the coach, questioned by neighbors about who the person is that has been coming to their home or apartment, or asked by family members what they are doing with the coach. As part of the plan, the coach and family can identify options that may include addressing the issue with the family member or friend, introducing the coach if approached by others while out in the community, or asking the coach to fade back if approached by a friend or acquaintance.

After Ron had adapted a bicycle seat for Tyler, James and Felicia planned to take Tyler for a quick ride up a mountain a few miles from their home. Loretta and Ron planned to meet them at the park near the base of the mountain to see if any modifications needed to be made to the seat. The park was typically frequented by a number of people in the community who knew James and Felicia. On the visit prior to the bike ride, Loretta talked with James and Felicia about going to the park.

"When we're all together at the park next week, we might run into some people you know."

"That's a possibility," James agreed. "It's a pretty popular place this time of year, and a lot of families with children go there in the evening."

"You know," Loretta said, "sometimes when Ron and I are out in the community with families and we run into people the family knows, it can be awkward for the family if the other people don't know that they participate in our program."

"Oh, I see what you're saying," Felicia said. "That may be an issue for some families who don't want others to know that they or their child might be involved with your program, but if this happens when we are with you guys at the park, we'll just introduce you as who you are. It's no problem. You have been a terrific support for us. We appreciate your wanting to be sure we can maintain privacy, but really it's no big deal."

"Okay," Loretta said. "I just always want to make sure we have a plan when we're out in the community together."

Loretta, Felicia, and James continued to discuss the upcoming mountain bike ride and how Tyler would ride with James while Felicia followed behind to see how Tyler rode in the new seat. In this way, Felicia could share her observations with Ron and Loretta as soon as they came back down the trail.

By supporting family time, lifestyle, and choices, honoring diversity, and protecting confidentiality, the coach demonstrates respect for the family and can help build the family's trust in the coach. Trust and respect are two key ingredients of an effective coaching relationship (Flaherty, 1999).

Addressing Critical Issues

The next coaching story (summarized in Figure 5.2) demonstrates how a coach can address the critical issues related to time, lifestyle, and diversity. Whereas some coaches may use their observations and interactions to make judgments about the family, the coach in the following story sees the richness of available activity settings as well as existing and potential learning opportunities. In this coaching story, Carlos, an occupational therapist in a rural community, sees the possibilities for activity settings and learning opportunities in a family context in which some might find challenging or limited at best. Carlos builds on family members' strengths, interests, and assets during an initial visit in the family context to identify rich opportunities for learning. As with the previous coaching story, the Coaching Worksheet is located in the chapter appendix.

LEARNING IN THE COUNTRY

On a hot day in June, Carlos made the first visit to a family referred to his early intervention program. As he turned down the dirt road leading to the house, three barking dogs chased his car until he came to a stop in front of the mobile home. While waiting for the dust to settle and someone to save him from the dogs, who were now peering in the driver's side window, he quickly scanned his surroundings. Carlos could see a tire swing hanging from a nearby tree, (*activity setting*) three chickens pecking at the ground near a tractor tire serving as a sandbox, (*activity setting*) and floral sheets flapping from the clothesline. A large woman stepped through the door and onto the wooden pallets that served as a porch. She called the dogs and chained each to the clothesline pole before she told Car-

Purpose of coaching:

To promote Kenny's participation and learning as a part of his family life

Outcomes of coaching:

1. Shirley and Opal will identify and use everyday activities as learning opportunities for Kenny.

2. Kenny will play with Jason and Amy during outdoor activities.

3. Jason and Amy will support Kenny's involvement in joint play activities.

Key partners	Child and family interests	Activity settings
Kenny—child *Shirley*—mother *Opal*—grandmother *Amy*—sister *Jason*—brother *Carlos*—occupational therapist	*Family*—caring for the animals, watching the children play outside, watching television *Child*—playing with his brother and sister, playing with the animals	Tire swing Sandbox Laundry basket Watching television Playpen Woods Feeding dogs and chickens

Figure 5.2.   Learning in the country.

los that he could get out of the car. *(Observation—observing environment and activity settings)*

Upon entering the home, Carlos could see a small, tidy living area. Children's toys were piled in a laundry basket *(activity setting)* by the television, *(activity setting)* which was tuned to a soap opera. As two school-age children ran past him and out the open front door, Carlos caught a glimpse of a young child who looked to be about 14 months old in a playpen in the corner. *(activity setting) (Observation—observing environment and activity settings)*

"That's Kenny," said the woman. "He's almost 2. I'm his grandma, Opal. His mama, Shirley, she's in the rehab. She's getting out next week. Amy and Jason are her kids, too, but they'll all be mine for a while now.

"The caseworker said I had to call you to look at Kenny. I'm not real sure why because he's a feisty little thing. Why, he's into everything if I don't keep it picked up, so I just have to put him in that playpen to get a break. I don't know why he's still so little. He's not too big on eating, and he can't tell me what he wants to eat or nothing else. He doesn't walk real good, but it doesn't stop him from getting around. He sure likes his sissy and brother.

He tries to do just about anything they do. (*child interest*) The caseworker said he might need therapy or something, and if they say that's what he needs, then that's what I've got to do. You know what I mean?

"Oh, I'm sorry. I didn't even offer you a seat. Sit down for a bit, but do you think you could tell me what you can do for him pretty quick? There's a show I like to watch that comes on in a few minutes, then I'll need to fix these kids something to eat or they'll be screaming they're hungry!"

Opal pushed clean laundry (*activity setting*) to the side of the couch for Carlos to sit down. "Now, if I need to take him to town for somebody to work with him, I can probably borrow a car or something because I'm gonna have to get his mama to her counseling appointment in town every week anyway. Maybe they could both go about the same time, and I could run by the store while they're both in therapy. That way, I could get everything done in town in one trip. Well, what do you need to know to get him signed up? Got a form you need me to fill out?" (*Initiation*)

"Well, as a matter of fact," Carlos responded, "I do have some forms to fill out, but we can take care of that later. Right now, I'd like to learn more about your family, especially Kenny. You said he likes to do whatever Amy and Jason do. What are some of the things they like to do?"

"Oh goodness! They feed the chickens and those darn dogs, play in the woods, swing on that tire swing down there. (*learning opportunities*) You know, they're just kids and they're always into something they think is fun."

"Sounds like the kids are busy being kids, and Kenny has lots of opportunities for having fun and learning new things at the same time. Opal, it looks like we could start with some of the activities you've mentioned and figure out how to support Kenny's participation so he can keep up with Jason and Amy."

"Okay," Opal said, "but when do you want me to bring him to town for his therapy appointment? He's got to learn to walk and tell me what he wants to eat. If I don't get some meat on his bones, the caseworker will be all over me!"

"Then, let's start with walking. What have you tried to help Kenny walk?" (*Reflection—determining what has been considered or tried*)

"Like I said, Kenny's getting around, but he could do more if he could walk better. You know, stand on his own two feet without somebody holding him up. So, I figure he needs walking lessons up at the clinic to get his legs stronger and teach him how to put one foot in front of the other. Know what I mean?"

Carlos nodded and said, "I hear what you're saying about getting around on his own. I'm also hearing that a lot is happening here at home, and it sounds to me from what you're saying that he's very motivated by trying to do what Jason and Amy do." (*Reflection—providing feedback*)

"So are you saying that what he does here at the house would count as his therapy? Why, if that's the ticket, then there's a whole mess of stuff I could have him doing around here. But all I've got to say is I don't have the time to do a bunch of therapy stuff myself. That's what I need you for!"

REFLECT ON THIS . . .
Learning in the country

- What are Opal's priorities for Kenny?
- What activity settings are present in this family context that could be used as learning opportunities?
- What does Kenny like to do?
- List at least three learning opportunities for each activity setting you identified above that would relate to Kenny's interests.
- What are Opal's interests as they relate to supporting Kenny in achieving her priorities for him?
- Imagine that you are Carlos. What probe questions would you ask Opal to prompt her reflection on how she can help Kenny keep up with Amy and Jason?

"You're right!" Carlos agreed. "I'll be here to support you, Shirley, Jason, and Amy, too. I'll be more like a coach to help you come up with ideas so Kenny can do the things that he wants and needs to do, just like you said." *(Reflection—affirming learner)*

"Well, when Amy was in speech therapy down at the school, they were always sending stuff home for me to do with her in the evening like homework. I'm counting on you to not give me more to do but to make use of what's already going on around this place." *(Reflection—comparing past to future)*

"Absolutely!" exclaimed Carlos with a smile.

Before Carlos even stepped out of the car, he demonstrated the observation stage of the coaching process by identifying a number of activity settings in which learning could occur. The activity settings he noticed included a tire swing hanging from a tree, a tractor tire serving as a sandbox, a laundry basket full of toys, a television, clean laundry, and a playpen in the corner of the room. He also learned that Kenny had an interest in anything his sister and brother liked to do. Some potential learning opportunities included feeding the chickens and dogs, playing in the woods, and swinging on the tire swing.

Carlos also demonstrated the reflection stage when he probed Opal for what she had already tried, rather than just giving her suggestions. Opal had definite ideas about the types of supports that Carlos should provide and what she was willing to do and not do. During the conversation, Opal shared Kenny's, Jason's, and Amy's interests as well as her priorities for Kenny. Carlos provided feedback on what Opal shared and affirmed her.

Notice how Opal demonstrated reflection by comparing her past experiences to her expectations for future actions. She also demonstrated initiation when she asked if there were any forms she had to fill out for Kenny to receive therapy.

The following coaching story takes place 3 months after Carlos's initial visit to Opal's house. Kenny's mother, Shirley, has been home from the alcohol and drug rehabilitation center since a week after Carlos's first visit. Both Opal and Shirley have been actively involved in the weekly conversations when Carlos visits. Carlos plans to engage Opal in a conversation about how the existing activity settings can be used for multiple and ongoing learning opportunities to assist Kenny in meeting the priorities she has for him.

When Carlos arrived, Opal and Shirley were sitting in the front yard while Kenny, Jason, and Amy were tossing feed to the chickens. Kenny had been using his walker for the last 3 weeks and seemed to be able to navigate the uneven terrain in the yard fairly well. Carlos noticed that when Kenny experienced any trouble, he grunted loudly and either Amy or Jason would quickly come to his rescue. If they didn't, Shirley would yell for them to go assist.

"So, looks like Kenny is still keeping up with his brother and sister," remarked Carlos. (*Observation—noticing siblings' actions*)

"Why, you can't keep him down!" exclaimed Opal. "That boy is running all over this yard with that thing!" (*Reflection—providing feedback on child's actions*)

"Last time I was here, we talked about how he still tried to crawl behind the walker when he used it inside the house," Carlos said. "In fact, Shirley, I think it was your idea to use it more in the yard because he'd be less likely to get down on his knees and crawl if he realized the walker would help him get around faster." (*Reflection—providing feedback on proposed actions*)

"Yeah, I think that was my idea," Shirley said. "But, you know, the kids came up with even a better idea. They tied one end of a rope around the neck of one of the dogs and the other end to Kenny's walker. Then, they stood Kenny up behind the walker. While Jason was following along behind Kenny, Amy would lead the dog around the yard. Funniest thing you've ever seen. Kenny hung on to that walker and marched right along behind!" Shirley slapped her knee then threw herself back in the chair and laughed, "Yeah, those kids, they think about making everything into a game. Why, I thought, 'Well, this isn't rocket science.' So after you and I talked last time, I came up with the idea of getting Kenny one of those bicycle baskets to put on the front of his walker. Then, I put the chicken feed in it and told him to get on out there and feed the chickens. He had to stand up because otherwise he couldn't get the food out. It worked like a charm!" (*Action—sharing practice opportunities*)

Carlos raised his eyebrows, then laughed. "Wow, you guys have really been putting our ideas last week into action! Sounds like Kenny's use of the walker is going well. (*Reflection—providing feedback, affirming family's actions*) How can we continue to have Kenny be successful in using the walker so he can keep up with Amy and Jason? Or, is there anything you'd do differently? Or . . ."(*Reflection—encouraging learners to generate ideas*)

Before he could finish his last question, Opal moved to the edge of her chair and interjected, "Well, I knew you were going to ask those questions, so I've been thinking about that very thing. You see that lawn mower over there?" Carlos nodded as she continued, "I mean the one with the big wheels on the back. Well, it's a lot easier to push than that mower over there with those wimpy little wheels that look like they came off of some pedal car. *(Reflection—sharing new ideas)* Well, I think if we could go down to the store and get him some bigger tires for the walker, it'd make it easier for him to move the walker around this big yard." *(Reflection—self-generating strategies)*

"Let me check into that, Opal. I think that's a really good idea." Carlos turned to Shirley and asked, "What about you, Shirley. How can we continue to make Kenny successful?" *(Reflection—probing for new ideas)*

"I think if he could talk more, then Amy and Jason would want to play with him even more. I've been watching him with the other little kids when I take him with me for my counseling sessions in town. They talk, and he just sits there or else he'll grunt or take their toys away from them. I . . ." *(Action—experience preceding discussion)*

Opal jumped in, "Why, I know what he's saying and so do Jason and Amy. He grunts and points, and they jump." *(Observation—observing siblings' reactions)*

"That's what I mean, Mama! Don't you remember last time Carlos was up here we talked about waiting and giving Kenny a chance to talk. He can't even get a word in edgewise with you!" *(Observation—observing grandmother's actions)*

"What could you try this week?" *(Reflection—considering what to try between sessions)* Carlos asked, as he looked at both Opal and Shirley.

"Well, I'm willing to wait a few seconds to see if he'll try to say a word. And I can talk to the other kids about doing that, too." *(Reflection—identifying strategies)* Shirley quickly responded, then looked at her mother.

"Okay, and what if he doesn't say anything or just grunts?" Carlos probed. *(Reflection—probing learners for response)*

Opal paused, looked at Carlos and Shirley, then said, "Well, I'd probably just give him what he wants."

Shirley turned to her mother, "Mama!"

"I don't care! What that baby wants, that baby gets!" Opal snapped.

"Well, what could you do or say if you wait and he doesn't say anything?" Carlos asked. *(Reflection—redirecting, checking for understanding)*

"I don't know exactly," answered Shirley.

"You heard what I'd do," Opal said as she recrossed her legs.

"Well, Opal," Carlos said. "I know what you could give Kenny if he doesn't say the word. But, it may not be what he wants, not just yet anyway." *(Reflection—sharing information)*

"Oh yeah, what's that?" she asked.

"You can give him the word that's the name for the thing he wants. If he wants a glass of milk, then you say 'milk' or if he wants up in your lap, then you ask him, 'want up?' So, you pause and wait for him to say the word, then if he doesn't say it, you model the word or words for him then wait again. If he doesn't say it that time, then go ahead and give him

what he wants. Do you want to try that this week?" *(Reflection—sharing information)*
"Yeah, yeah, I do," Shirley said. "And I'm going to teach Jason and Amy how to do it, too. How about you, Mama?" Shirley asked. *(Reflection—self-generating idea and plan)*

"Oh, all right then!" she quipped as she turned to Carlos with a crooked smile on her face.

"When would be some times that you could do this?" *(Reflection—identifying opportunities)*

"Well, that's a good question!" Opal said.

"When does he grunt to ask for things most often?" Carlos queried. *(Reflection—probing with more specific question)*

"Well, it's certainly not when we eat," Opal answered. "He still doesn't like to eat much." *(Observation—sharing observation)*

"I think it's when he wants something to play with or he wants you to do something is when . . ." *(Reflection—identifying opportunity)* Shirley said as she stood to look for the children. "Oh, there they are. Look they've got Kenny up in the tire swing!"

The three adults stood up so they could see the three children playing on the tire swing. Carlos began to ask a question, "Do you think . . ." Before he could finish the question, Shirley jumped in.

"Well, there's a fine time when it would be natural for the kids to wait for him to use his words. Amy and Jason are always saying 'push me' or 'higher.' They should expect Kenny to do the same! They swing in that swing about a million times a day!" *(Reflection—self-discovering opportunity and plan)*

"Sounds like a plan to me," Carlos said. "It's just part of their game and part of what we would expect in order for Kenny to get what he wants."

Both Opal and Shirley nodded as they sat back down in their lawn chairs to finish their conversation that day with Carlos.

In this portion of the coaching story, Carlos observed actions by Kenny's brother and sister, and Opal provided feedback on Kenny's actions since the last visit. Then, Carlos encouraged Opal and Shirley to reflect on how Kenny was using his walker. As a result, Shirley employed the action phase to share the practice opportunities that had taken place between coaching sessions. Using reflection-on-action, Carlos provided feedback and affirmed what the family had done. Then, rather than listing his own ideas for what they could do next, Carlos probed Shirley and Opal to generate ideas. Opal used the reflection phase to share new ideas with Carlos and to self-generate a strategy to address one of her concerns, making it easier for Kenny to use the walker in the yard.

Carlos continued to probe Opal and Shirley to generate more ideas for what they might try. In response, Shirley used the action phase to describe an experience that preceded the coaching discussion. She had noticed how other children Kenny's age were already talking, and she wished Kenny could express himself

TRY THIS . . .
Tips for providing supports in family and community contexts

· Look for what the child and family like to do and do well.

· Join the family in identifying opportunities for learning within the context of what the child and family are already doing, want to do, or have to do as part of family and community life.

· Provide opportunities for reflection by the parents related to using child interests as learning opportunities and how they can support their child's participation.

· Share feedback, information, and resources only after parents have the opportunity to reflect and only if necessary.

this way, too. Opal responded with her observation that she, Amy, and Jason understood what Kenny wanted. This comment upset Shirley, and she revealed her observation that Opal was not giving Kenny a chance to talk. To help settle the debate, Carlos probed Shirley and Opal to consider what they might try or do differently between coaching sessions. Opal used the reflection phase to identify strategies to promote use of words, and she began to develop a plan for what to do between coaching sessions.

Carlos continued to use the reflection phase by proposing situations and asking Opal and Shirley what they would do. When they got off topic, Carlos redirected them and probed them again to check if they understood what to do. Opal and Shirley said they did not have any additional ideas, so rather than continuing to probe, Carlos chose to share information. He ended with an invitation to the family to accept, modify, or reject his suggestions. In response to Carlos's suggestions, Shirley was able to use the reflection phase to self-generate a way to expand on his idea and plan for what to do between visits. She added to Carlos's suggestion by coming up with the idea to also teach Kenny's siblings how to support his communication development. Carlos encouraged Shirley and Opal to identify opportunities to employ this strategy. He asked a more specific question when necessary to help them reflect. Opal shared her observation that Kenny still did not like to eat, so meals would not be a good setting to employ the strategy. Shirley reflected and identified playtime as an opportunity. She self-discovered an opportunity to use the strategy during playtime on the swing and planned to use this opportunity between coaching sessions.

Notice how Carlos used the coaching process with Opal and Shirley to the extent that Opal even anticipated Carlos's questions, and both shared their self-reflections made since Carlos's last visit. Carlos asked Opal and Shirley to reflect, then as appropriate within the context of this conversation, he provided additional information and feedback. As the three adults moved to the planning portion of this coaching discussion, Carlos had Opal and Shirley consider high-frequency learning opportunities within one of the children's typical activity settings. Carlos continued to use and build on what was important to this family and worked to support them in promoting Kenny's development within the context of their everyday lives.

MOVING FROM A TRADITIONAL SERVICE APPROACH

As evidence-based practice has emerged in early childhood intervention and related fields as the framework for early childhood practitioners to make decisions about conceptualizing and implementing supports and interventions, Dunst (2000) has encouraged revisiting and rethinking early intervention. This analysis compares a more traditional approach to intervention with a newer paradigm of evidence-based practices. A traditional paradigm is defined as a professionally centered model focused on remediation of a child's identified deficits by experts who provide services as they deem appropriate and needed. The new, evidence-based paradigm is a family-centered model focused on enhancing an adult's competence and creating opportunities to promote existing and new skills based on recognized interests and assets within a broad range of supports and experiences. Based on this information, the research supporting the use of coaching (see Chapter 2) and the recommendations from leaders in the fields of early childhood special education (Dinnebeil et al., 2001), occupational therapy (Hanft & Pilkington, 2000), physical therapy (Campbell, 1997; Shelden & Rush, 2001), and speech-language pathology (Coufal, 1993; Rush, 2000), the role of the early childhood practitioner can be described as that of a coach supporting family members and other caregivers.

The process for moving from a traditional service approach to using coaching in family settings involves

1. Identifying the role of the early childhood practitioner as coach
2. Identifying the primary learners in the family and community context
3. Redefining hands-on intervention
4. Reconsidering frequency and intensity of support

Most families are accustomed to a traditional service delivery approach in which practitioners work directly with the child to remediate some type of deficit or problem. The role of the early childhood practitioner changes as he or she becomes a coach because he or she will not spend time alone with the child. Instead, the early childhood practitioner will promote parent competence and confidence and mobilize resources within the community, all of which will support the family's desired outcomes for the child. The practitioner will also promote the family members' and other caregivers' capacity to increase child participation in family and community life. (Page 36 includes a script for introducing this approach to family members during the initiation component of the coaching process.)

In the coaching approach, an early childhood practitioner must identify the primary learners in the family and community, which is different from the traditional approach in which the primary learner is the child. Primary learners in the coaching approach include mothers, fathers, brothers, sisters, aunts, uncles, grandparents, family friends, neighbors, guardians, and foster parents. Early childhood practitioners also must redefine hands-on intervention as something only used when necessary. Instead of a pull-out approach—in which an early childhood practitioner has the child practice decontextualized therapy activities, such as exercises or articulation drills during a therapy or play session—intervention focuses on support for the family and other caregivers within the context of family and community activity settings. Coaches use hands-on intervention for two purposes: assessment (e.g., when exploring options for the best strategy for the caregiver to use such as positioning in a highchair) and modeling a technique for a caregiver (e.g., feeding the child using a new spoon for the first time).

Finally, early childhood practitioners must reconsider the frequency and intensity of support. In a traditional approach, regardless of how much or how often, all of the early childhood practitioners involved see the child at a frequency and intensity based on past experiences, best guesses, billable hours, and availability. In the coaching approach, frequency and intensity are based on the amount of involvement required to support the family members and other caregivers (i.e., the learners) across settings in achieving their desired outcomes for the child. The amount of support will vary depending on the desires, interests, and priorities of the family members and other caregivers.

The following coaching story (summarized in Figure 5.3) illustrates how to move from a traditional service delivery approach to using coaching in the family context. Asia, an early childhood education teacher, goes to her first visit with a family previously seen by Jan, a physical therapist. Pay particular attention to how Asia engages Jackie, the mother, in the conversation to lay the foundation for coaching as they discuss activity settings, learning opportunities, interests, and important people in the life of this child and family. The Coaching Worksheet is located in the chapter appendix.

RETHINKING THERAPY

Asia was eager to meet Jackie and Lawrence and their son, Marcus, who had just turned 13 months old. Although Jackie and Lawrence were musicians who worked at night, Jackie had stayed up very late after work straightening the house in preparation for Asia's visit. Jackie's mom, Wanda, had stopped by for coffee and was also present when Asia arrived.

Upon her arrival, Asia noticed a pallet on the floor (*activity setting*) and Jackie preparing to go to the basement to do the laundry. Jackie and Wanda warmly greeted Asia, and

---

Purpose of coaching:

> To support Marcus's participation and learning during family life activities

Outcomes of coaching:

> 1. Marcus's family will recognize and use everyday activities as learning opportunities.
>
> 2. Marcus's family will use his interests to promote his participation during church activities.

Key partners	Child and family interests	Activity settings
Marcus—child *Jackie*—mother *Lawrence*—father *Wanda*—grandmother *Cecil*—grandfather *Fuzzy*—dog *Asia*—early childhood special educator	*Family*—listening to music, going to church, participating in family activities *Child*—listening to music, dancing, playing with other children and grandparents' dog, being outside, playing ball	Children's choir practice at church Birthday parties Family gatherings Going to the store

Figure 5.3. Rethinking therapy.

Wanda indicated that she would slip out so Asia and Marcus could do their work without any distractions.

"I'll just be downstairs if you need me," Jackie called to Asia as she bounded down the stairs. "Have fun with your new teacher, Marcus! Mama will be back up in about an hour after you finish your exercises, then Gramma and Grandpa will come back, and we'll go to the store!"

Asia thought to herself, "Okay, what do I do now? Obviously, this family is used to something that I don't provide. Now, how am I going to handle this?" Although Jan had been assigned as the primary coach from the early intervention program, it appeared that she had been using hands-on therapy in the family's home to remediate Marcus's identified impairments. Jackie thought Jan's services were solely for Marcus, rather than a way to support the whole family in promoting Marcus's participation in life activities.

Asia took a deep breath as she focused on how she was going to engage Jackie in a conversation about considering a different approach. This approach would be based on Marcus's interests and assets to support Jackie's capacity to promote Marcus's involvement in activities that are important to the family.

At that moment, Jackie stuck her head around the corner, "Oh, Asia, I'm sorry. You must think I'm terribly rude. I'll stay with Marcus while you run out to your car to get your bolster, therapy ball, and toy bag. You're really going to have to match the great toys that Jan always brought. Can't say much for the therapy ball, but Marcus always loved playing with Jan's toys!"

"Jackie, can we talk for a few minutes while Marcus plays with some of his toys?" asked Asia. *(Initiation—identifying coaching opportunity)*

"Sure," Jackie responded. "I have a few minutes before that load of laundry is dry."

"I need some time to get to know you and your family. Sounds like your mom and dad, Wanda and Cecil, are a big support for you. Would you mind telling me more about your family and the types of activities you like to do?"

"Well," Jackie proceeded, "we like to go to church, *(community context)* and since we have a large extended family, we participate in a lot of different activities. My daughter leads the children's choir at church, *(activity setting)* and Marcus loves to go be around the other children. *(child interest)* He especially loves to play outside, and he loves music, too. Sometimes, we take him to work with us for a little while, and one of my sisters or brothers picks him up and takes him home. We also look forward to family gatherings for birthdays and holidays. *(contexts for multiple activity settings)* They always give Marcus an opportunity to play ball with his cousins. *(activity setting, child interest)* Oh, and Marcus loves my parents' dog. I can't keep him away from Fuzzy!"

"You've given me a wealth of information," Asia said. "How has the therapy that Marcus has been receiving helped him be involved in the types of activities you have mentioned and enjoy the things he like to do?" *(Reflection—probing learner to reflect)*

"Well, therapy is separate from what we do as a family. It's what Jan did when she came. I guess you could say it's getting him to a point where he can learn to walk and not develop bad habits that would prevent him from moving more normally." *(Reflection—sharing expectations)*

"Do you feel like you have the supports and information you need to help Marcus participate right now?" Asia asked. *(Reflection—probing learner about usefulness)*

"The therapy is a support. He's made great progress in therapy, and we loved Jan. He can sit up now, and he couldn't until Jan came to work with him. Have you talked to her about everything he's accomplished? He needs you to stretch his legs by rolling him over the ball, even though he may not like it," Jackie quickly added.

Asia responded, "Have you thought about ways that you and other family members could encourage Marcus's learning and participation all the time based on the activities he likes to do and with the people that are most important to him, instead of doing things he doesn't like or he only did when Jan was here?" *(Reflection—determining reception of new ideas)*

Jackie raised her eyebrows and looked away from Asia, "We may not have specific ideas about what to do, but we have wondered if we couldn't be doing something ourselves."

"Could you be more specific?" *(Reflection—clarifying learner's expectations)*

"Well, for instance, he loves to dance to music, *(learning opportunity, child interest)* so wouldn't that help his legs get stronger? He loves eating marshmallows. *(learning opportu-*

REFLECT ON THIS . . .
Rethinking therapy

- What type of approach was previously being used with Marcus and his family?
- How is the coaching approach different from the traditional approach?
- How did Asia begin to explore activity settings and learning opportunities with Jackie?
- What are Marcus's interests? What does he like to do? What interests Jackie and Lawrence?
- What are some of this family's activity settings?
- Within these activity settings, list Marcus's learning opportunities.
- Formulate three questions that you could use to stimulate Jackie's reflection regarding how Marcus can take Fuzzy for a walk.

---

nity, child interest) Wouldn't feeding himself marshmallows give him practice using his fingers to pick things up? He'd do just about anything to play with the dog. I'd sure like to figure out some way for Marcus to help take him for a walk." *(activity setting, child interest)* *(Reflection—self-discovering ideas)*

"These are some of the same thoughts and questions that came to my mind," Asia agreed. "I'm really excited about your ideas. *(Reflection—providing feedback, affirming ideas)* Together, we can come up with some strategies for helping Marcus walk the dog."

Asia identified a coaching opportunity and initiated a conversation with Jackie in the beginning of the coaching story. Through this conversation, Asia was able to learn family activity settings, child learning opportunities, and child and family interests. Marcus's activity settings included a pallet on the floor, the children's choir at church, and family get-togethers. His interests included playing ball with his cousins, playing with his grandparents' dog, eating marshmallows, dancing, and being around the children in the choir. Some community contexts included church and family gatherings.

In order to promote Jackie's capacity to support Marcus's participation in the family context, Asia encouraged her to be reflective. She probed Jackie to reflect on what had been happening in light of what she wanted and needed to do with Marcus. Jackie then shared what she wanted Marcus to do and her feelings about the usefulness of Jan's services. Next, Asia used the reflection phase to probe Jackie to see if she would be open to other ideas, and Jackie admitted that she would like to do more things herself for Marcus. Asia probed Jackie to be more specific about what she wanted to do for Marcus, and Jackie self-discovered ideas for how to support Marcus in the family context and provide an opportunity for him to practice new skills. Finally, Asia provided feedback and affirmation for Jackie's ideas.

CONCLUSION

In early childhood intervention, family and community settings provide the content for coaching conversations versus the use of decontextualized therapy activities designed and implemented by multiple practitioners in unnatural settings (e.g., therapy clinics, segregated classrooms, hospitals). Using coaching as a primary strategy for supporting families in home and community settings builds the capacity of the people who are important in the life of the child to enhance child learning and participation in real-life activity settings.

This chapter focused on how an early childhood practitioner as coach can support families in promoting child participation in family and community contexts in accordance with Part C of the IDEA 1997. As described, family and community contexts are rich in learning opportunities for young children. The role of the coach in these contexts is to facilitate parent identification and use of existing and potential learning opportunities that are interesting and engaging to the child and, in turn, provide environments for the child to practice existing skills and master new abilities. Being in the family and community contexts alongside parents and other family members can present challenges that were not evident when providing clinic-based services. In natural environments, practitioners must consider the family's time and lifestyle, recognize and respect family diversity, and prepare for potential confidentiality issues. This chapter also provided four considerations for a process of moving from a traditional service approach to using coaching in family and community settings because this approach is different from what most families may know.

Each of the coaching stories illustrated how to identify interests, activity settings, and learning opportunities within the family and community contexts. In the first story, Loretta, the coach, brainstormed with the parents so they could continue a favorite family activity. This story was also used to illustrate the three critical issues when working in the family and community contexts. The critical issues included supporting family time, lifestyle, and choices; honoring the diversity of families; and preparing for circumstances in which confidentiality could be compromised. In the second coaching story, Carlos could have observed and listened to the mother and grandmother through the filters of his own personal values, beliefs, and experiences, which could have led to the conclusion that the natural environment for this child held few activity settings and limited learning opportunities; however, when looking through the lens of family strengths and assets, Carlos saw many opportunities. The competence of this family in supporting the child's learning was further illustrated by their ability to self-reflect and generalize learning opportunities across activity settings. The final coaching story demonstrated how a practitioner acting as coach might support a family in moving from a traditional model of service delivery to a coaching approach.

TRY THIS . . .
Prompting reflection by parents

A parent tells you that she reads books to her daughter before bedtime every night. Write down three questions that you could use to promote the parent's reflection related to increasing child participation in this bedtime ritual.

1.

2.

3.

    Select a family that you are currently supporting as part of your role in an early intervention or early childhood program. The next time a family member asks you for ideas or you want to share your ideas about a particular topic, practice your coaching skills by inviting the family member to reflect on his or her ideas first. Support the family in identifying ideas and strategies based on the child's interests that could occur within planned family activities or spontaneously as a part of family life.

    Supporting parents in promoting child participation in family and community contexts through coaching challenges how families and early childhood practitioners have viewed early childhood intervention. Not only has the "where" changed, but the "how" is very different as well. The early childhood practitioner must know how to clearly explain the approach and the rationale. When implementing the coaching approach, the practitioner must:

- Recognize and build on the existing knowledge and skills of the family members

- Avoid the tendency to immediately tell the family member what he or she should do, and take the time to explore what they are already doing to support their child

- Become familiar with the family's activity settings and jointly identify typical as well as spontaneous learning opportunities as part of these settings

- Remember that moving to a coaching approach means learning from the family just as they may learn from the coach

- Begin this change one family at a time

    As you conclude this chapter, reflect on these questions:

- Think about a family you support. How familiar are you with their typical activity settings and interests?

- Do families see you as an expert who comes in and tells them what to do, or do they see you as a resource who can support them in promoting their child's participation in ordinary family life?

- If you were to choose one family with whom to begin using a coaching approach, what family would you select, and how would you explain this approach to them?

RESOURCES

Dunst, C.J., Bruder, M.B., Trivette, C.M., Raab, M., & McLean, M. (2001). Natural learning opportunities for infants, toddlers, and preschoolers. *Young Exceptional Children, 4*(3), 18–25.
This article provides an overview and examples of activity settings and natural learning opportunities. In addition, the authors outline the steps for identifying a child's learning opportunities and interests as well as how to increase learning opportunities.

Dunst, C.J., Trivette, C.M., Humphries, T., Raab, M., & Roper, N. (2001). Contrasting approaches to natural learning environment interventions. *Infants and Young Children, 14*(2), 48–63.
This article provides three dimensions for considering how to provide supports in natural learning environments. These dimensions include whether the setting is contextualized or decontextualized, whether the type of activity is child-initiated or adult-directed, and whether learning opportunities can occur only when the practitioner is present.

REFERENCES

Bronfenbrenner, U. (1992). Ecological systems theory. In R. Vasta (Ed.), *Six theories of child development: Revised formulations and current issues.* Philadelphia: Jessica Kingsley.
Bronfenbrenner, U. (1993). The ecology of cognitive development: Research models and fugitive findings. In R.H. Wozniak & K.W. Fischer (Eds.), *Development in context: Acting and thinking in specific environments.* Mahwah, NJ: Lawrence Erlbaum Associates.
Bronfenbrenner, U. (1999). Environments in developmental perspective: Theoretical and operational models. In S.L. Friedman & T.D. Wachs (Eds.), *Measuring environment across the life span: Emerging methods and concepts.* Washington, DC: American Psychological Association.
Bruder, M.B., & Dunst, C.J. (December 1999/January 2000). Expanding learning opportunities for infants and toddlers in natural environments: A chance to reconceptualize early intervention. *Zero to Three,* 34–36.
Campbell, S. (1997). Therapy programs for children that last a lifetime. *Physical and Occupational Therapy in Pediatrics, 7*(1), 1–15.
Chen, J.Q., Krechevsky, M., Viens, J., & Isberg, E. (Vol. Eds.). (1998). *Project Zero frameworks for early childhood education: Vol. 1. Building on children's strengths: The experience of Project Spectrum.* (H. Gardner, D.H. Feldman, & M. Krechevsky, Series Eds.). New York: Teachers College Press.
Coufal, K. (1993). Collaborative consultation for speech-language pathologists. *Topics in Language Disorders, 14*(1), 1–14.
Dinnebeil, L., McInerney, W., Roth, J., & Ramaswamy, V. (2001). Itinerant early childhood special education services: Service delivery in one state. *Journal of Early Intervention, 24*(1), 35–44.
Dunst, C. (2000). Revisiting "Rethinking Early Intervention." *Topics in Early Childhood Special Education, 20,* 95–104.

Dunst, C.J., Bruder, M.B., Trivette, C.M., Raab, M., & McLean, M. (2001). Natural learning opportunities for infants, toddlers, and preschoolers. *Young Exceptional Children, 4*(3), 18–25.

Dunst, C.J., Hamby, D., Trivette, C.M., Raab, M., & Bruder, M.B. (2000). Everyday family and community life and children's naturally occurring learning opportunities. *Journal of Early Intervention, 23*(3), 151–164.

Dunst, C.J., Trivette, C.M., Humphries, T., Raab, M., & Roper, N. (2001). Contrasting approaches to natural learning environment interventions. *Infants and Young Children, 14*(2), 48–63.

Flaherty, J. (1999). *Coaching: Evoking excellence in others.* Boston: Butterworth-Heinemann.

Gallimore, R., & Goldenberg, C. (1993). Activity settings of early literacy: Home and school factors in children's emergent literacy. In E.A. Forman, N. Minick, & C.A. Stone (Eds.), *Contexts for learning: Sociocultural dynamics in children's development.* New York: Oxford University Press.

Gallimore, R., Goldenberg, C.N., & Wesiner, T.S. (1993). The social construction and subjective reality of activity settings: Implications for community psychology. *American Journal of Community Psychology, 21,* 537–559.

Goncu, A. (Ed.). (1999). *Children's engagement in the world: Sociocultural perspectives.* Cambridge, England: Cambridge University Press.

Hanft, B., & Pilkington, K. (2000). Therapy in natural environments: The means or end goal for early intervention? *Infants and Young Children, 12*(4), 1–13.

Individuals with Disabilities Education Act (IDEA) of 1990, PL 101-476, 20 U.S.C §§ 1400 *et seq.*

Individuals with Disabilities Education Act Amendments of 1997, PL 105-17, 20 U.S.C §§ 1400 *et seq.*

Lave, J. (1996). The practice of learning. In S. Chaiklin & J. Lave (Eds.), *Understanding practice: Perspectives on activity and context* (pp. 3–32). Cambridge, England: Cambridge University Press.

Rush, D.D. (2000). Invited perspective. *Infants and Young Children, 13*(2), vi–ix.

Shelden, M.L., & Rush, D.D. (2001). The ten myths about providing early intervention services in natural environments. *Infants and Young Children, 14*(1), 1–13.

Wolery, M., & Bailey, D. (1989). Assessing play skills. In D.B. Dailey & M. Wolery (Eds.), *Assessing infants and preschoolers with handicaps* (pp. 442–447). Columbus, OH: Charles E. Merrill.

Appendix

Coaching Worksheet: A New Ride for Tyler

Learner: _James and Felicia_   Coach: _Loretta_   Date: _May 15_

INITIATION

Coaching opportunities observed or presented

Referral to early intervention program

The purpose of the coaching relationship is

To support Tyler's participation in family outdoor activity settings

Intended learner outcomes resulting from the coaching relationship

Tyler's family will identify alternative interest-based activity settings.

James, Felicia, and Tyler will resume outdoor activities as a family.

Barriers to the coaching process	**Strategies to address barriers**
Both parents work full time.	Loretta also supports Tyler's child care provider. She visits Felicia on her day off work during the week, and she visits James and Felicia after work.

Ground rules

Discuss potential confidentiality issues prior to any trip into the community in which Loretta will join the family

OBSERVATION

	What/where	When
Coach observes learner's actions and interactions		
Learner observes coach model actions		
Learner observes self		
Coach/learner observe environment		

ACTION	What/where	When
Coach models for learner (coach present)		
Learner practices an action (coach present/absent)		
Learner describes experience (coach absent)		
Coach/learner observe environment	James and Felicia are thinking about discontinuing their hikes in the mountains because Tyler is too heavy to carry.	May 15

REFLECTION	Description		
Learner reflects on action or observation	James and Felicia considered a stroller or not taking Tyler, but being in the mountains is an activity they enjoy as a family. James and Felicia remembered that Tyler's godfather had suggested they consider mountain biking.		
Coach gives feedback about observation or action following reflection			
Learner uses resources (e.g., print, video, peer)	James will borrow a couple of mountain bikes. Loretta will ask Ron to adapt the child seat on the bicycle or make an insert.		
Coach confirms learner's understanding and summarizes			
Coach/learner plan next steps	Who	What	When
Observations	Loretta and Ron will go to the mountain bike trail at the park with James, Felicia, and Tyler on Friday to see how well the adapted child seat on the bike works.		
Practice			
Resources	Ron will adapt the child seat on the mountain bike on Friday.		

EVALUATION

Coach Self-Reflection

1. Is the learner accomplishing his or her goals?

   Yes

2. What changes, if any, do I need to make in the coaching process?

   Be more affirming of James's and Felicia's ideas

3. Should I continue as this learner's coach? (If not, who would be more effective?)

   Yes

Coach Asks Learner

1. Shall we continue coaching or have your goals been accomplished (continuation)?

   Yes, continue coaching

   If continuing coaching:

   - What changes need to be made in the coaching plan?

     Continue with the current coaching plan

   - What observations and/or actions should take place between coaching sessions?

     James and Felicia will use the mountain bikes with the adapted child seat and share the results during the next coaching visit.

   - How will we communicate in between sessions?

     James and Felicia can call Loretta if needed between coaching sessions. If they need to change the child seat on the bicycle, they will contact Loretta, and she'll get in touch with Ron.

   - Do we have a plan for the next session?

     Yes

2. If goals have been reached (resolution):

   - Is the learner committed to and capable of self-assessment, self-correction, and self-generation?

   - Has a plan for reinstituting coaching been discussed?

Coaching Worksheet: Learning in the Country

Learner: _Opal and Shirley_   Coach: _Carlos_   Date: _September 3_

INITIATION

Coaching opportunities observed or presented

Referral to early intervention program

The purpose of the coaching relationship is

To promote Kenny's participation and learning as a part of his family life

Intended learner outcomes resulting from the coaching relationship

Shirley and Opal will identify and use everyday activities as learning opportunities for Kenny.

Kenny will play with Jason and Amy during outdoor activities.

Jason and Amy will support Kenny's involvement in joint play activities.

Barriers to the coaching process	Strategies to address barriers
At beginning of coaching experience, Kenny's mother was away. His grandmother was the primary care provider until his mother returned.	When his mother returned, she was included in the coaching conversations. Kenny's grandmother assisted in bringing her up-to-date.

Ground rules

Coaching visits will last about an hour. Coach will work with grandmother to determine best time. Kenny's brother and sister are encouraged to be part of the coaching visits.

OBSERVATION

	What/where	When
Coach observes learner's actions and interactions		
Learner observes coach model actions		
Learner observes self		
Coach/learner observe environment		

ACTION

	What/where	When
Coach models for learner (coach present)		
Learner practices an action (coach present/absent)	Shirley waits to give Kenny opportunity to talk at mealtimes and during play.	August 15 to September 3
Learner describes experience (coach absent)	Opal put chicken feed in basket attached to walker to help Kenny feed chickens using walker.	August 17
Coach/learner observe environment		

REFLECTION

	Description		
Learner reflects on action or observation	Opal suggests larger wheels for walker. Shirley reports Kenny grunts to get toys instead of using words.		
Coach gives feedback about observation or action following reflection			
Learner uses resources (e.g., print, video, peer)			
Coach confirms learner's understanding and summarizes			
Coach/learner plan next steps Observations Practice	Who	What	When
Practice	Shirley and Opal will provide opportunity for Kenny to use words by waiting and modeling word for him during play September 3–17. Shirley will teach brother and sister how to wait and model when playing on tire swing September 3–17.		
Resources	Opal will get larger tires for walker September 5.		

EVALUATION

Coach Self-Reflection

1. Is the learner accomplishing his or her goals?

   Yes

2. What changes, if any, do I need to make in the coaching process?

   Continue to support mother and grandmother and use their ideas

3. Should I continue as this learner's coach? (If not, who would be more effective?)

   Yes

Coach Asks Learner

1. Shall we continue coaching or have your goals been accomplished (continuation)?

   Yes, continue coaching

   If continuing coaching:

   - What changes need to be made in the coaching plan?

     Continue with the current coaching plan

   - What observations and/or actions should take place between coaching sessions?

     Mother, grandmother, brother, and sister are going to increase opportunities for Kenny getting what he wants during play by giving him time to say the word. Then, if he does not, they will model the word, then wait for him to attempt the word.

   - How will we communicate in between sessions?

     Because the family does not have a phone, the mother and grandmother prefer to stop by the office to leave a message when they borrow a car to come into town, or the coach will take a message to them if necessary.

   - Do we have a plan for the next session?

     Yes, follow-up on strategies discussed during previous visit

2. If goals have been reached (resolution):

   - Is the learner committed to and capable of self-assessment, self-correction, and self-generation?

   - Has a plan for reinstituting coaching been discussed?

Coaching Worksheet: Rethinking Therapy

Learner: _Jackie_   Coach: _Asia_   Date: _November 29_

INITIATION

Coaching opportunities observed or presented

Referral to early intervention program

The purpose of the coaching relationship is

To support Marcus's participation and learning during family life activities

Intended learner outcomes resulting from the coaching relationship

Marcus's family will recognize and use everyday activities as learning opportunities.

Marcus's family will use his interests to promote his participation during church activities.

Barriers to the coaching process	Strategies to address barriers
Both parents work nights.	Asia will call before visiting to ensure it is a good time.
	Some visits will be made with grandparents and aunt, who are also caregivers.

Ground rules

Visits will last about an hour.

Asia will call before making a visit.

Because extended family members play an active role in Marcus's life, they are encouraged to participate in visits, and visits will occasionally be scheduled at times and locations so they may attend.

OBSERVATION

	What/where	When
Coach observes learner's actions and interactions		
Learner observes coach model actions		
Learner observes self		
Coach/learner observe environment		

ACTION

	What/where	When
Coach models for learner (coach present)		
Learner practices an action (coach present/absent)		
Learner describes experience (coach absent)		
Coach/learner observe environment		

REFLECTION

	Description		
Learner reflects on action or observation	Jackie reflects on how she and other family members can support Marcus's learning and participation as part of family activities. Jackie identifies Marcus's interests and opportunities for learning.		
Coach gives feedback about observation or action following reflection			
Learner uses resources (e.g., print, video, peer)			
Coach confirms learner's understanding and summarizes	Asia affirms Jackie's ideas about learning opportunities and ways to support Marcus's involvement in the family.		
Coach/learner plan next steps Observations	Who	What	When
Practice		Jackie will continue to think about ideas to support Marcus in the family context and provide him with opportunities to practice his skills November 29–December 6.	
Resources			

EVALUATION

Coach Self-Reflection

1. Is the learner accomplishing his or her goals?

   Will discuss further during the next visit

2. What changes, if any, do I need to make in the coaching process?

   Need to discuss during next visit

3. Should I continue as this learner's coach? (If not, who would be more effective?)

   Yes

Coach Asks Learner

1. Shall we continue coaching or have your goals been accomplished (continuation)?

   Yes, continue coaching

   If continuing coaching:

   - What changes need to be made in the coaching plan?

     Will discuss further during the next visit

   - What observations and/or actions should take place between coaching sessions?

     To be discussed

   - How will we communicate in between sessions?

     Asia will call Jackie

   - Do we have a plan for the next session?

     Follow up on what Jackie has tried

2. If goals have been reached (resolution):

   - Is the learner committed to and capable of self-assessment, self-correction, and self-generation?

   - Has a plan for reinstituting coaching been discussed?

6

COACHING IN GROUP SETTINGS

This chapter focuses on the role of the early childhood practitioner as a coach supporting families and their young children in group settings, such as preschools, child care programs, library story hours, and toddler playgroups. The critical issues associated with coaching in group settings are explored, and coaching stories are used as a mechanism for depicting the coaching process in action. Readers are encouraged to compare the practices delineated in the stories to their own and to reflect on how coaching could be incorporated into their interactions with the important people in group settings where families and their children are participating or desire to do so. As in Chapter 5, matching child and family interests to existing or desired activity settings is used as the basis for promoting participation in group settings.

Chapter 5 discussed the framework for looking at the family and community settings for opportunities for coaching. This chapter looks at group settings in early childhood as another venue for use of the coaching process. Group settings can provide increased learning opportunities for young children with disabilities to interact and develop alongside similar age peers without disabilities that may be different from the learning opportunities they may experience in family and community contexts (Appl, Fahl-Gooler, & McCollum, 1997; Wolery & Odom, 2000).

Research shows positive effects for all children in the setting when staff are properly supported to include children with disabilities (Bricker, 2000; Bruder, 1993; Bruder & Brand, 1995; Odom, 2000). Odom, following an exhaustive review of the literature, noted positive outcomes for all children in inclusive settings and reported research supporting the fact that teachers and families generally have positive attitudes about including children with disabilities in their classrooms. In addition, the quality of the inclusive settings was comparable to the quality of the traditional settings in programs where only typically developing children were supported. In this review, the most replicated finding in the literature indicated that in inclusive settings, children with disabilities engage in social interaction with peers less often than the children without disabilities. This information is important from a coaching perspective because a major role of the coach in a group setting will most likely be focused on supporting adults in that setting to implement and possibly learn strategies to promote the social interaction and participation of the child with disabilities.

For a group setting to be inclusive, two critical features of the setting must be present—critical mass and physical membership (Odom, 2000). Critical mass indicates that at minimum, the number of children with disabilities in the group does not outnumber the children without disabilities. The term *physical membership* means that in a group setting, a child with a disability is more likely a true member of the group if he or she spends the same amount of time in the same location and participating in the group activities as children without disabilities (Brown, Odom, Li, & Zercher, 1999). Many early childhood practitioners, however, have served children in segregated programs or pulled them out of or to the side of a classroom to provide isolated therapy and instruction using decontextualized activities. Although supporting young children with disabilities in public and private preschools, child care programs, and other group settings may bring new challenges for many early childhood practitioners, coaching will facilitate communication and collaboration to develop effective partnerships for child learning across settings.

The information presented in Chapter 5 on moving from a traditional service delivery approach to the use of the coaching process applies also in early childhood group settings. Again, the process involves

• Identifying the role of the early childhood practitioner as coach

• Identifying the primary learners in the group context

• Redefining "hands-on" intervention

• Reconsidering frequency and intensity of support

For example, in a more traditional service delivery approach, it would be typical for a child to receive multiple therapy services in a preschool setting. The child might be taken to a special therapy room or pulled aside within the classroom to practice skill acquisition based on identified impairments. In doing so, the child

REFLECT ON THIS . . .
Environmental observations and reflective questions

- Do the children/family members appear happy and actively involved with each other and materials?
- Does the program appear to consider the child and family interests as a way to structure learning opportunities?
- What is the ratio of adults to children in the group setting?
- Does the room arrangement allow for freedom of movement?
- How does the group leader or teacher promote participation of the children in activities?
- Does the group leader or teacher follow the child's lead?
- Are the activities that are planned for the children fun, engaging, and based on their interests?
- Are families' ideas and opinions valued and considered in planning for the group? (Oklahoma State Department of Education, 2001; Wolery & Odom, 2000)

---

misses valuable opportunities for practicing existing as well as new skills within the context of the group activity setting. The child or caregiver is then responsible for applying learned skills within the context of the group activity. When using coaching within a group setting, the teacher or leader is the learner and supports the child's participation, resulting in motivation, reinforcement, and generalization occurring naturally within the activity.

ROLE OF THE COACH IN GROUP SETTINGS

The role of the coach is to support learners in group settings by developing relationships with key people in these environments. The coach should recognize that learners in these settings have unique strengths but perhaps differing needs and expectations. The coach should strive to involve these partners in assessment and development of the IFSP or IEP rather than using the process to compel an early childhood program or child care provider to engage in a certain type of programming or level of activity. Through coaching conversations, the IFSP or IEP is jointly developed by the people who can have the most significant impact on the child's participation and learning.

As a coach and learner enter into a new coaching relationship, the coach must understand the setting-specific issues that may be facing the learner, such as fluctuating staff–child ratios in a child care setting or frequently changing leaders of community-based groups. With appropriate permission, the coach should initially plan on spending time observing the early childhood setting. The coach should not solely focus on the child within the setting, but instead focus on understanding the general environment, expectations, and philosophy of the setting. The interaction styles, and if appropriate, the teaching styles of the people in the setting are also important for the coach to recognize and understand. The Reflect on This activity on page 127 presents some possible environmental observations for the coach to consider and some questions to be thinking about while in the environment.

The following coaching story (summarized in Figure 6.1) illustrates a coach supporting a local librarian as he is challenged to promote the participation of a young girl and her father in a toddler story hour. The story demonstrates the coach reflecting with the learner, developing new ideas, and learning new skills. A Coaching Worksheet with the appropriate sections completed for this coaching story is located in the chapter appendix. You may find it helpful to use the worksheet to follow the coaching process while reading the story.

TODDLER READ-ALONG GROUP

Archie, a local librarian, looked forward to his next conversation with Lisa, the teacher from the early intervention program. He was excited to discuss Desiree's participation in the toddler read-along group *(activity setting)* last week. Desiree's father, J.H., had approached Archie a couple of months back and asked if he could bring Desiree to the toddler group on Tuesday and Thursday mornings. Archie told him that it was open to all 2- and 3-year-old children and their parents or child care providers, and he would gladly welcome them. Archie remembered J.H.'s hesitation as he explained that his 2-year-old daughter had cerebral palsy and used a breathing machine attached to her wheelchair. J.H. had wanted to make sure that Archie wouldn't be opposed to them joining the group.

Archie recalled feeling unfamiliar with and somewhat nervous about the situation, but he wanted J.H. to feel welcome and encouraged him to bring Desiree to the next story hour. J.H. then further explained the local early intervention program and told Archie about Lisa, an early childhood special education teacher who served as his coach. J.H. asked if he and Lisa could meet with Archie before attending the group. Archie readily agreed to a meeting.

Rrrrring . . . Archie was abruptly returned to the present as he answered the ringing phone on his desk.

"Hi, Archie. It's Lisa. How are you?"

"I'm great," Archie exclaimed.

"Wow! You sound pumped!" Lisa said. "Is this a good time for you to talk? I had in my book to call around 8:15."

"This is perfect," Archie replied. "I've actually been sitting here waiting for the phone to ring. I tried some of the ideas we came up with last week, and I'd like to get your thoughts on some other things I've been thinking about." *(Action—situation preceding discussion)*

Purpose of coaching:

> To support Desiree's participation in the local library toddler read-along group

Outcomes of coaching:

1. Archie, the librarian who leads the story hour, will learn new skills related to promoting Desiree's participation in group activities.

2. J.H. will gain increased confidence in participating with his child in a group setting.

3. Desiree will have fun and interact with other children and parents in the group setting.

Key partners	Child and family interests	Activity settings
Desiree—child *J.H.*—father *Archie*—librarian *Lisa*—early childhood special education teacher	*Family*—giving child opportunity to play with other children *Child*—playing with other children, reading books, listening to music	Library story hour

Figure 6.1. Toddler read-along group.

"Great," replied Lisa. "I'm all ears."

"The first thing I'm excited about is that almost all of the parents and other children have been open, warm, and friendly to Desiree and J.H. Most of the kids go up to her and ask questions about her wheelchair and the breathing machine. J.H. handles the questions beautifully. I've learned a lot listening to him. I feel like I can answer similar questions more effectively and confidently now." *(Reflection–confirming understanding)*

Lisa interjected, "Have you shared this information with J.H.? *(Reflection)* It would be great feedback for him to hear that he has been helpful to you."

"That's a great idea, Lisa. I'll do it tomorrow before group begins. We use Thursday mornings before the group to touch base. It's working out really well. I am wondering, though. We do have a lot of activities that involve the parents and children sitting and playing on the floor together. I've worked pretty hard to establish a comfortable and inviting area—you know, big pillows and beanbag chairs. I've even put most of the books at eye level for the children in brightly colored cubbies and small bookshelves. This is awkward for Desiree. Because she is in her wheelchair all of the time, she isn't able to get down on the floor or even look at the choices of books. J.H. does a great job of choosing several books to present to Desiree, but it's just not the same thing."

"What are your thoughts, Archie?" Lisa asked. *(Reflection–determining what learner thinks)*

"Well, I'd like to get her out of that wheelchair. I mentioned it to J.H. He seemed hesitant but said we could do it and he could show me how. I just wanted to check with you to make sure I wasn't doing something wrong. What do you think?" asked Archie. *(Action—anticipating and discussing an experience)*

"I think it's a great idea to get her out of the wheelchair, and this may help with several issues, including those few reluctant children who seem extra cautious of the wheelchair. I also think it's a great strategy to have J.H. be the one to get Desiree out of her wheelchair, but I agree that you should learn how to help in case you're needed. *(Reflection—providing feedback, sharing information)* If you're planning on doing this tomorrow, would it be helpful for me to come and observe the group at that time?" *(Reflection—planning new actions)*

"Lisa, that would be great. Let's plan on it."

"Are there other specific strategies that you'd like me to be watching for tomorrow?" Lisa asked. "I know you'd mentioned adapting a few books with Popsicle sticks glued to the pages to help Desiree turn the pages on her own. *(learning opportunity)* Have you tried that yet?" *(Reflection—determining what has been tried)*

Archie quickly replied, "I rigged a few books yesterday afternoon and am ready to try them out tomorrow." *(Action—trying new strategy)*

The next day, Lisa observed the toddler read-along group. *(Observation—observing learner in action)* She arrived early and joined Archie and J.H. in their planning conversation. The three of them decided to take Desiree out of her wheelchair and position her comfortably on a beanbag chair in the center of the group reading area. As the parents and children arrived, they were surprised and excited to see Desiree out of her wheelchair. Several children ran up to her and sat down beside her on the bean bag.

During the reading group, Archie attempted to use the newly adapted books and was struggling with how to help Desiree turn a page. Archie motioned for Lisa to come over to him and asked, "Hey, Lisa, can you help us out here? We can't figure out how to hold the book, keep it where Desiree can see it, and help her to turn the page all at the same time." *(Action—self-observation)*

Lisa gave Archie and J.H. a few pointers, including demonstrating how to help Desiree move her arm herself to turn the page. *(Action—modeling actions)* J.H. and Archie gave it a try and after a few practice attempts Desiree was successful and turned the page herself. *(Action—practicing new skill)* She was obviously pleased and laughed out loud at her accomplishment. Archie, J.H., and the other parents and children joined in the celebration.

A few days later, Lisa received a phone call from Archie to discuss the group's activity from the previous week.

"Lisa, this is Archie. Do you have a few minutes to talk?"

"Sure, Archie, I've got about 20 minutes before I need to head out for my next appointment. Will that work?"

"Great! I appreciate your time," replied Archie. "I just wanted to thank you for your help last week. I think we've really overcome a major obstacle and the entire group seems excited about our collective progress. I'd like some feedback from you, though."

"I was excited about the progress, as well," Lisa said. "Tell me why you think the group was so successful?" *(Reflection—determining what learner thinks)*

Archie thought a minute and said, "I think getting Desiree out of her wheelchair was a major success. The children and other parents were more responsive to her right away. It was also very helpful having you there to show me how to use the adapted book the first time. Now, I feel comfortable using it and teaching others how to use it on my own." *(Reflection—self-reflecting on new strategies)*

"I agree, Archie. Your idea to get Desiree out of her chair was successful. Also, you caught on really quickly to the ideas I shared regarding book placement and cues to assist Desiree in turning the page herself. *(Reflection—providing feedback, confirming understanding)* Have you thought of some other ways that Desiree could exert additional independence during the read-along group?" *(Reflection—determining what learner thinks)*

"I'm glad you asked, Lisa." Archie proceeded to share some new ideas with his coach.

This coaching story demonstrates the reciprocal nature of coaching and the effectiveness of supporting a learner in generating and implementing ideas that match priorities in a timely manner. Although Archie was eager to accept J.H. and Desiree into the group, he needed support in figuring out how the group could be a meaningful environment for Desiree and her father.

The coaching story began in the action phase of the coaching process. Archie had tried a few ideas in the toddler group and contacted Lisa for her feedback. He then used the reflection phase when he confirmed that he understood what he had learned from J.H. Lisa then used reflection to encourage Archie to share his thoughts with J.H. and to generate ideas to solve the problem of Desiree not being able to reach books. Archie used the action phase when anticipating taking Desiree out of her wheelchair and discussed it with Lisa prior to implementation. Next, Lisa gave Archie feedback and planned to attend the session. She continued to encourage Archie to reflect on things he had tried with Desiree and things he would like to try.

The following day, she observed Archie in action during the toddler group. Archie also observed himself and recognized that he needed Lisa's help using the adapted book with Desiree. Lisa used the action phase of the coaching process to model how Archie could assist Desiree in turning pages of the book. Archie in turn used the action phase to practice turning the pages.

During a phone conversation after the toddler group, Lisa encouraged reflection by asking Archie why he thought the group was successful. Archie self-reflected on the new strategies he had tried during the toddler group, and Lisa gave feedback confirming his understanding. Finally, Lisa encouraged reflection by assisting Archie in discovering how Desiree could be even more independent during the toddler group.

Not all coaching situations are as simple as this one. Sometimes a child care provider is not as interested in joining a coach or parent in identifying new learn-

Purpose of coaching:

> To identify possible learning opportunities for Jody in Ms. Phoebe's child care home

Outcomes of coaching:

> 1. Jody's interests will be identified and matched to existing or desired activity settings within the child care home.
>
> 2. Amber will enter into a formal coaching relationship with Ms. Phoebe.
>
> 3. Jody will have fun, play with other children, and participate in newly identified learning opportunities.

Key partners	Child and family interests	Activity settings
Jody—child *Melody*—mother *Ms. Phoebe*—child care provider *Amber*—physical therapist	*Family*—giving child opportunity to play with other children *Child*—playing with other children, reading books, playing with balls	Free play in living room of child care home Television time Mealtimes

Figure 6.2. Ms. Phoebe's house.

ing opportunities for a young child. The following coaching story (summarized in Figure 6.2) illustrates a coach, parent, and child care provider discussing possible learning opportunities for Jody, a child being cared for in the child care provider's home. After an in-depth discussion, the child care provider, Ms. Phoebe, makes it clear she is not interested in entering a coaching relationship with Amber, Jody's physical therapist from the early intervention program. Amber reflects on alternatives following the discussion.

Ms. Phoebe's House

Melody loved to rave about Ms. Phoebe. When Amber came to visit Melody and Jody at Ms. Phoebe's house, Melody couldn't stop praising Ms. Phoebe.

"My family lives 2 hours away, so Ms. Phoebe has been a real angel to me!" she said. "Jody stays with Ms. Phoebe during the day, then I pick him up when I get off work—usually about 7:00 P.M. Since my schedule changes and I usually have to work evenings, I was lucky to find someone who is flexible with me and keeps him in the evening."

Ms. Phoebe smiled, "Oh, honey, you and Jody are just a joy to me!"

Amber listened as Melody and Ms. Phoebe described Jody's experiences in child care. Then, she asked Ms. Phoebe, "What does Jody like to do best at child care?" *(Reflection—determining what learner knows)*

"Well," Ms. Phoebe thought for a moment, "you know, he's a pretty active 2-year-old, so I came up with the idea to make him a little play area over there in the corner of my living room." *(activity setting)*

Amber turned to look at the corner of the living room that Ms. Phoebe had cleared of furniture and circled with a plastic fence. Inside the area, Amber could see three plastic cars and a small ball sitting on a quilt. Two other children, who appeared to be close to Jody's age, sat on the sofa watching a videotape of cartoons.

Melody added, "She put up the little plastic fence to keep him and his toys away from her cats and collection of Snow Baby figurines."

"Oh yes, he would just love to get into my pretties AND the cat's litter box! He does like playing with cars *(child interest)* though. Sometimes, he throws them over the fence, so I just keep them until he simmers down. There's been a time or two when he carried on so long that I just didn't give them back! I always tell Melody when this happens. In fact, if I decide I can't handle him anymore, she's going to have to find another place to go." *(Reflection—describing current situation)*

Melody quickly interjected, "But we're trying to work on that. I don't know what I'd do if he couldn't stay here. With my job, I just can't afford one of the bigger day care centers. And besides, he wouldn't get as much attention there either."

"Jody loves to watch the game shows on television *(activity setting)* with me," Ms. Phoebe added. "Why I could just sit and watch those things for hours, but Jody can't watch for more than 30 minutes at a time!" *(Reflection—describing current situation)*

As Ms. Phoebe spoke, Amber thought to herself, "Ms. Phoebe is affordable for Melody, and she's afraid that she can't find another child care provider if she chooses to leave or if Ms. Phoebe asks her to take him somewhere else. On the other hand, I do have some concerns about the quality of care Jody is receiving here at Ms. Phoebe's. I need to ask some questions to get at Ms. Phoebe's level of knowledge about learning opportunities for young children."

Amber said, "Ms. Phoebe, a child care provider can provide many sources of learning opportunities for young children. How about if we take a few minutes to think about some opportunities that maybe are occurring here or could occur here with you and Jody during the day? How do you plan the day for the children in your care?" *(Reflection—probing learner to consider new options)*

"Oh, honey, I don't really do any planning other than meals. *(activity setting)* I just take it as it comes. They play, we watch television, and sometimes I read books *(activity setting)* to them. Are you saying I should have some planned activities? This isn't a preschool, you know, it's just a day care home." *(Reflection—describing current situation)*

"Well," Amber took a deep breath, "you know Jody pretty well. You know he likes to play with the cars and the ball *(child interests)*, and you said that he likes to watch television with you for up to 30 minutes at a time. You know that he is a little boy that likes to be active."

"Right."

"You also told us about how he throws his toys sometimes," Amber continued, "What could be some of the reasons he throws his toys?" *(Reflection—discovering possible reasons)*

"Oh, he's just ornery sometimes, I guess," Ms. Phoebe replied.

"What else?" *(Reflection—probing learner again)*

"Well, I guess he could be trying to get my attention or maybe he's trying to tell me that he doesn't want to play with the car anymore." *(Reflection—discovering explanation)*

"I've noticed he does that with me, too!" Melody said. "When I give him another toy, he usually always calms right down and begins to play." *(Action—experience preceding discussion)*

Ms. Phoebe sat back in the chair and looked at her hands. She felt uncomfortable with the way the conversation was going.

"Ms. Phoebe," Amber said. "I'm wondering if it would be helpful to you if we set up some time for us to talk further about Jody's interests and what to do when he throws his toys. Maybe we could even come up with some ideas of other toys or activities he would be interested in even more than your Snow Babies and the cat's litter box. Of course, this would be at times when it's convenient for you. I'm sure with three young children in your care that it can be hectic here at times." *(Initiation—identifying coaching opportunities, inviting learner into coaching relationship)*

Ms. Phoebe paused, then said, "No, I don't think that's necessary. I've taken care of kids probably longer than you've been born. I feed them, keep them clean, and love them like their grandma. I'm too old to be learning anything new now."

"Well, Ms. Phoebe," Amber said, "I appreciate your honesty and taking the time to visit with me. If you think of any questions, I sure hope you'll give me a call. In fact, I think I'll touch base with you in a few weeks to see if anything has come up. Is that all right with you?"

Ms. Phoebe nodded her head yes.

Melody thanked Amber for coming to Ms. Phoebe's house. As Amber left, Melody stayed behind to say goodbye to Jody.

In the car on the way to her next visit, Amber reflected on the conversation with Melody and Ms. Phoebe. She felt that her conversation with Ms. Phoebe had gone well, even though she didn't achieve the outcome that both she and Melody had intended. She appreciated that Ms. Phoebe was frank about not wanting suggestions for how to promote opportunities for Jody to learn while under her care. In retrospect, Amber wished that she had talked with Melody more about what happened at Ms. Phoebe's and maybe even prepared Melody for the potential outcomes of the conversation. *(Evaluation—reviewing coaching process)* Amber acknowledged to herself that Melody was in a difficult position. Melody believed that she has no other options for child care that were affordable, gave individualized attention, and provided the type of supports that would be most beneficial to Jody.

As she reflected, Amber identified four possible options that she would like to discuss with Melody at their next scheduled visit. First, Amber could follow up with Ms. Phoebe in a couple of weeks to see if she has changed her mind about discussing ways to support Jody. Second, Amber could coach Melody to talk to Ms. Phoebe about allowing Amber to come talk with her about Jody. Another option would be for Amber to teach Melody how to coach Ms. Phoebe about activities that would be interesting to Jody and promote his communication, learning, and positive behavior. Finally, Amber could talk with Melody about what she wants and needs in child care, then she could work with her as she evaluates her options and other potential resources for child care within the community. This last option would probably be the most difficult for Melody.

This coaching story began with reflection. Amber assisted Ms. Phoebe in discovering what she already knew about Jody. Ms. Phoebe used reflection when she described Jody's current behavior, and Amber learned Jody's activity settings (e.g., play area in Ms. Phoebe's living room, meals prepared by Ms. Phoebe, watching television and reading books) and interests (e.g., playing ball, playing with cars, watching game shows). Then, Amber used reflection when she probed Ms. Phoebe to consider what she could be doing to promote Jody's participation in learning opportunities. Ms. Phoebe used reflection to describe what takes place at her home. Amber invited Ms. Phoebe to discover reasons for Jody's behavior in the hopes of leading her to identify interest-based learning opportunities as a means of positive behavioral support. Ms. Phoebe reflected and discovered an additional explanation for Jody's behavior. Melody added to the conversation by explaining an event that occurred prior to this discussion. She used the action phase to describe how she had given a new toy to Jody and had been able to calm him down. Next, Amber used the initiation phase when she identified possible coaching opportunities and invited Ms. Phoebe into a coaching relationship. After Ms. Phoebe declined to offer, Amber used the evaluation phase of the coaching process to review what she could have done differently.

This coaching story illustrates several of the critical issues involved when supporting children and their families in a group setting. The following section outlines these issues in greater detail.

CRITICAL ISSUES IN GROUP SETTINGS

The critical issues faced in group settings are certainly individualized to the particular environment, people, context, and so forth; however, the following section focuses on seven issues that deserve careful consideration and planning on the part of the early childhood practitioner prior to supporting a child in a group setting:

- Identifying current group settings or desired activity settings for the child and family

- Respecting the group setting
- Developing partnerships with learners in group settings
- Supporting other children in a group setting
- Finding time for the coaching relationship
- Maintaining confidentiality in group settings
- Sustaining support in group settings with staff retention challenges

Identifying Current Group Settings or Desired Activity Settings

When engaging in initial conversations with families, the coach should explore whether the child and family are currently or would like to be involved in a group setting activity. If the child is currently involved in a group setting, the coach should determine if the family is interested in having the coach support the adults in this group setting. If so, the coach must obtain permission from the family to engage with care providers in the various child group settings to see if they are interested in participating in a coaching relationship. When the child is not involved in a group setting and the family is interested in pursuing this type of activity, the coach should participate with the family in community resource mapping to identify the possible options that match the child's and family's interests (Daley & Poole, 1985; Katz, 1984; Kretzman & McKnight, 1993; McKnight, 1987; McWilliam, 1992; Trivette, Dunst, & Deal, 1997).

Community resource mapping is a process that involves identifying particular kinds of resources that match the interests of the family and child. The coach engages in the community mapping process alongside the parents and explores the community by knowing what is available and assisting the family or caregiver in identifying resources and learning about how to access and use the resources in a helpful and meaningful way. Trivette and colleagues (1997) identified four major sources of formal and informal support: personal social network members, associational groups, community programs and professionals, and specialized professional services. Their research indicates the most valuable resources may often be the more informal supports (e.g., a neighbor caring for a child while the mother runs errands) as opposed to more formal supports (e.g., respite care from a paid provider).

Coaching is an excellent strategy to support parents and other caregivers in learning how to identify and use community resources of interest to them. The coach is valuable because of his or her knowledge of community resources, but even more important is the coach's use of reflection, observation, and feedback to promote the parent's ability to identify, evaluate, and use resources when the coach is not present or no longer involved.

Prior to entering into the toddler read-along group at the local library, Lisa explored multiple community options with J.H. before he decided that he was interested in joining the library group. Lisa, in her combined role as service coordinator and early childhood special educator in the early intervention program, was responsible for identifying resources in the local community. She used J.H.'s and Desiree's interests to help J.H. navigate possible options already available near his home. Instead of just making a list of what was available, Lisa used community resource mapping as a resource-based practice, which provided the opportunity for J.H. to develop his skills in seeking other possible resources when he so desired. Lisa, although familiar with the community, mapped the community along with J.H. He then experienced not only the benefit of the resources they discovered but also learned how to engage in the process himself.

> **REMEMBER THIS . . .**
> **Definition of community resource mapping**
>
> "Community resource mapping is a process of developing a complete list of particular kinds of resources and the location of these resources within a physical space. Community resource mapping literally identifies target community resources and pinpoints the location of these resources on a large map of the catchment and surrounding areas of the early intervention program." (Trivette, Dunst, & Deal, 1997, p. 85)

Respecting the Group Setting

Initially, the coach must develop an understanding of the philosophy of the group or preschool program. Philosophies vary among programs and sometimes within a program. The coach's ability to provide support is contingent on an in-depth understanding of the guiding principles of the teacher, group, or program. Without an understanding of the philosophical framework, the coach may inadvertently make contradictory suggestions. For example, consider a Montessori preschool program in which the curriculum relies heavily on child use of specific materials. If a coach were to make a suggestion to use a specific type of toy or discouraged use of current materials, this could create a conflict for the teacher by asking him or her to put aside designated curriculum and preferred materials. Rather, the role of the coach in this environment would be to support the teacher in developing ways to adapt the current materials or activities to promote child use and exploration of the available toys or objects. Similarly in a preschool that uses a teacher-directed or academic approach, if a coach suggested a series of child-initiated activities during a time that the teacher typically focused on direct instruction, the teacher might have a difficult time understanding or appreciating the coach's recommendations.

In addition to these specific approaches, other preschool philosophies that are frequently discussed in the literature include, but are not limited to, coopera-

TRY THIS . . .
Community resource mapping

Next time a family identifies an interest in participating in a new group setting and they have asked you for ideas, think about the four major sources of supports identified by Trivette and colleagues (1997):

- Personal social network members (family members, friends, neighbors, co-workers, church or synagogue members, babysitters)

- Associational groups (civic groups, interest clubs, political organizations, self-help groups, charitable groups, veterans groups)

- Community programs and professionals (schools, child care programs, family resource programs, community colleges, hospitals, fire departments, housing programs)

- Specialized professional services (early intervention programs, special education programs, family preservation programs, therapy programs, substance abuse programs, respite care)

Can you identify several choices in each of the four major areas in your local community and surrounding area?

Could you teach someone else how to identify these resources (e.g., using phone book, calling associations, informal discussions with others)?

---

tive, play-centered, Waldorf, Reggio-Emilia, and combination approaches (Wood, 2000/2001). Each philosophical approach mentioned is unique and deserves the attention and understanding of the coach when supporting a learner in a group setting that maintains specific philosophical tenets.

As quickly as possible, the coach must also develop an awareness and understanding of the expectations of the environment for all of the children and the care providers. Information about timelines, routines, and child–staff ratios is critical regarding when the coach could observe the group, reflect with the staff, and provide feedback as appropriate. Contact with the group leaders or program staff must be prearranged and occur at times conducive to quality interactions.

Developing Partnerships with Learners in Group Settings

A family's agreement to participate in an early intervention program does not ensure that care providers from group settings will automatically be interested as well. During the assessment process and IFSP meeting or preparing for a transition IEP, the coach is responsible for ensuring that family members and care providers or teachers from group settings have realistic opportunities to participate. It is critical that all parties that will be affected by the IFSP or IEP be involved in the development of the document. Minimally, each person should be aware of the outcomes being written and have consented to participating in the plan. Identifying the multiple activity settings, learning opportunities, and key people within the group con-

TRY THIS . . .
Strategies for supporting other children in group settings

- Coach the adults to support all children in a group setting by reflecting on opportunities to engage them in activities, and if needed, model strategies for the coaching partner to implement.

- Answer any questions the other children have honestly and directly. For example, if a particular child happens to use a wheelchair and the other children wonder why, then you might say, "Desiree needs the wheelchair to help her get around, kind of like you use your legs to get around."

- Invite individual children to join an activity that might be of interest to them. For example, you can say, "Jessica, Desiree and her dad are reading a story about a little raccoon starting school. Would you like to join them?"

- Assist children in inviting other children to play with them. For example, say, "Grace, it looks like you'd enjoy playing with Desiree. Would you like to ask her to listen to the music with you?"

- Assist children in learning about personal space boundaries. For example, you can say, "Daniel, I think it's really nice that you wanted to give Desiree a hug. Remember that we talked about hugging her in a gentle, soft way. Let's try it again, and tell her what you'd like to do."

- Encourage children to ask questions and talk about their feelings. For example, say, "José, you seem to be interested in Desiree's breathing machine. Do you have a question about it?"

---

text sets the stage for a discussion about the potential benefits for the adult learners within the group setting. The coach and family identify who will be participating in the coaching process in addition to any other primary care providers. Participants may include a program director, supervisor, and other responsible parties.

For instance, Melody expressed an interest in having Amber talk with Ms. Phoebe about supporting Jody's participation at her home. Neither Amber nor Melody, however, assumed that Ms. Phoebe would participate in the process. Because Ms. Phoebe was not interested in entering into a coaching relationship with Amber, Amber developed a plan for discussion during her next conversation with Melody.

Supporting Other Children in a Group Setting

Once the coach has established his or her involvement in the group setting, additional opportunities for coaching will arise with other adults and children who participate in that setting. If the other children in the group setting have questions or need support, the coach's focus should be on mobilizing the abilities of the adult (e.g., teacher, group leader, child care provider) to assist the children. As with any coaching relationship, following discussion and joint planning, the coach could model strategies with the other children involved in the group setting as a support to the learner. For example, Archie asked some questions about supporting Desiree in the toddler read-along group. He also, however, asked many questions and developed multiple strategies along the way to support the other children and families involved in the group (e.g., answering questions honestly and directly, inviting other children to join a specific activity, encouraging other children to discuss their feelings).

Consider the following conversation between Lisa and Archie as Desiree and J.H. continue to participate in the library toddler read-along group.

"Lisa, I'd like to talk to you a few minutes about some of the other children and parents who attend the read-along group that Desiree and J.H. have joined," Archie said. "I'm getting some pretty tough questions, and I'm not so sure I'm handling them well." *(Action—experiencing situation to discuss with coach)*

Lisa quickly replied, "Sure, Archie, tell me what's on your mind." *(Reflection—determining what learner knows)*

"Well, the other day, one of the parents hung around after group time and obviously wanted to talk with me. I approached her and asked her how she thought the group was going. She told me she loved the group, but she was worried that Desiree might be frightening her child and some of the other children, as well." *(Action—experiencing situation to discuss with coach)*

"What was your response?" asked Lisa. *(Reflection—determining what happened)*

"To be quite blunt, I was shocked at first. Frightening, I thought! How could Desiree be frightening to anyone? But then, I thought back to when I first met Desiree and J.H., and I had to recognize that I'd been uncomfortable, too." *(Reflection—self-reflecting on feelings)*

"Archie, that is an honest reflection," Lisa said. "I'm impressed that you were able to put your emotions aside so quickly and think back to your initial response to Desiree." *(Reflection—sharing information)*

"I can't say that I completely put my emotions aside, but I did give it a good try," stated Archie with a smile. "So I thought to myself, 'This mother could use some coaching,' and I asked her if she would like to sit down and talk about her concerns. *(Initiation—identifying coaching opportunities)* She agreed, and we had a great discussion."

"Would you like to talk more about it?" asked Lisa. *(Reflection—planning new actions)*

Archie thought for a minute and then replied, "I feel pretty good about the end result. Let me tell you what the resolution was, and then I'd like some feedback."

Lisa thought to herself about the coaching process with Archie. His confidence in approaching the other parent was great to see. Lisa also thought that Archie's increased understanding of the coaching process was apparent as he demonstrated the ability to successfully invite another parent into a coaching relationship. She agreed. *(Evaluation)*

Archie continued, "I asked her some questions to get at her real concerns, and we got down to the fact that she was having a hard time explaining Desiree to her own daughter.

(Reflection—determining what learner knows) She wasn't really frightened of Desiree, she just didn't have the words to use. She also admitted that she was having a difficult time not feeling sad around Desiree. *(Reflection—self-reflecting on feelings)* We talked about this for a while, and I asked her a lot of questions. We then came up with a plan that included me doing some modeling for the mother and helping her and her daughter get to know both J.H and Desiree better. *(Reflection—joint planning new observations and actions)* I figured if she had these questions and feelings, others in the group probably would, too. We did talk specifically about how to answer her daughter's questions. *(Reflection—sharing information)* She had some good ideas. I think she just needed some feedback to see if they were good ideas . . . kind of like you and me, huh?"

"Archie, I'm very impressed. You've found some strategies for supporting the parent, her child, and most probably other parents and their children as it relates to promoting Desiree's and J.H.'s participation in your group. Your decision to use coaching as the way to support this mother was timely and effective. *(Reflection—feedback, sharing information)* You mentioned before that you've resolved the situation. Will you continue the coaching process with this mother?" *(Evaluation—review of coaching process)*

"Definitely," replied Archie. "We both agreed that it would be helpful for us. We're going to talk a few minutes after group at least once a week for a while."

Lisa then asked, "How about we include your coaching conversations with this parent as a formal part of our discussions?" *(Reflection—planning new strategies)*

Archie smiled. "Sounds like a great plan to me."

Notice how this coaching story began with the action phase. Archie experienced a situation with a parent in the toddler group and decided to discuss it with Lisa. Lisa used reflection to encourage Archie to tell her what happened. Archie described what happened with the woman in the toddler group and how her comments encouraged him to self-reflect on his initial feelings about Desiree. Then, Lisa provided feedback on Archie's ability to put his feelings aside in order to reflect honestly.

Archie told Lisa how he had identified a coaching opportunity and initiated a relationship with the new coaching partner. Lisa used the reflection phase to ask if he would like to discuss the situation. Archie indicated that he would like to discuss it further and get Lisa's feedback. He recounted how he had used the reflection phase to assist the parent in identifying what she already knew about Desiree. The parent in turn was able to self-reflect on her feelings. Both Archie and the parent planned new observations and actions to do before the next coaching session. Archie also shared some information about how the woman could answer her daughter's questions. After Archie told his story, Lisa used the reflection phase to provide feedback as Archie had requested. Lisa used the evaluation phase when she asked Archie if he would continue the coaching process with the parent. She also used the reflection phase when she asked Archie if they should use the discussions with the parent as a topic for their coaching conversations.

Through the coaching process, Archie identified opportunities to promote another parent's ability to support her child's participation during the toddler read-along group. Archie encouraged the mother to be open and honest with her child, promoted her ability to share her feelings and discuss her daughter's feelings, and discussed specific ways both the mother and daughter could be more involved with Desiree during the group.

Finding Time for the Coaching Relationship

Probably one of the most challenging issues facing the coach and learner in a group setting is finding time to have conversations. Most teachers, child care providers, and other leaders of group activities are very busy, and their time is completely occupied with direct involvement with the children or other critical support activities, such as planning activities, preparing food, cleaning up, or organizing materials. Coaches must be flexible and sensitive to these issues and plan creatively alongside the learner to identify viable opportunities for the coach and learner to share information. Of course, face-to-face discussions are essential to a developing relationship; however, other activities can be beneficial and productive as well. Using telephone calls, e-mail, and question logs to communicate are effective coaching strategies for promoting ongoing, timely dialogue. If coaches can be available for blocks of time versus a scheduled appointment (e.g., Tuesday morning versus 10:00 A.M. to 11:00 A.M.), this may provide more opportunities for interaction and offer the added benefit of real-life observations and just-in-time coaching support.

The following coaching story (summarized in Figure 6.3) provides a realistic example of the challenges facing a busy child care provider and a few of the strategies used by the coach to successfully use available moments as coaching opportunities. Maria, a busy child care provider, and Ross, a nurse from the local early intervention program, partner together to support the participation of Angel in program activities. The story demonstrates the coach reflecting with the learner, developing new ideas, and learning new skills. A Coaching Worksheet with the appropriate sections completed for this coaching story is located in the chapter appendix. You may find it helpful to look at the worksheet as you read this story.

MARIA'S BUSY DAY

Ross had been providing support to Angel and her family as part of the early intervention program for the past 6 months. Angel's mother, Anita, previously worked nights while a relative took care of Angel; however, she was starting a new job and would be working during the day. For the first time, Angel would be in a child care facility weekdays from 7:30 A.M. until 5:30 P.M. Ross would provide support to both Anita and the new child care provider,

---

Purpose of coaching:

> To promote Angel's participation in learning opportunities in a child care center

Outcomes of coaching:

1. Maria will learn how to identify Angel's interests and match them to existing or desired activity settings within the child care center.

2. Maria will learn to promote Angel's participation in interest-based learning opportunities.

3. Angel will have fun, play with other children, and participate in newly identified learning opportunities.

Key partners	Child and family interests	Activity settings
Angel—child *Anita*—mother *Maria*—child care provider *Ross*—nurse	*Family*—giving child opportunity to play with other children *Child*—playing with other children, participating in art activities	Free play in child care center Arts and crafts center time

---

Figure 6.3. Maria's busy day.

Maria. Ross, Anita, and Maria participated in a review of Angel's IFSP and added ways that Ross could be available for Maria in the child care facility.

On Thursday, as scheduled, Ross arrived at the child care facility to meet with Maria.

"Hi, Maria!" Ross called as he entered the room.

Maria looked up from the table where she was watching three children, including Angel, finger-paint with colored pudding. *(activity setting)* "Ross, so good to see you!" Maria replied. "I remember you said that you wanted to talk with me, but I went ahead and cleared out the room next to mine as a place for you to work with Angel after we finish talking. I'm a little short on toys, so I had hoped you would bring your own. Angel, start cleaning up so you can go with Mr. Ross for therapy."

Ross felt confused because he thought he had clarified his role to Maria during the IFSP meeting. He thought she understood that his role would be to coach her rather than do therapy with Angel.

"Maria, thanks for taking the time to clean out a room for me. I think to help me get started, I'd like to just hang out with you a while and watch Angel do what you've already got planned. *(Observation—observing environment)* We can sit down and talk when it's convenient for you."

"I guess that's okay. I might feel pulled in too many directions if I think the kids need me and you're trying to talk with me, too."

"Well, for today how about if I just hang out, watch, and gather my thoughts. Then, I'll call you to schedule the next visit at a time that's convenient for you," offered Ross.

Maria agreed, and Ross observed that day. A few days later, Ross called Maria and said, "Hi, Maria, it's Ross from the early intervention program. Is this a good time for you to talk?"

"Sure," Maria answered. "I'm just finishing my break and have a few minutes to talk."

"I believe we were going to schedule the next visit at a time when you and I could talk for a few minutes."

"I think that's the problem," Maria admitted. "I just don't have time to talk to you when the children are here, and that's from 6:00 A.M. until 6:00 P.M."

"Hmmm," Ross said and paused. "Let's take a few minutes to think about our options. My role is not to add more work for you or to take you away from the other children to do something 'special' with Angel. As I recall, when we talked before Angel's IFSP meeting you told me about your daily schedule at the center. You mentioned that during the morning you have free play, arts and crafts time, and outdoor activities (*activity settings*)." *(Reflection—sharing information)*

"That's right, and during the free play, I'm getting set up for arts and crafts time and keeping an eye out for what the children are doing."

"If I come to the center during free play, then I could help you set up for arts and crafts time, and we could talk then," Ross replied. "How does that sound?" *(Reflection—planning new observations and activities)*

Maria thought about what generally occurs during free play and her set-up time. "Well, I've already been thinking about some ways to get Angel more active during free play, so maybe you'll have some ideas, too." *(Reflection—self-reflecting on ideas)*

Ross smiled and said, "That sounds like a good plan. How about we start there when I visit on Tuesday?"

"Sounds good! Talk to you then," Maria said as they ended their conversation.

On the following Tuesday, Ross entered Maria's classroom at the child care center and noticed that Angel was sitting in a chair holding a doll and watching two boys build a tower with blocks. Maria was setting out a variety of materials for the children to use to make collages. When Maria saw Ross, they exchanged greetings, and he crossed the classroom to join her at the arts and crafts table. Ross asked Maria how he could help, and she asked him to put the glue sticks and bottles on the table.

"I noticed Angel is kind of watching from the sidelines. You mentioned before that you had some ideas of ways to get her involved. What are you thinking?" Ross asked. *(Reflection—determining what learner already knows)*

"I don't want to be directive with her, but it seems if I ask her a question or tell her to do something, she will, but after a little bit she is sitting back down again." *(Reflection—describing current situation)*

As he finished arranging the glue bottles, Ross turned to Maria, "Asking her a question about what she'd like to do sounds like a good idea. *(Reflection—providing feedback, shar-*

ing information) Why do you think she sits back down?" *(Reflection—probing learner to reflect)*

"I don't know. I do wonder if she's having a hard time figuring out what to say or how to approach the other children. I've tried asking some of the other children to invite Angel to play with them. She usually does join them, but then after a while she's back in a chair just watching." *(Reflection—sharing ideas)*

"I think you're right. I'd keep trying to involve the other children, and if the activity is something that she seems to be interested in doing, then see if you and the other children can keep her involved for longer periods of time. *(Reflection—providing feedback, sharing information)* Any ideas for how to do it?" *(Reflection—determining what learner knows)*

Maria sat down in one of the chairs at the arts and crafts table. As she began empty-ing the bag of cotton balls, she responded by saying, "I've been thinking about this ever since you asked me before the IFSP meeting what Angel likes to do and is good at doing here. She's good with her hands and really seems to like arts and crafts. *(child interest)* Now that I think about it, most of the free play activities are movement oriented or involve sit-ting on the floor. Angel seems to prefer seat work." *(Reflection—self-reflecting on current situation)*

Ross nodded and asked, "What type of table activity could you make available during free play in the morning?" *(Reflection—assisting learner to generate ideas)*

"Let's see," Maria sat down the bag of cotton balls and leaned forward on the table, "I could try setting up a little post office center with cards, play stamps, envelopes, and pack-ages. *(new activity setting)* That would also tie-in with our study of community helpers. I think I have everything I need to set it up this afternoon during nap time." *(Reflection—planning new actions)*

"I had a cancellation for tomorrow morning. Would it be helpful if I called to see how it goes? Then, if we need to, we could think about ways to adapt the post office center to get her more involved."

"Sounds like a good idea."

This coaching story illustrates some of the demands on a child care provider in a busy setting committed to implementing recommended practices for quality child care settings. Ross demonstrated flexibility, creativity, and a willingness to assist Maria in multiple ways as they reflected together on strategies for increas-ing Angel's participation in the activity settings at the child care center. Through coaching probes and thoughtful reflection on Maria's part, Maria decided to intro-duce a new activity setting that was based on Angel's interests and strengths.

Notice how the coaching story began in the observation phase. Ross arrived at the child care center and took time to observe the environment. He recognized the colored pudding finger paints, free play, arts and crafts time, and outdoor ac-tivities as activity settings. Ross used the reflection phase to share information

TRY THIS . . .
Activities for supporting a child care provider

- Suggest scheduling blocks of time in the center instead of a specific appointment (e.g., Tuesday morning instead of 10–11 A.M.).
- Schedule visits during staff preparation time (e.g., clean up, food preparation, activity set up) and work alongside the child care provider as he or she performs his or her duties.
- Ask the child care provider for a preferred meeting time. Be prepared to meet very early or late in the day.
- Once a relationship is established (if convenient for the child care provider) use phone calls, e-mails, notebooks, and communication logs for sharing ideas.
- When observing a child care provider interacting with a specific child, offer to be responsible for the rest of the children under the provider's care during that observation. For example, if you are observing the child care provider demonstrate a new feeding strategy for a child during snack or meal time, then take responsibility for ensuring the other children are eating, minding manners, enjoying themselves, and cleaning up any spills that happen so the child care provider is free to feed the other child.
- Reflect often (every visit) with the child care provider regarding the convenience of the meeting time and helpfulness of the strategies.

with Maria about his role as a coach. He also used reflection to plan new observations and activities with Maria; he recommended that he come during free play and help Maria set up for free play. Before Ross left for the day, Maria self-reflected on her ideas for getting Angel to be more active during free play.

The next Tuesday, after both Maria and Ross observed Angel during free play, Ross assisted Maria in identifying what she already knew about Angel's behavior. Ross provided feedback and shared information with Maria. With Ross's encouragement, Maria was able to generate new ideas to try. She used the reflection phase to plan a new activity to try before the next coaching session.

Maintaining Confidentiality in Group Settings

The issue of confidentiality as a right of parents and children involved in an early intervention program is no different in group settings. It can, however, be more complicated. The coach must take the initiative and responsibility of talking up front with all people involved about the issue of confidentiality. The initial conversations must be with the parents to ask them how they would like to handle possible situations where being in public could bring attention to them and their child being involved with an early intervention program as a formalized support. Discussing possible scenarios before they happen is an excellent strategy for avoiding uncomfortable situations later.

The coach and parents must also decide who will discuss confidentiality with group leaders, teachers, and other staff. These same safeguards apply as well, however, to the other children and adults involved in the group setting. Most often, these individuals will not be aware of the requirement of maintaining confidentiality as part of Parts B and C under the IDEA 1997 (PL 105-17). It is imperative, however, that all involved in the IFSP and IEP process understand and take responsibility for confidentiality issues in group settings.

Before the meeting with Amber was scheduled, Melody asked Ms. Phoebe for permission for Amber to come to the house. Once Ms. Phoebe agreed, Melody also asked that Ms. Phoebe not talk about Jody's involvement with the early intervention program with the parents of other children who stay with Ms. Phoebe. Once Ms. Phoebe understood Melody's feelings on the matter, she readily agreed to support Melody's wishes. Upon Amber's arrival to Ms. Phoebe's, she explained that her visit there was a confidential one as a representative from the local early intervention program and that she would not talk about her discussion with Ms. Phoebe, or about any of the children under her care, with anyone else.

TRY THIS . . .
Supporting a busy child care provider

Next time you are having difficulty meeting with a child care provider to support a child in that environment, ask the child care provider to suggest the most convenient time to meet. If the child care provider states that he or she is too busy or that no convenient time exists, then ask him or her to share less hectic times at the center. If the child care provider still is having a tough time finding any time to meet with you, offer to spend a chunk of time in the center, and explain that you can take advantage of any spontaneous opportunities to talk and share information.

Sustaining Support in Group Settings with Staff Retention Challenges

Supporting young children and their families in group settings that have frequent staffing changes is an issue that most community-based, early childhood practitioners have encountered. High staff turnover rates are probably the most common in child care centers (Bruder, 1993; Buysse, Wesley, & Keyes, 1998; Janko & Porter, 1997; Odom, 2000). When using the coaching process to support a child and family in a child care center, the coach must be prepared for the possibility or likelihood of staff leaving or changing groups within the center. Due to the nature of the relationship, coaches and learners must have open and honest conversations that involve continuous planning, action, and reflection.

The roles of the coach and learner in a coaching relationship necessitate involvement of the child care provider on each visit. The early childhood coach goes to the child care center to see the child care provider, not just the child. Therefore, a child care provider planning to quit before the next scheduled contact with the coach would be likely to mention his or her departure. The possibility of the coach showing up for the next scheduled meeting with a child care provider and finding out he or she no longer works there is greatly decreased. Using the coaching process, therefore, is a strategy that inherently helps prepare early childhood practitioners and other site staff for the possibility of a child care provider leaving. When the learner no longer works at the child care facility, the coach must be prepared to develop a new relationship and start over with a new initial coaching conversation with another staff member. Understanding that staff turnover is a natural process of working in group settings should help prepare the coach for the possibility of the event. If retention rates seem to be a major obstacle in a particular group setting, the coach may also find it helpful to have a discussion with the center director about possible reasons for this problem.

Although many issues can complicate supporting young children and their families in group settings, coaching is an effective strategy that can provide the foundation for working through many of these issues. Commitment to the coaching process can result in promoting successful participation of the child and family in activities that are interesting and important to them. In summary, let's revisit Archie and Lisa to see how the toddler read-along group has progressed.

"Hey, Archie!" exclaimed Lisa. "It's great to see you. How have things been progressing with the toddler read-along group?" *(Reflection—determining current situation)*

"Hello, Lisa. I've been anxious to talk with you about some new ideas I have . . . and some worries," replied Archie. *(Reflection—sharing thoughts)*

"Well, let's get started. Where would you like to begin?"

Archie smiled and said, "You know me. Let's start with the tough stuff. I've been worried about how I can get Desiree more involved during the read-along group. Most of the other children either play with one another or their own parents. Desiree does not reach out to the other kids, and since they've gotten used to her wheelchair, they don't seem to take notice unless she coughs or something. *(Action—situation preceding conversation)* I knew you were going to ask me what I had tried, so I made a list (see Figure 6.4). Here, take a look at my notes." *(Reflection—anticipating questions, self-reflecting)*

Lisa reviewed Archie's notes and was impressed with his thorough account of the different strategies he had implemented to promote Desiree's involvement in the group. As Lisa thought about the strategies, she noticed that J.H. was not mentioned much on the paper. Lisa looked up at Archie and said, "Archie, thank you for taking the time to write all of this down. It's very helpful to me as we talk about your ideas. Tell me about how you've included Desiree's father in these strategies." *(Reflection—determining current situation)*

Archie sat silent for a moment then replied, "I haven't. I guess I just got so excited about how I could help, that I failed to include J.H. in the process." *(Reflection—reflecting on actions, sharing ideas)*

Read a book with Desiree, and invite others to join us.

Push Desiree's wheelchair next to another parent or child, and ask if we can join the group.

Ask a specific child to invite Desiree to join him or her in play.

Talk to another parent about asking his or her child to invite Desiree to read a story with them.

Include a new activity during group where we have a child selected as leader for the day, and that child gets to choose the book and special reading partners (another parent and child) for the morning. I'll start with Desiree as the leader.

Position Desiree strategically next to the popular books, and hope for a serendipitous interaction to unfold.

Figure 6.4. Archie's list of strategies for promoting Desiree's participation in the toddler read-along group.

"Don't be so hard on yourself. I've spoken with J.H. about their participation in the read-along group, and he is very pleased. He is happy with how the children are accepting Desiree. How often have you been talking with J.H. about their participation in the group?" *(Reflection—providing feedback, sharing information)*

"Well, we speak every week about the group, but as I think back on those discussions, it's mostly me talking about my ideas," reflected Archie. "I'm getting my thoughts organized, but it seems like some of the strategies I've tried might have a chance with J.H. using them instead of me. For instance, if he approached another parent reading to her own child and asked if they could join in, the parent might respond more naturally than if it were me asking for him. Or if J.H. asked another parent and child to join him and Desiree rather than me asking for him, it might go more smoothly. What do you think, Lisa?" *(Reflection—reflecting on actions, self-generating ideas)*

"Archie, you've got some great ideas. Can you give them a try next week?" asked Lisa. *(Reflection—joint planning of actions)*

Archie replied, "Sure thing."

"I'd also encourage you to schedule a special time with J.H. to talk about your ideas and see what he thinks. I'll bet he'll be as excited as you are," said Lisa with a smile. *(Reflection—providing feedback, sharing information)*

In this story, Archie demonstrated creativity, enthusiasm, and flexibility to create many development-enhancing learning opportunities for Desiree and her father. He also was interested in learning about coaching and was motivated to reflect on his own and to develop new ideas.

Notice how the coaching story began in the reflection phase when Lisa assisted Archie in identifying the current situation. Archie shared his thoughts about what he had tried and used the action phase when he described a situation that occurred prior to the coaching conversation. He also used the reflection phase when he anticipated the questions Lisa would ask and self-reflected on his response. After reviewing Archie's notes, Lisa probed Archie to find out how he had included J.H. in his strategies. Archie in turn reflected on his actions and shared his ideas. Then, Lisa provided feedback and probed Archie for more information. Archie was able to use the reflection phase to reflect on his actions and self-generate ideas for how J.H. could be more involved in the toddler playgroup. Next, Archie and Lisa planned the actions that would take place between coaching conversations. Finally, Lisa provided feedback and suggested a specific action to take place before the next coaching session.

Although not all community group leaders may demonstrate the motivation depicted in this story, the strategies Lisa used were simple, straightforward, and adaptable to most any situation. Lisa was responsive to Archie's questions, promoted his ability to generate new solutions, and observed increased confidence and mastery as Archie chose coaching as the strategy to support another parent in the toddler read-along group.

CONCLUSION

Group settings provide opportunities for young children to interact and learn with similar age peers. The coach can support families in identifying and enhancing their child's involvement in existing group settings and explore new options in desired group settings that either match or develop the child's assets and interests. This chapter provided suggestions and guidance on strategies for successfully supporting young children and their families in group settings where other children participate. Important research surrounding preschool inclusion was included to emphasize the responsibility early childhood practitioners have in supporting implementation of the IDEA and promoting the participation of children in natural settings, not those created especially for children with disabilities and their families. The role of the coach in group settings was emphasized, particularly noting critical issues that are setting specific for formal and informal group activities. Following discussion of each critical issue, we provided suggestions for success in a wide variety of group activity settings.

Through the use of detailed coaching stories, we have illustrated the role of the coach in specific situations and identified the coaching process in progress. Each coaching story brings to life real situations that early childhood practitioners will most likely encounter as they support young children and their families in community-based activities. The coaching stories provide examples of specific strategies for supporting children who have previously had little or no opportunity to play with other children, implementing ideas to partner with busy caregivers and group leaders, and a discussion with a child care provider who is not interested in establishing a coaching relationship.

As you support families and young children as they participate in existing activity settings and identify new activity settings of interest to them in their neighborhoods and communities, your coaching skills will continue to improve with each new relationship, situation, and accomplishment. We challenge you to reflect on a previous relationship with a child care provider, preschool teacher, or leader of a group activity that may not have been successful. Consider how the relationship might have developed differently if you had used coaching as the framework for your support. Can you identify specific conversations and strategies that could have changed the course of the relationship and proved to be a more positive opportunity for the child and family? As you focus energy on moving forward supporting families and their children in a wide variety of group opportunities, concentrate on the coach's role in group settings—to partner with parents, group leaders, teachers, and other staff to support the child and family in building skills, furthering interests, and establishing friendships.

- The next time you meet a child care provider who feels too busy to engage in a coaching relationship, think of three strategies you could try to assist the child care provider in feeling supported.

- If you are introduced to a family interested in becoming involved in some formal group activity settings, what are two new strategies you could try to help them discover options that match their interests and assets?

- Consider families you are currently supporting. Identify a family that would be interested in establishing a coaching relationship to increase their child's participation in a group activity with other children. What would you need to do to prepare for trying this out on your next visit?

RESOURCES

To learn more about inclusion see the following:

Janko, S., & Porter, A. (1997). *Portraits of inclusion through the eyes of children, families, and educators.* Early Childhood Research Institute on Inclusion, University of Washington.
This report provides a summary of many of the findings of the Early Childhood Research Institute on Inclusion.

Wolery, R.A., & Odom, S.L. (2000). *An administrator's guide to preschool inclusion.* Chapel Hill: University of North Carolina, Frank Porter Graham Child Development Institute, Early Childhood Research Institute on Inclusion.
This book provides a summary of current research supporting inclusion of preschoolers and detailed information on implementing strategies for supporting young children with disabilities in community preschool settings.

To learn more about eco-mapping see the following:

McWilliam, R.A. (1992). *Family-centered intervention planning: A routines-based approach.* Tucson, AZ: Communication Skill Builders.

This book provides information on how to use eco-mapping as a strategy for assisting families in identifying resources and supports.

To learn more about community resource mapping see the following:

Trivette, C.M., Dunst, C.J., & Deal, A.G. (1997). Resource-based approach to early intervention. In S.K. Thurman, J.R. Cornwell, & S.R. Gottwald (Eds.), *Contexts of early intervention: Systems and settings* (pp. 73–92). Baltimore: Paul H. Brookes Publishing Co.

This chapter provides research supporting use of a resource-based approach for assisting families and their children. The chapter also defines informal and formal supports and describes how to use resource community mapping as a specific strategy for building the capacity of families to identify and use resources of interest to them.

REFERENCES

Appl, D.J., Fahl-Gooler, F., & McCollum, J.A. (1997). Inclusive parent–child play groups: How comfortable are parents of children with disabilities in the group? *Infant-Toddler Intervention, 7*(4), 235–249.

Bricker, D. (2000). Inclusion: How the scene has changed. *Topics in Early Childhood Special Education, 20*(1), 14–19.

Brown, W.H., Odom, S.L., Li, S., & Zercher, C. (1999). Ecobehavioral assessment in inclusive early childhood programs: A portrait of preschool inclusion. *Journal of Special Education, 33,* 138–153.

Bruder, M.B. (1993). The provision of early intervention and early childhood special education within community early childhood programs: Characteristics of effective service delivery. *Topics in Early Childhood Special Education, 13*(1), 19–37.

Bruder, M.B., & Brand, M. (1995). A comparison of two types of early intervention environments serving toddler-age children with disabilities. *Infant-Toddler Intervention, 5*(3), 207–218.

Buysse, V., Wesley, P., & Keyes, L. (1998). Implementing early childhood inclusion: Barrier and support factors. *Early Childhood Research Quarterly, 13*(1), 169–184.

Daley, J., & Poole, D. (1985). Community development insights for planning public social service innovations. *Research in Rural Sociology and Development, 2,* 143–157.

Individuals with Disabilities Education Act Amendments of 1997, PL 105-17, 20 U.S.C. §§ 1400 *et seq.*

Janko, S., & Porter, A. (1997). *Portraits of inclusion through the eyes of children, families, and educators.* Early Childhood Research Institute on Inclusion, University of Washington.

Katz, R. (1984). Empowerment and synergy: Expanding the community's healing process. In J. Rappaport, C. Swift, & R. Hess (Eds.), *Studies in empowerment: Steps toward understanding and action* (pp. 201–226). New York: Haworth Press.

Kretzman, J., & McKnight, J. (1993). *Building community from the inside out.* Evanston, IL: Northwestern University, Center for Urban Affairs and Policy Research.

McKnight, J. (1987, Winter). Regenerating community. *Social Policy,* 54–58.

McWilliam, R.A. (1992). *Family-centered intervention planning: A routines-based approach.* Tucson, AZ: Communication Skill Builders.

Odom, S. (2000). Preschool inclusion: What we know and where we go from here. *Topics in Early Childhood Special Education, 20*(1), 20–27.

Oklahoma State Department of Education. (2001). *Transition at age 3: Steps for success transition guide.* Oklahoma City, OK: Author.

Trivette, C.M., Dunst, C.J., & Deal, A.G. (1997). Resource-based approach to early intervention. In S.K. Thurman, J.R. Cornwell, & S.R. Gottwald (Eds.), *Contexts of early intervention: Systems and settings* (pp. 73–92). Baltimore: Paul H. Brookes Publishing Co.

Wolery, R.A., & Odom, S.L. (2000). *An administrator's guide to preschool inclusion.* Chapel Hill: University of North Carolina, Frank Porter Graham Child Development Institute, Early Childhood Research Institute on Inclusion.

Wood, S. (December 2000/January 2001). Pick the right preschool. *Sesame Street Parents,* 45–49.

Appendix

Coaching Worksheet: Toddler Read-Along Group

Learner: _Archie_   Coach: _Lisa_   Date: _June 4_

INITIATION

Coaching opportunities observed or presented
J.H. wanted to participate in the library read-along group with his daughter, Desiree. J.H. approached Archie, the librarian, and asked if he and Lisa, the early childhood coach, could talk with him before joining the group.

The purpose of the coaching relationship is
To support Desiree's participation in the local library toddler read-along group

Intended learner outcomes resulting from the coaching relationship

Story-hour group leader will learn new skills related to promoting Desiree's participation in group activities.

J.H. will have increased confidence and competence in participating with Desiree in a group setting.

Desiree will have fun and interact with other children and parents in a group setting.

Barriers to the coaching process	Strategies to address barriers
Concerns and fears of other parents in the toddler group (identified after J.H. and Desiree joined the group).	Archie initiated a coaching relationship with one very concerned parent and modeled strategies (e.g., how to greet Desiree and talk with Desiree without startling her, how to get on her level) for all of the parents in the group.

Ground rules
J.H. and Archie meet every Thursday before the group for 15 minutes to talk about how things are going with Desiree in the group.
Archie will solicit feedback from Lisa at times convenient for both.

Note: All observations occur at the library during the toddler read-along group.

OBSERVATION	What/where	When
Coach observes learner's actions and interactions	Lisa observed Archie and J.H. getting Desiree out of her wheelchair and using the adapted book.	June 4
Learner observes coach model actions	Lisa demonstrated how to use the book and help Desiree turn the pages herself.	June 4
Learner observes self		
Coach/learner observe environment		

ACTION	What/where	When
Coach models for learner (coach present)	J.H. showed Archie how to get Desiree out of her chair.	July 5
Learner practices an action (coach present/absent)	Archie and J.H. practiced helping Desiree use the adapted book, and Desiree was successful! (coach present)	July 5
Learner describes experience (coach absent)	Archie told Lisa that a parent was concerned Desiree was frightening her child.	July 10
	Archie was frustrated because he wanted Desiree to be an active participant in the group.	July 11
Coach/learner observe environment		

REFLECTION	Description		
Learner reflects on action or observation	Archie shared what made the June 4 session so successful. He can replicate this or support others in doing so in future group meetings. The strategies Archie had been using to prompt parents and children to interact with Desiree and J.H. would have been more successful if he'd coached J.H. to use them. Archie realized he'd been doing all the talking when he met weekly with J.H. instead of having J.H. share his ideas.		
Coach gives feedback about observation or action following reflection	Lisa praised Archie for initiating a coaching relationship with the concerned parent.		
Learner uses resources (e.g., print, video, peer)			
Coach confirms learner's understanding and summarizes	Lisa confirmed Archie's idea to get Desiree out of her wheelchair and use adapted books.		
Coach/learner plan next steps	Who	What	When
Observations	Lisa will observe toddler group on June 4 to support Archie and J.H. in getting Desiree out of the wheelchair and using the adapted book.		
Practice	Between July 10 and July 17, Archie will coach J.H. to show other children how to greet Desiree, talk with Desiree without startling her, get on her level, and invite other children to read with them.		
Resources			

EVALUATION

Coach Self-Reflection   *(completed by Lisa)*

1. Is the learner accomplishing his or her goals?
   Yes

2. What changes, if any, do I need to make in the coaching process?
   In conversations with Archie, Lisa will make a point to bring up his coaching discussions with J.H. and the concerned parent.

3. Should I continue as this learner's coach? (If not, who would be more effective?)
   Yes—progress toward outcomes is still being made

Coach Asks Learner   *(learner is Archie)*

1. Shall we continue coaching or have your goals been accomplished (continuation)?
   Yes, continue coaching relationship

   If continuing coaching:

   - What changes need to be made in the coaching plan?
     Lisa will make a point to bring up his coaching discussions with J.H. and the concerned parent.

   - What observations and/or actions should take place between coaching sessions?
     Lisa will observe Archie coaching J.H. to shift responsibility of promoting Desiree's participation in the group from Archie to J.H.

   - How will we communicate in between sessions?
     Archie will call Lisa between scheduled visits if needed.

   - Do we have a plan for the next session?
     Yes, see above.

2. If goals have been reached (resolution):

   - Is the learner committed to and capable of self-assessment, self-correction, and self-generation?

   - Has a plan for reinstituting coaching been discussed?

Coaching Worksheet: Maria's Busy Day

Learner: _Maria_   Coach: _Ross_   Date: _September 6_

INITIATION

Coaching opportunities observed or presented

Maria was interested in promoting Angel's active participation in activities at the child care center and was willing to make the time to exchange ideas with Ross.

The purpose of the coaching relationship is

To support Angel's participation in child care center activities and promote more social interaction with other children

Intended learner outcomes resulting from the coaching relationship

Maria will learn how to identify Angel's interests and match them to existing or desired activity settings.

Maria will learn how to promote Angel's participation in interest-based learning opportunities.

Angel will have fun, play with other children, and participate in newly identified learning opportunities.

Barriers to the coaching process	**Strategies to address barriers**
Limited time for Maria to meet with Ross and plan new activities of interest to Angel _Maria initially thought Ross would be working only with Angel._	_Ross asked permission to stay in the main room and observe the routines, interactions, and activity settings. Ross re-explained his role as a support to Maria, and they planned a convenient time for coaching._

Ground rules

Ross and Maria will meet during preparation time for morning activities. Ross will assist Maria in preparing for the activities. Ross knows that Maria may need to interact with the children multiple times during their coaching conversations.

OBSERVATION

	What/where	When
Coach observes learner's actions and interactions		
Learner observes coach model actions		
Learner observes self		
Coach/learner observe environment	_Ross observes Angel sitting alone and not involved during free play._ _Ross and Maria observe Angel sitting alone holding a doll during the free play activity._	_September 6_ _September 20_

ACTION	What/where	When
Coach models for learner (coach present)		
Learner practices an action (coach present/absent)		
Learner describes experience (coach absent)	Maria explains what she has tried in the past to encourage Angel to be more participative. She questions being too directive.	September 20
Coach/learner observe environment		

REFLECTION	Description		
Learner reflects on action or observation	Maria shared an idea of why Angel may not be playing with other children. She had tried encouraging other children to play with Angel, but Angel sat down again. Maria had been thinking about Ross's question at the IFSP meeting about what Angel liked to do and was good at. Angel really enjoyed arts and crafts and was good with her hands. Maria also thought about free play. Most of the learning opportunities are gross motor in nature, not fine motor. Maria came up with the idea to add a play postal center during free play for coloring, writing, cutting, and sending letters.		
Coach gives feedback about observation or action following reflection	Ross praised Maria for her good observations and probed her for ideas about adapting free play. He supported her postal center idea and asked what support she might need in getting it up and going.		
Learner uses resources (e.g., print, video, peer)			
Coach confirms learner's understanding and summarizes	Ross supported Maria in developing her new ideas about getting Angel to participate more during free play time and how to use her interests as a way to do it.		
Coach/learner plan next steps	Who	What	When
Observations	Ross will observe the new activity setting tomorrow morning during free play time.		
Practice	Maria will prepare for the new activity this afternoon during the children's nap time.		
Resources			

EVALUATION

Coach Self-Reflection

1. Is the learner accomplishing his or her goals?

   In progress

2. What changes, if any, do I need to make in the coaching process?

   Too early to tell. Ross will continue to make sure that meeting times are convenient for Maria.

3. Should I continue as this learner's coach? (If not, who would be more effective?)

   Yes—progress toward outcomes is still being made

Coach Asks Learner

1. Shall we continue coaching or have your goals been accomplished (continuation)?

   Yes, Ross and Maria are making progress. They have a plan.

   If continuing coaching:

   - What changes need to be made in the coaching plan?

     They have developed a plan and are moving forward.

   - What observations and/or actions should take place between coaching sessions?

     Maria is preparing the new post office center for free play.

   - How will we communicate in between sessions?

     Ross will call Maria, and Maria will call Ross between scheduled visits if needed.

   - Do we have a plan for the next session?

     Yes, see above

2. If goals have been reached (resolution):

   - Is the learner committed to and capable of self-assessment, self-correction, and self-generation?

   - Has a plan for reinstituting coaching been discussed?

7

COACHING COLLEAGUES

This chapter focuses on the special issues of coaching colleagues who work in the same or related agencies to share knowledge and strengthen collaborative relationships in order to support families and their children. Colleague-to-colleague coaching, also known as peer coaching, has been employed since the early 1980s in education settings to help teachers integrate new information within their instructional practices (Joyce & Showers, 1982; Mello, 1984). One definition of peer coaching that is particularly relevant for early childhood practitioners and administrators emphasizes the collaborative nature of a coaching partnership:

> Peer coaching is a confidential process through which two or more professionals work together to reflect on what they are currently doing, refine current skills and build new ones, share ideas with one another, or solve problems. (Robbins, 1991, p. 1)

An early childhood practitioner can assume a coaching role in interactions with colleagues to prompt their reflection on their daily practice, such as the effectiveness of their support for families and other adults caring for very young children. In addition, some early childhood programs use coaching as part of their professional development and encourage practitioners to formalize opportunities for coaching one another to learn specific skills and incorporate evidence-based practices in their daily work (Gallacher, 1997; Hendrickson, Gardner, Kaiser, & Riley, 1993; Miller, 1994; Vail, Tschantz, & Bevill, 1997).

The following story illustrates important points to consider when planning to use coaching as part of professional development for early childhood practitioners. Josie and Katarina are members of a 55-person staff of an early intervention program located in an urban setting. Josie has been a parent-to-parent support coordinator for an early intervention program the past 6 years; Katarina has recently joined the staff.

An Orientation to Peer Coaching

As part of Katarina's orientation to their program, Josie described their program's philosophy regarding continuing competency: All staff members consider themselves to be lifelong learners with expertise that they are willing to share with one another through peer coaching. Katarina was invited to look over a survey developed by the staff to help her identify her interests and skills related to peer coaching. Completing this survey prompted a number of questions about how she thought peer coaching worked.

"Does everyone really participate in coaching?" Katarina inquired.

"Well, we all value learning about new research and practices as something that all effective practitioners do," Josie said. "Before we started peer coaching, people would go off alone or in small groups to a workshop and come back with great ideas. But actually implementing those ideas was a lot harder! Coaching gives us a concrete way to learn from colleagues who experience the same challenges and successes we deal with every day. Only they have figured out a way to make things work better. This might be because they have more experience, or learned from someone else, or have a different set of skills."

"I know what you mean," agreed Katarina. "I've learned from watching my colleagues, to see what they do when they are loaded down with paperwork or how they support a family. But that's very different than coaching a colleague or having a coach observe me."

"There are ways to start out so it's not overwhelming," explained Josie. "We set up a committee to consider key factors, like having support from program administrators and making coaching a voluntary activity separate from evaluating job performance. We included practitioners from five disciplines, two program administrators, and another parent in addition to me to form the committee."

"What kind of training did you have to learn to coach?" Katarina asked. "You just didn't decide to start coaching one another, did you?"

"That's a really important question. Our committee spent several months reading about coaching and sharing articles with us at staff meetings about what they thought would work. One of the things we decided to do was to start looking for spontaneous opportunities for coaching one another in staff meetings and other less formal times. We brought in a consultant to help us learn to ask open-ended questions to prompt reflection. Then, we tried it out for the next 2 weeks and had a follow-up conference call with her to answer our questions."

"Did you coach one another to use the consultant's suggestions?"

"We sure did!" exclaimed Josie. "Four of us decided to schedule some time to observe one another and reflect about it afterward. Other people wanted to join our coaching sessions when they saw how helpful it was to apply the training."

Katarina's questions and comments highlight six critical issues, discussed in detail next, that can help establish and sustain effective peer coaching among colleagues (Ackland, 1991; Gersten, Morvant, & Brengelman, 1995; Hasboruck & Christen, 1997; Kohler, McCullough, & Buchan, 1995; Robbins, 1991; Showers, 1985):

REMEMBER THIS...
Peer coaching helps colleagues

• Reflect on their actions/ attitudes

• Acquire and refine behavior/skills

• Share ideas and problem-solve

• Create a community of learners who support coaching as a way to acquire new skills and knowledge

• Develop a flexible format to meet the needs of all learners

• Promote spontaneous, as well as planned, opportunities for coaching

• Adapt peer coaching topics to address early childhood practitioner interests and experience

• Consider how to align coach and learner experience and knowledge

• Acknowledge and support early childhood practitioners' efforts to learn new skills

CREATE A COMMUNITY OF LEARNERS

Establishing a supportive climate for peer coaching provides the essential foundation for collegial relationships as part of a "companionship with peers" (Brandt, 1987). As Josie described in the initial coaching story in this chapter, learning from a respected peer who understands a learner's daily context is very different from attending an in-service or reading about a new practice in a professional journal. Contrast peer coaching with what frequently happens after an in-service training, as Josie recounted for Katarina. Early childhood practitioners struggle on their own to apply their new learning as time permits. As they strive to remember exactly what was said and/or demonstrated, their enthusiasm subsides, and it becomes difficult to sustain the new practice.

Mutual respect and nonjudgmental support among early childhood practitioners and administrators with various professional and personal perspectives provide the critical atmosphere for voluntary participation in peer coaching (Gingiss, 1993; Robbins, 1995). Observing one another and reflecting together is a natural, although more public, way to interact with and learn from others. Despite the benefits of receiving on-site support for learning a new practice, some early childhood practitioners may feel anxious about being observed by a colleague and may need to watch others engage in coaching before trying it themselves (Donegan, Ostrosky, & Fowler, 2000). Educators and therapists historically have provided isolated intervention and instruction alone in a therapy room or classroom. Although they may not be familiar with coaching, early childhood practitioners value the opportunity

REFLECT ON THIS...
Positive peer coaching environment

Create a positive climate for peer coaching in early childhood by promoting:

1. Respect for various professional practices and personal perspectives

2. Belief in life-long learning for continuing competency

3. Desire to incorporate evidence-based practice in all interactions and support services

4. Willingness to be observed, to observe others, and to engage in reflective dialogue with colleagues

5. Administrative support for shared problem solving and creative scheduling for coaching sessions

to identify effective strategies for supporting a family and enhancing a child's development. Many professions whose members work with children and their families promote life-long learning for continuing competency (American Nurses Association Early Intervention Consensus Committee, 1993; American Occupational Therapy Association, 1999; Sandall, McLean, & Smith, 2000).

Early childhood practitioners are likely to keep and use new strategies and concepts if they participate in coaching while trying out these new ideas and practices. Personal enthusiasm, knowledge of theory, and watching a demonstration are not sufficient reinforcers to ensure that practitioners can use new information to change their professional behavior. Repetition, with reflection and feedback about one's actions, are also critical components of the process of transferring training to daily practice (Gordon, Nolan, & Forlenza, 1995; Showers, Joyce, & Bennett, 1987). For example, a voluntary peer coaching program, designed by teachers in a small school district near a large urban city, followed a staff in-service program for all teachers to promote a specific decision-making model (Desrochers & Klein, 1990). In order to ensure that the training was incorporated in the educators' daily instructional practices, coaching teams of outstanding teachers observed their colleagues in their classrooms. They then met together in a conference session to prompt the observed teacher's analysis of successful and unsuccessful decisions related to the decision-making model.

Support from program leaders is essential in establishing a learning climate where team members are encouraged to share their knowledge as well as reflect on a program's mission and how it incorporates recommended practices (Pellicer & Anderson, 1995; Robbins, 1991; Strother, 1989). An active leader (e.g., administrator, early childhood practitioner, program supervisor) promotes colleague-to-colleague coaching as an effective strategy to decrease the isolation that comes from providing itinerant intervention, facilitating an independent group, or teaching in a classroom. Peer coaching is also effective in helping groups come up with creative options to program challenges. Rather than "muddle" through challenges alone when they inevitably arise, coaching encourages early childhood practitioners to seek others who have experienced the same issue or are currently facing similar challenges. Colleague-to-colleague coaching can help early childhood practitioners:

- Ensure that initial interviews are family friendly
- Involve family members in a child's evaluation and assessment in a variety of active roles
- Assist parents in identifying functional outcomes for their children
- Support a parent's or child care provider's efforts to help a child participate in daily activities at home and in the community
- Incorporate a program's guiding principles within all interactions with colleagues and families

Early childhood leaders can promote coaching to practitioners and demonstrate how coaching supports and improves professional practice. Orienting new early childhood practitioners to peer coaching, as Josie did for Katarina when she joined their early intervention program, is a first step once peer coaching is embraced by a group of practitioners. Program leaders also can help practitioners understand coaching by:

- Sharing introductory articles about coaching among practitioners (for suggestions, see the resource list at the end of this chapter)
- Listening to practitioners' coaching stories on this topic over a brown bag lunch
- Routinely incorporating a short period of time (10 or 15 minutes) at the beginning or end of staff meetings to share coaching experiences
- Organizing a panel discussion, including pairs of learners and coaches, to talk about the benefits from participating in coaching for both practitioners and families
- Including a statement of support in program policies and principles for peer coaching as a valued part of lifelong learning

DEVELOP A FLEXIBLE FORMAT

When peer coaching is valued as a worthwhile strategy for continued professional development, attention can then be focused on deciding how to deliver it to best meet early childhood practitioner needs and experience. Two approaches to peer coaching identified in the literature, expert and reciprocal, provide opportunities for varying levels of coach expertise in a specific area of practice (Ackland, 1991;

Robbins, 1991). Both approaches can be used separately or in combination and complement the coaching process presented in this book.

Expert Approach

In the *expert approach*, peer coaching is provided by a practitioner with acknowledged content expertise in a specific area, such as experience with young children with autism or supporting children and families in natural learning environments. An early childhood practitioner who assumes the role of an expert peer coach has specialized knowledge and may be a member of a particular group of practitioners or may be brought in as an external consultant. In the coaching story introduced previously, Josie and Katarina's program contracted with a consultant as the expert coach to help staff become competent in asking and responding to open-ended questions.

An experienced practitioner serving as an "expert coach" observes a colleague who would like to improve skills in the coach's area of expertise, then encourages self-reflection, shares feedback and information as appropriate, and provides encouragement as the colleague practices new actions (Ackland, 1991; Swafford, 1998). One school district designated an experienced teacher as an expert coach to facilitate collaboration and communication between special educators, general education teachers, and therapists as they implemented an inclusion project in a second-grade classroom (Kovic, 1996). Another used an early childhood special education consultant as the expert coach to provide initial follow-up support to attendees of a staff development workshop on including children with autism in a community child care center (Donegan et al., 2000). Still a third coaching project in a large inner-city elementary school used two expert coaches, special educators with expertise in reading, to coach classroom teachers to teach students to read using research-based teaching strategies (Gersten et al., 1995). Lessons learned from these coaching projects emphasize that:

- New strategies require significant time for early childhood practitioners to master. A learner typically experiences plateaus, peaks, and valleys as he or she integrates unfamiliar techniques into practice. Coaches must understand that changing behavior takes time and assist the learner in finding ways to stay on task despite any setbacks.

- Early childhood practitioners are not always comfortable about being observed and often feel they are being evaluated because their coaches are helping them change their behavior. Coaches have to help learners become comfortable with observation by noting and encouraging all positive behaviors observed and taking time to help learners analyze the effectiveness of their actions in making a difference for a family and child.

- Differences in perspectives and expectations between a coach and a learner must be acknowledged, particularly when the partners are from different disciplines. Reflection is invaluable in helping colleagues look at their deeply held convictions and assumptions about their practices before suggesting actions for behavior change.

Reciprocal Approach

In the *reciprocal approach* to peer coaching, a pair or small group of early childhood practitioners observe one another, reflect afterwards, and share their feedback regarding a specified topic (Sparks & Bruder, 1987). The reciprocal approach is most effectively used by early childhood practitioners who decide to refine their skills in a defined area of evidence-based practice. Colleagues are at similar levels in learning and applying the specified practice. This does not mean practitioners must have equal early childhood experience and knowledge to engage in reciprocal coaching or be from the same discipline. For example, Josie and Katarina's early intervention program used reciprocal coaching as an on-site follow-up to training regarding open-ended questions. Although staff experience in early childhood varied from 6 months to 15 years, none had specific training in this communication skill, so they were at similar levels in implementing the training. Additional examples include using specific instructional strategies to promote preliteracy, facilitating social interaction in child care and preschool settings, or using parent desires and child interests to identify IFSP outcomes with families.

Reciprocal peer coaching uses scheduled sessions for early childhood practitioners to periodically exchange coach and learner roles. Each spends time being observed as well as observing others. In one education program, two or three practitioners who desired to work on similar strategies set up reciprocal observation, reflection, and feedback sessions with one another (Rogers, 1987). In another, "peer observation teams" of two people met periodically as a support group to discuss strategies and challenges encountered in their daily teaching (McREL, 1983; Mello, 1984). Three interdisciplinary staff members in a third early childhood program agreed to use spontaneous coaching among themselves as opportunities arose during the day to prompt predetermined behaviors; they met in weekly support meetings to discuss their observations and provide feedback to one another (Miller, 1994).

The following coaching story illustrates how three colleagues created a plan for reciprocal coaching to help them apply new information following an in-service session. The story demonstrates how one early childhood practitioner took advantage of an opportunity for spontaneous coaching to prompt a colleague to reflect on new ideas. Figure 7.1 provides an overview of the key partners involved in this coaching story, the purpose for coaching, and the learners' anticipated out-

Purpose of coaching:

> To use reciprocal peer coaching for early childhood practitioners to apply information from an in-service session

Outcomes of coaching:

> 1. Daniel, Sue, and LaVerne will learn how to assist families in identifying natural learning opportunities for their children.
>
> 2. Daniel, Sue, and LaVerne will support and encourage one another while integrating training into daily practice.
>
> 3. Families will be supported in helping their children participate in home and community activity settings.

Key partners	Practitioner interests	Context
Daniel—coach/learner *Sue*—coach/learner *LaVerne*—coach/learner	Develop new skills. Gain support and respect from colleagues.	Interactions with families and colleagues in early intervention program

Figure 7.1. Conference ideas in action.

comes. A Coaching Worksheet with the appropriate sections completed for this coaching story is located in the chapter appendix. You may find it helpful to use the worksheet to follow the coaching process while reading the story.

CONFERENCE IDEAS IN ACTION

Three early childhood practitioners attended a workshop on promoting natural learning opportunities for young children at their annual state-sponsored early intervention conference. On their way home, the practitioners, Daniel, Sue, and LaVerne, talked enthusiastically about the information and research presented. They agreed that the presenters' emphasis on how early intervention is implemented, not just where, really made them rethink their ideas about working in natural environments. However, they felt stumped about how to proceed next.

"Most of the families expect me to conduct a therapy session," fretted Sue, an occupational therapist who had worked in early intervention for 9 years. "They think their kids won't make progress unless I lay my 'magic hands' on them in as many sessions per week as I can schedule."

"Do you recall what the presenter said about how traditional sessions might feel like from a child's perspective and look like from a parent's view?" asked Daniel, a psychologist

TRY THIS . . .
Initiating spontaneous peer coaching

Spontaneous peer coaching is initiated by an early childhood practitioner who is skilled in recognizing both an opportunity for reflection and a colleague's willingness to engage in reflective dialogue. Look for opportunities to ask a *wh-* question during

- Staff meetings
- Informal discussion over lunch or breaks
- Case conferences
- Planning sessions
- In-service and other professional development events, including travel time

---

in private practice who provided contract services to Sue and LaVerne's early intervention program. *(Reflection—initiating spontaneous coaching, asking open-ended question)*

"Well, she talked about looking at the percentage of time we spend directing the child versus coaching parents to use activity settings that have multiple learning opportunities," Sue responded. "That way, I can help families ensure that key actions and interactions for a child occur over and over." *(Reflection—relating new strategy to past actions)*

"The point that sticks in my mind is whether practitioners are conducting sessions in their own comfort zone or are figuring out how to enter a family's story rather than star in it," observed LaVerne, the Family Network Coordinator. "Parents are often ambivalent about having practitioners come into their lives. They want help with their kids but don't want their lives turned inside out. I'd like to help practitioners understand a family's story without disrupting it." *(Reflection—relating new idea to current responsibilities)*

Daniel, Sue, and LaVerne continued their reflections about the conference. They decided to spend time over the next month tracking their interactions with one family. Specifically, they agreed to look at how much time they spent directing a child's actions, even in a "natural" environment, such as a child's home, versus looking for natural learning opportunities with family members within activity settings in their home or community. Each practitioner agreed to make an audiotape of one interaction with a family (with the family's permission) to review and reflect about in a group meeting the next month and to schedule time to observe one another coaching family members. The trio also decided that they would share a summary of the conference highlights about natural learning opportunities at their next lunch meeting and would report on their experiences with peer coaching at their monthly staff meeting.

In this coaching story, the three practitioners used the reflection phase of the coaching process. Daniel reflected on Sue's comment and decided to initiate spontaneous coaching. He prompted her to reflect by asking her an open-ended *wh-* question. Sue reflected on what she heard at the conference and related it to what she already knew. LaVerne also reflected on what she heard at the conference and related it to her current responsibilities. Daniel, Sue, and LaVerne obviously were familiar with peer coaching and felt comfortable enough with one another to:

- Ask *wh-* questions (who, what, where, when) in a way that prompted reflection about their attitudes and practices

- Define what they wanted to do differently in their professional practice (use natural learning opportunities to support family members and children in home and other community settings)

- Create a plan for how to proceed—that is, use reciprocal coaching to practice desired actions, observe one another via audiotape, and reflect together at a specified time

- Look for ways to inform colleagues about the benefits of peer coaching

PROMOTE SPONTANEOUS AND PLANNED OPPORTUNITIES FOR COACHING

Expert and reciprocal peer coaching can occur as either a planned or spontaneous practice (see Figure 7.2). *Planned* peer coaching grows out of an early childhood practitioner's desire to expand his or her knowledge and skills in a specific area. This is accomplished by scheduling observation and reflection sessions with a colleague who possesses the desired expertise (expert approach), or by arranging for colleagues to observe one another implement a new practice or modify a current one, then reflect together on its impact (reciprocal approach). Daniel, Sue, and LaVerne planned to use audiotapes and on-site observations of their interactions with families in planned peer coaching sessions.

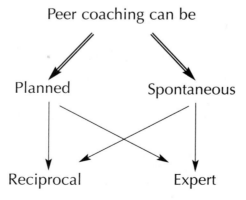

Figure 7.2.   Peer coaching.

When an atmosphere of trust has been established among colleagues, *spontaneous* peer coaching is possible—and desirable—for implementing and sustaining changes in practice. Spontaneous occasions for coaching colleagues provide valuable opportunities for shorter rounds of reflection and dialogue than planned coaching sessions. Spontaneous coaching is initiated by one practitioner who is skilled in recognizing both an opportunity for reflection and a colleague's willingness to engage in reflective dialogue. Such opportunities typically occur when one team member poses a question for a teammate's consideration, thus initiating a time for reflection and feedback. This can simply be a 10-minute discussion in a formal setting, such as a team meeting, or an informal "coming together" in an office, parking lot, or lunch room.

A practitioner or program administrator sees an opportunity for reflection and initiates a coaching interaction with a colleague. Often, this is accomplished by asking a probing question (see Chapter 4), typically a *wh-* question, to encourage a colleague to reflect on his or her intention and/or practices. For example, Daniel seized the moment to initiate spontaneous coaching as he and his colleagues drove home by asking his colleagues, "Do you recall *what* the presenter said about how intervention might feel from a child's perspective and look like from a parent's viewpoint?"

The following coaching story illustrates how an early childhood practitioner used spontaneous coaching to prompt a colleague's reflection about supporting a young boy's participation in play situations with his brother, rather than directing structured sessions with the child. After several spontaneous coaching conversations, planned sessions were scheduled to provide structure to the learner's desire to acquire new skills. The Coaching Worksheet for this story in the chapter appendix includes completed sections based on the coaching conversation. It may be helpful to use the worksheet to follow the coaching process while reading the coaching story. Figure 7.3 provides an overview of the key partners involved in this story, the purpose for coaching, and the learner's anticipated outcomes.

JASON'S PLAY TIME

Joanie, a physical therapist, had been working for the past 3 months with 18-month-old Jason in traditional therapist-directed sessions in his home to prompt his motor development. Jason was a quiet little boy who loved his 9-year-old brother, Aaron, and dog, Rusty. (*child interests*) Joanie was part of an early intervention team that covered a large metropolitan area, and she reported on Jason's progress at her team's bi-weekly team meeting.

"After all these months, Jason finally crawled when his older brother, Aaron, stayed with us in the living room instead of going downstairs to play video games!" exclaimed Joanie.

Purpose of coaching:

To guide Joanie to support Alma in using natural learning opportunities with Jason in their home

Outcomes of coaching:

1. Joanie will help Jason's family (and others) identify their interests and potential/current activity settings so that they can use natural learning opportunities to prompt Jason's development.

2. Jason will expand his play behaviors with his brother to other situations and environments.

Key partners	Child and family interests	Activity settings
Jason—child Aaron—brother Alma—mother Joanie—practitioner/learner Phyllis—practitioner/learner	Family—encouraging Jason to play with Aaron and neighborhood children Brother—playing video games, pretending to be superheroes Child—playing with his brother, petting his dog	Playing in the living room with his brother Playing in the backyard with neighborhood kids Rolling a ball to the dog in the kitchen

Figure 7.3.   Jason's play time.

"What a great way to motivate him, Joanie!" responded Phyllis, a speech-language pathologist who was a member of Joanie's early intervention program. "What was his mom's response when she saw Jason crawl?" *(Reflection—reinforcing learner's actions, asking a wh- question)*

"She's thrilled but also worried that Aaron might disrupt Jason's therapy time," Joanie said. "I pointed out that it was Aaron's involvement that triggered Jason's crawling. After I suggested to Aaron that he could help us make up a story about his favorite video characters, he started talking and jumping all over. *(activity setting)* Before we knew it, Jason started crawling to follow him."

"As you've discovered, using family and child interests is far more motivating than structuring a session for a child that is separate from real life. So, Aaron likes to act out stories about his video characters! *(family interest)* What does Jason's mom like to do with him during the day when you are not there?" *(Reflection—asking a wh- question)*

"You know, I don't know what Alma does with Jason other than what I suggest she try when I leave," admitted Joanie. *(Reflection—considering coach's question)*

"Maybe that is the place to start. Ask Alma what she and Jason would be doing if you weren't there. What would happen if you suggest that you take a look together at the kinds of things she would like Jason to be involved in both in and out of their home?" *(Reflection—providing feedback, suggesting actions)*

"Maybe that's something I should think more about," Joanie replied thoughtfully. "I know that Jason doesn't move around much on his own, but I've never really looked at how that affects him in different situations throughout his day."

In this coaching story, Phyllis assumed the role of coach to support Joanie's attempt to encourage interaction between Jason and his brother. As a speech-language pathologist, she knew that one of the best ways to promote Jason's language skills was to encourage his interaction with his mother and brother, some of the key people in his life. As a supporter of natural learning opportunities, Phyllis wanted to prompt Joanie to find out more about family and child interests as the focus for her interactions with Jason and Alma.

Phyllis saw an opportunity for spontaneous coaching when Joanie expressed her observation that Jason really was motivated to follow his brother. By Joanie's own assessment, Jason was not making much progress with her current approach (i.e., holding play sessions with Jason to work on gross motor skills while Alma observed and carried out suggestions between sessions). Phyllis listened to what Joanie said, acknowledged Jason's successful crawling and encouraged Joanie to extend her thinking on this topic by asking "What does Jason's Mom like to do . . . " and "What would happen if . . . " Phyllis chose her words carefully so that her questions would be interpreted by Joanie as helpful, not accusing.

Notice how the coaching story involved the reflection phase of the coaching process. First, Phyllis reinforced Joanie's actions in an effort to help her focus on child interests. She did this by asking a *wh-* question. Joanie used reflection when she considered Phyllis's question. Phyllis provided feedback and suggested actions for Joanie to consider. Note that Phyllis asked Joanie to consider "What would happen if . . . " in order to help her connect past and future actions.

Phyllis found several more opportunities to use spontaneous coaching with Joanie in the following weeks. Two months later, Joanie asked Phyllis to help her become more skillful in coaching Alma. As part of their coaching plan, Joanie decided to 1) observe Phyllis coach a mother and 2) review two video segments of a physical therapist and mother using natural learning opportunities (e.g., Edelman, 2001) as a basis for her coaching discussion with Phyllis. The following discussion took place after Joanie observed Phyllis coaching a mother, Cassie, and her daughter, Mara.

Phyllis began, "Cassie wants to help her daughter, Mara, become more independent by increasing the number of choices she makes. I'm coaching Cassie to help her find ways to add choices during her daily play and care routines with Mara. What did you notice about how I prompted her to do this?" (*Reflection—eliciting learner's observations, asking open-ended question*)

"The first thing I noticed that you did was to ask Cassie to tell you about the successes she's had with making choices since your last visit." (*Reflection—sharing observation*)

"Yes, you noticed something very important," Phyllis agreed. (*Reflection—confirming learner's observation*) "I want to build on Cassie's successes and figure out what is going right for her before jumping in to give her my ideas. It's a lot more helpful to encourage someone to do more of a successful action than it is to direct them to change their actions. What was Cassie's reaction to my question?" (*Reflection—sharing information, asking open-ended question*)

"Well," Joanie said, "she smiled and told you in great detail how many choices Mara made during mealtimes—whether she wanted a drink or another bite, to sit in a big or little chair, and eat pretzels or raisins next."

"How could you do something similar during your session with Alma?" Phyllis asked.

"I could support Alma by addressing her concern that Jason withdraws from playing with his brother when the big kids next door come over."

"Another action I use as a coach is modeling. Could you model actions for Alma in a way that doesn't imply you've got all the answers?" Phyllis asked.

"Hmmm," Joanie said. "I don't know off-hand what I could do."

"Well," Phyllis said, "what do you think about how I asked Cassie if she wanted to watch me try some new ideas with Mara for making choices, or would she prefer that I prompt her to try them with Mara while I observed their interaction?"

"I noticed you asked that," Joanie responded, "and wondered why. Were you trying to help Cassie make choices herself?"

"Not choices, decisions. I wanted to give her an opportunity to decide how to proceed and didn't want to imply that I have all the answers," Phyllis explained. "Modeling can be tricky sometimes. What have been your experiences with demonstrating your ideas for others?" (*Reflection—determining learner's perspective*)

"Well, some people want to try it out right away and other are hesitant and want to watch me do it. So, I sometimes hold off on demonstrating if I think the person might be put off," Joanie said.

"It sounds like this topic is something you might like to explore further," Phyllis said. "Would you like to plan another coaching session? I have an excellent videotape that shows therapists modeling actions for families. You could borrow it, and we can talk about it next Tuesday during lunch, if that's a good time for you."

"That would be great," Joanie said.

"So far, we've discussed prompting and modeling. Is there anything else you would like to talk about?" Phyllis asked.

"Yes, I've been thinking about something for a while now," Joanie shared. "I've been working with Alma and Jason for almost 6 months. I am still pretty much directing what happens when I see Jason, and Alma still looks to me to plan what we'll be doing. I'm not sure how to change my approach midstream. What should I do?"

"Tell me some more about what you want to change and why," prompted Phyllis. *(Reflection—probing learner to generate ideas)*

"Alma says that there are many instances that Jason is left out of play times because he still sits in her lap rather than get into the thick of things. I read an article in my journal recently about motor learning and was impressed with the author's point that motor skills have to be practiced over and over again in the actual context before they are owned and can be used in another situation. So, I'm wondering how to help Alma use natural learning opportunities for Jason to practice crawling."

"Yes," Phyllis said and nodded her head to encourage Joanie to continue.

"I guess what I'd like to say to Alma is that I don't think that my doing a therapy session is the answer to helping Jason be more active in his play like Alma wants. But I'm not sure I should admit that to her."

"What would happen if you did?" Phyllis asked.

Joanie paused in thought, then replied emphatically, "I think using natural learning opportunities would go a whole lot further helping Jason develop his motor skills while he enjoys playing with other kids. I guess that's not such a bad thing to say—in fact, it's pretty positive!"

"Do you want to role-play some different versions of this conversation until you are comfortable with how you could share your ideas with Alma?" Phyllis asked.

"Absolutely!" Joanie said, and the two went on to practice several conversations.

Notice how this coaching story has many examples of the reflection phase at work. First, Phyllis used an open-ended question to orient Joanie and elicit her observations. Joanie used the reflection phase to share her observation. Phyllis then used the reflection phase to confirm Joanie's observation and offer reinforcement. She shared information, then returned to an open-ended question to prompt further reflection on Joanie's observations. Note that Phyllis did not ask a closed-ended question, such as "Could you do something similar?", which might have easily led to a yes or no answer. She wanted to prompt Joanie to link her observations of Phyllis's actions to her own. She also sought information from Joanie to understand her perspective on modeling before giving too much instruction. Finally, Phyllis used another open-ended question to help Joanie discover what she could and wanted to do differently in her work with Jason and his family. Observe that Phyllis used verbal and gestural signs to indicate she was listening to Joanie as she talked about her ideas.

In this coaching story, Phyllis resisted the temptation to suggest what to do or say until she and Joanie explored what was really on Joanie's mind—how to change her approach midstream with a family. Joanie discovered through her own reflections what Phyllis already embraced. The difference between doing a therapy session and using knowledge of child development and experience as a therapist to coach parents is significant.

ADAPT PEER COACHING TO PRACTITIONER INTERESTS AND EXPERIENCE

Coaches who use either an expert or reciprocal approach to peer coaching must have effective communication skills to establish rapport with learners, help them develop a coaching plan, then prompt their reflection and self-discovery while learning new skills (Rush, Shelden, & Hanft, 2003). While there is no perfect way to implement peer coaching, it is important to take the time to identify the roles and define the interests of a particular group of practitioners, as well as plan for when and how to schedule coaching sessions. When coaching colleagues, a coach must consider the roles (e.g., clinical coordinator, supervisor, friend) that either a coach or learner may assume outside of their coaching relationship. Colleagues who interact as coach and learner are equals with different spheres of knowledge. Surveying early childhood practitioner interests and skills helps target areas for peer coaching by identifying those areas in which practitioners could possibly coach a colleague and/or participate in as a learner. Three categories to start this discussion are identified below:

- Child/family (e.g., helping families to identify their child's interests and assets; assisting parents in identifying functional outcomes for their children)

- Programmatic (e.g., understanding the federal/state requirements of the IDEA or Early Head Start related to transitioning from early intervention to community-based preschool programs)

- Coaching specific (e.g., developing listening skills or sharing helpful feedback; understanding how to interact with adults and incorporate the principles of adult learning)

Once potential coaching topics are identified, the educational background and experience of early childhood practitioners, their communication skills, and their

Visual learning	Auditory learning	Kinesthetic learning
Learner observes coach	Learner summarizes feedback from coach	Learner keeps a journal of actions and reflections
Learner observes others	Learner narrates actions on video	Learner practices actions
Learner watches video	Learner listens to audiotape	Learner demonstrates actions to others

Figure 7.4. Suggestion of multisensory options for learners to integrate new information and actions with what they already know and do.

understanding of the principles of adult learning should also be considered. Effective peer coaching is dependent on a thorough understanding of the principles of adult learning (discussed in Chapter 2). The observation, action, and reflection process that is the cornerstone of coaching depends on a coach's interpersonal communication and ability to apply the basic principles of adult learning to developing collegial relationships with another adult. In particular, a coach must possess skill in integrating new information and practices with what an adult learner already knows in a way that honors individual learning styles. Figure 7.4 suggests strategies for a coach to discuss with a learner when deciding how to individualize coaching to incorporate a learner's preferences for acquiring new information.

For learners who prefer *visual* strategies, a coach can suggest articles and other print resources to read, professional and "homemade" videos to watch, and of course, times for a learner to observe a coach and/or peers. New practices are more likely to be imitated when the observer sees that a respected role model has a positive experience with an innovation or new practice (Rogers, 1983). For early childhood practitioners, seeing a child improve his or her participation in a desired environment as a result of supports provided to other adults is very reinforcing. Auditory learners benefit from discussion and explanation of what they see others do. Because auditory learners can be reinforced by their own verbalizations, encourage them to summarize key points and new understandings made during reflection sessions. For kinesthetic learners, practicing actions becomes the focal point for their learning; viewing their actions via a videotape is also helpful. Some kinesthetic learners enjoy keeping a journal to reflect on their thoughts and actions. This can become part of the reflection sessions, or may be kept private.

ALIGN COACH AND LEARNER EXPERIENCE AND KNOWLEDGE

Regardless of whether a coach and learner in early childhood share disciplinary backgrounds and professional experiences, they must explore what a learner already knows during the initiation component of coaching as a baseline for acquiring new knowledge and skills. This discussion must include an analysis of what a learner hopes to learn or do and how both a coach and a learner will know that a learner's goals have been accomplished. Sometimes, a coach and/or learner will realize during this discussion that a coach's expertise is not sufficient for helping a learner realize his or her objectives. Several options are then available: 1) a learner can request a different coach, 2) a learner can modify his or her objectives, or 3) both a coach and learner can decide to learn the new skill together, essentially switching from an expert to a reciprocal approach to coaching.

A coach must understand what knowledge or skills a learner wants to acquire and how she or he will use the particular information or practice. A coach has the additional responsibility of translating his or her knowledge and experience to provide alternative perspectives and strategies for a learner, appropriate to his or

TRY THIS . . .
Peer coaching questions

When planning peer coaching sessions with a learner, be sure to discuss the following points:

- What exactly does the learner hope to learn or do, and what evidence is there that this additional knowledge or skill will lead to improved outcomes for young children and their families?
- How will both the coach and learner know that the learner has acquired the desired knowledge or skill?
- What is the learner's baseline knowledge and experience?
- What foundation knowledge and experience does the learner need, and how will it be obtained?
- How will the learner use the new knowledge and skill in his or her early childhood practice?

---

her knowledge, experience, and role with a particular child and family (Hanft & Place, 1996). How a coach translates his or her knowledge and experience requires a careful analysis with a learner of the following contextual variables:

- *What the learner would like to learn or do:* What evidence is there that the learner's desired goals (i.e., to acquire additional knowledge and skills) will lead to improved outcomes for children and families? What is a learner's baseline experience/knowledge? What foundation knowledge or experience is needed, and how will it be obtained? How will a learner use the desired knowledge or skill in his or her early childhood practice?

- *Confirmation that a coach is the right choice for a specific learner:* Does the coach know what the learner really hopes to master? Does the coach understand the learner's context for using the knowledge or skills the coach plans to share and/or prompt him or her to acquire? Does the coach have the expertise (both knowledge of evidence-based practices and experience using them) to guide a learner?

- *How to assist a learner in acquiring knowledge or skill:* What frequency and intensity of coaching sessions are needed to help a learner reach his or her goals? How will the principles of adult learning be addressed for each learner? (See the previous section on adult interaction and also Chapter 1.) What mix of coaching strategies, such as demonstration, observation (in person or via video), and review of print resources, will help a learner? How often will a learner need follow-up once his or her goals are met?

In the following coaching story (summarized in Figure 7.5), an occupational therapist coaches an early childhood educator to learn how to use an evaluation

Purpose of coaching:

> To engage Kim in planned coaching sessions with a colleague to refine her professional skills

Outcomes of coaching:

> 1. Kim will learn how to use an evaluation tool to determine a child's eligibility for early intervention.
>
> 2. Kim will participate on the early intervention program's evaluation team.
>
> 3. Colleagues and families will benefit from Kim's expertise in observation.

Key partners	Practitioner interests	Context
Kim—learner *Bijul*—coach	*Kim*—improving professional skills, receiving support from a colleague *Bijul*—sharing expertise with a colleague, gaining respect from colleagues	Team evaluations for eligibility to infant and toddler program

Figure 7.5. Kim's professional development.

tool to determine a child's eligibility for Part C (of the IDEA 1997, PL 105-17) early intervention services. The story highlights a coach's considerations for sharing specific knowledge with a colleague and depicts a discussion initiated by a coach to develop a coaching plan that guides a learner to use new information appropriately. Kim, an occupational therapist, had worked in adult rehabilitation for 15 years before joining the county early intervention program a year ago. She asked Bijul, an early childhood special educator with 10 years' experience in early intervention, to teach her how to administer and interpret a norm-referenced evaluation for infants and toddlers as part of the process of determining a child's eligibility for early intervention. A Coaching Worksheet with the appropriate sections completed for this coaching story is located in the chapter appendix. You may find it helpful to use the worksheet to follow the coaching process while reading the story.

KIM'S PROFESSIONAL DEVELOPMENT

"First of all, thank you for asking me to be your coach," Bijul said. "Before we go over the evaluation, I'd like to understand what you already know about infant evaluations and how you hope to use this one. That way, we can be sure I'm the right coach to guide your learning. We need to be sure that I can help you achieve your goals." *(Initiation—clarifying purpose and outcomes)*

"Well, you know that I have a master's degree in occupational therapy," Kim said. "I learned to administer norm- and criterion-referenced tests for people of all ages. I also can use observation to assess a child in a specific activity, like eating or creative play with peers. I had a course in tests and measurement but did not have much experience during my fieldwork actually testing a very young child suspected of having a developmental delay."

"It sounds like you would like to learn how to use a norm-referenced evaluation to help you look at a child's development when he or she is referred to early intervention," Bijul summed up. *(Initiation—clarifying outcomes)*

Kim nodded. "Yes, there will be an opening on the evaluation team in 2 months when Sidney goes on maternity leave, and I would like to be considered when an OT's expertise is needed. If I could learn the evaluation you use and practice with kids in my neighborhood, then I'll be prepared to use it with infants and toddlers who are suspected of having a delay." *(Initiation—expanding on desired outcomes)*

"Sounds like a good idea," Bijul said. "But let's take a second to think about what you need to know beyond how to administer and interpret this one evaluation tool. For starters, you have to understand the IDEA requirements for evaluation and assessment and know how to share results with families using language that is easy to understand. Then, the real assessment skill comes into play—making the link between a child's abilities and the settings the family hopes to see the child participate in on a daily basis."

"That sounds like a lot," Kim said. "I'd like to work on all of those things and would like to start with using this evaluation with young children. Do you think you can help?" *(Initiation—invitation for coaching relationship)*

"It won't be difficult to develop a specific coaching plan for you," Bijul said with a smile. "I'm confident that I have the expertise in the areas you want to learn about and can help you learn to use this evaluation tool so that you can be an effective member of our evaluation team. You'll also bring some important skills to the position. Evaluation is just the first step in the process of understanding a child's abilities. Once eligibility is determined, your observation skills can really help pinpoint ways for promoting a child's participation in desired activity settings." *(Reflection—providing feedback and encouragement)*

In this coaching story, Bijul used the initiation phase of the coaching process when she clarified the purpose and outcomes of coaching with Kim. Bijul's summary prompted Kim to expand on her desired outcomes, also part of the initiation phase. Bijul noted that Kim already had a basic plan for practicing actions outside of coaching sessions. Kim invited Bijul into a coaching relationship when she asked if she could help her use the evaluation with young children. With reflection and discussion, Bijul gave Kim some feedback and encouragement.

Because defining the context in which the learner wants to use new knowledge and skills is important in colleague-to-colleague coaching, Bijul and Kim continued to identify the exact knowledge and skills that Kim needed to acquire in order to function competently on the evaluation team. They also spent more time talking about how Kim learns, and they identified several coaching strategies for her, including observing an occupational therapist in the adjoining county as well as Kim making a videotape of two practice sessions with typically developing children to review with Bijul and, of course, reading the test manual from cover to cover.

Bijul wound up this initial planning session by talking with Kim about what they discussed and the coaching actions they agreed on to help Kim reach her goals. As Bijul drove to her next appointment, she employed the evaluation phase of the coaching process. She analyzed her actions related to developing a coaching relationship and plan with Kim and asked herself the following questions:

- Did I clarify what Kim wanted to learn?
- Do I understand the context in which she will use her new information?
- Do I have the skills needed to coach Kim to reach her goals?
- What other actions could I take to help Kim reach her goal?

Bijul was careful to ascertain that Kim had the background training necessary to administer a norm-referenced tool (e.g., education degree, course in tests and measurement, observation skills, opportunities for practice). She was also satisfied that she had the expertise needed to be an effective coach for Kim (e.g., 10 years experience using norm-referenced tools in early intervention, an understanding of the IDEA 1997 [PL 105-17] and state requirements for evaluation and assessment, an appreciation of the limitations of standardized tools in understanding a child's ability to participate in specific activities in home and community settings).

ACKNOWLEDGE AND SUPPORT EFFORTS TO LEARN NEW SKILLS

Learning a new practice such as coaching requires that early childhood practitioners find time to observe it, try it out, then evaluate its impact on their own personal and professional lives (Gersten et al., 1995). Strategies for encouraging early childhood practitioners to engage in coaching will vary according to practitioners' availability, encouragement from administrators and other program leaders, and interest and willingness of practitioners to modify their current practices.

Availability

Availability of the coach and learner to schedule time for observation and reflection sessions is sometimes a major issue during coaching. While peer coaching offers a low cost and effective method for providing practitioners with additional knowledge and skill to support children and families, it does require time and effort by both the coach and learner to

- Observe each other's actions and/or those of other colleagues

- Reflect, analyze, and discuss a learner's anticipated and past actions, including what occurred while a learner practiced specific actions between coaching sessions

- Evaluate the coaching process, assess a learner's progress toward achieving his or her goals, and readjust the coaching plan as necessary to continue moving forward

Administrative support for the coaching process is key to exploring creative options for finding the time to coach (Garmston, 1987). One early intervention program schedules all staff in the office for 1 hour per month for colleague consultation. This strategy could also be used for peer coaching. A sign-up sheet is posted beforehand with names of the specific "staff-on-call" listed at 15-minute intervals. Anyone can sign up in one of these slots to discuss a particular issue with the identified colleague. Staff rotate being on call for each session so that all early childhood practitioners have the opportunity to gather feedback from colleagues about a particular issue (E. Feinberg, personal communication, April 1, 2003).

In group settings, such as child care and preschool programs, reflection sessions between a coach and learner can be scheduled while children play, eat their lunch or snack, or rest and nap or before children arrive and after they leave for home (Donegan et al., 2000). In some programs, a program administrator and volunteer will take responsibility for leading or teaching a group of children in order to free a coach and learner to meet with one another and reflect on their observations and actions. Some programs hire a floating substitute at regular intervals for the same purpose (Ackland, 1991; Joyce & Showers, 1987).

When schedules are very tight and a coach cannot observe a learner's actions and interactions with certain individuals in a designated setting, video and audiotape can be used to record actions. Obviously, it also takes time to set up and record a video, but this can be accomplished by enlisting assistance from a learner's colleague or program administrator who supports peer coaching. Telephone conferencing for reflection and feedback, if used judiciously, can also be scheduled to augment in-person sessions.

Administrative Support for Coaching

Colleague-to-colleague coaching takes place within early childhood practitioners' work environments during the course of their workday. Peer coaching must have the endorsement of program administrators and leaders because coaching sessions may take time away from contact with family members and other caregivers when a coach and learner meet for reflection and feedback. Coaching takes place during the workday, unlike other options for professional development (e.g., evening and weekend seminars and workshops, independent study), which all can generally be fulfilled outside of the workday. Program leaders, including administrators, supervisors, coordinators, and respected practitioners, are also important role models and set professional standards for a particular group of early childhood practitioners. If these leaders engage in coaching themselves, both as coaches and learners, early childhood practitioners will have the opportunity to observe how these leaders benefit from their coaching experience and will be more likely to give coaching a try themselves (Rogers, 1983).

Practitioner Interest

Early childhood practitioners' interest and willingness to learn new practices is crucial. Both learners and coaches must voluntarily engage in coaching if a learner is going to acquire or refine specific knowledge and skill to use in daily professional interactions with colleagues and families. Coaches contribute support and information to the coaching process; learners also play a proactive role in coaching and must believe that they can ultimately learn and implement new evidence-based practices. Even when a learner indicates great interest in acquiring new skills, the nature of the behavior change will have a dramatic impact on how quickly he or she implements a new practice, particularly if it is different from the status quo. Disenchantment can easily occur if the process of changing practice is not understood and accepted.

The Concerns-Based Adoption Model (CBAM), a seven-stage framework for managing change in professional development programs, emphasizes that learning brings change, and change creates different kinds of stress (Hall & Hord, 2000; Hall, Hord, Rutherford, & Huling-Austin, 1987; Hall & Loucks, 1978). The CBAM reminds early childhood administrators and program leaders to pay attention to early childhood practitioners' needs for information, assistance, and emotional support when considering and adopting coaching as part of professional development. The seven stages of CBAM—awareness, information, personal, management, consequences, collaboration, and refocusing—emphasize the need for different kinds of information and support as early childhood practitioners experience change in their professional practices.

Initially, early childhood practitioners may become aware of coaching by hearing or reading about it. Program leaders can actively promote *awareness* of peer coaching as a valuable tool for professional development by sharing information at staff meetings or in-service days, passing around journal articles, or posting notices about upcoming lectures or resources about coaching. In the *information* stage, early childhood practitioners actively seek out resources about coaching through discussing it with a peer or supervisor, reading print resources, or attending presentations and conferences. Early childhood practitioners who have been exposed to coaching will need more detailed information to answer basic questions about what coaching looks like, its benefits, and how to develop skills as a coach.

Next, *personal* concerns arise, and early childhood practitioners may question how much time and effort may be required to learn something new and change their professional behavior. Concerns about confidentiality and competency issues may arise about being observed by a colleague or outside consultant. Practitioners may wonder, "Will a coach talk about my actions to anyone else and will coaching affect my performance evaluations?" At a very personal level, practitioners may worry, "What if I don't measure up?"

Once early childhood practitioners understand that a new practice is beneficial, *management* or logistical issues arise related to schedules, availability, and how to choose a coach and acquire basic coaching skills. Hearing successful coaching stories and querying learners and coaches about their experiences scheduling coaching sessions and learning to coach can be helpful. After early childhood practitioners understand the mechanics of coaching and how to use it within their practice, they may consider the *consequences* of not engaging in coaching, for themselves and the families they support. At this point, early childhood practitioners can develop a more in-depth appreciation for the benefits of changing a professional practice.

During the *collaboration* stage, early childhood practitioners are engaged in trying out the coaching process and begin to talk about what else they need to do to successfully manage changing their practice. They may request help in individualizing coaching to their particular situation. For example, "How can we use expert or reciprocal peer coaching to address our needs?" and "How can we be more judicious with our time to schedule coaching sessions?"

Refocusing is the final stage in the change process and is broached when early childhood practitioners begin to answer their own doubts and share insight about how to make coaching work effectively for others as well. This occurs after a core group of practitioners has engaged in coaching, and they become the role models for other practitioners. Their stories highlight the benefits of coaching; even negative experiences, when they occur, prompt reassessment and refinement, rather than abandonment of the innovation in practice.

CONCLUSION

This chapter describes the key logistical and support issues that provide the foundation for effective peer coaching by early childhood practitioners (summarized as a self-assessment in the chapter appendix). Peer coaching is a professional development strategy that incorporates the same process described in Chapter 3 for supporting families and other adult caregivers. In peer coaching, however, both a coach and learner are colleagues who interact with varying regularity in early childhood settings. Administrators, early childhood practitioners, child care providers, preschool and nursery school personnel, and family advocates can all use this process to share their knowledge and experience with their colleagues. Voluntary participation, a key characteristic of all coaching, develops from the respect and trust shared by a particular group of individuals who are comfortable in translating their knowledge and experience to help one another grow professionally. This means that a coach considers how and what personal and professional knowledge and experience to share with a learner, as appropriate to a learner's role, training, and experience.

Peer coaching builds on the expertise of team members who are supported by program leaders in their efforts to coach, and be coached, by colleagues. Two approaches to peer coaching, reciprocal and expert, provide options for practitioners to learn new knowledge and skills together (reciprocal) or work with a colleague who has already mastered the desired practice (expert). Peer coaching can also occur as a planned interaction with scheduled sessions focused on initiation, observation, action, reflection, and evaluation. It can also be initiated as a spontaneous exchange by an early childhood practitioner who sees an opportunity to assume a coaching role with a colleague to prompt his or her reflection about current practices.

The coaching stories presented illustrate different approaches to peer coaching, as well as the unique issues to consider when coaching early childhood colleagues. In the first story, Katarina joined an early childhood program that embraced peer coaching as part of lifelong learning. An orientation discussion with an experienced team member, Josie, raised questions for Katarina about the basics of coaching including, "Who participates in coaching?" "Why coach or be coached?" and "How do you learn to become an effective coach?" The second coaching story showed how a group of practitioners, Daniel, Sue, and LaVerne, developed a plan to use reciprocal coaching to help them implement information from a conference about supporting families in new ways. This story also provided an example of spontaneous coaching and showed that early childhood practitioners can use peer coaching even when they do not all work in the same agency. The third story demonstrated how spontaneous coaching leads into planned coaching to help Joanie, a therapist who would like to redirect her traditional therapist-directed sessions with a child to support families to use natural learning opportunities. Joanie and her colleague-coach, Phyllis, used coaching strategies that included Joanie observing Phyllis coach a parent and then reflecting with Phyllis to relate her observations to her own practice. The last coaching story highlighted a coach's considerations about sharing specific knowledge with another practitioner and illustrated the evaluation component of the coaching process. Bijul, an early childhood special educator, agreed to coach Kim, an occupational therapist, to use an evaluation tool to help determine a child's eligibility to early intervention. Their discussion led to the development of a coaching plan that addressed how Kim could appropriately use this new information.

Peer coaching is a valuable part of a continuum of professional development activities that include summer coursework at a university, weekend workshops and conferences, in-service sessions during the work week, and independent study. The essential qualities of peer coaching—learning from and with colleagues—also highlight the unique opportunities provided to help practitioners transfer learning from formal training into daily practice. Early childhood practitioners are likely to keep and use new strategies and concepts if they engage in either expert or reciprocal coaching while they try out new strategies and skills (Showers et al., 1987). Effective professional development links theory, research, and demonstration with on-site opportunity for a learner's observation, action, and reflection about new strategies and practices.

RESOURCES

Donegan, M., Ostrosky, M., & Fowler, S. (2000). Peer coaching: Teachers supporting teachers. *Young Exceptional Children, 3*(2), 9–16.
This article illustrates peer coaching in early childhood and describes a coaching process focused on joint planning, observation, and feedback used by practitioners in an inclusive child care center. Guidelines for establishing a peer coaching program and sample forms are also included.

Gallacher, K. (1997). Supervision, mentoring and coaching. In P.J. Winton, J.A. McCollum & C. Catlett (Eds.), *Reforming personnel preparation in early intervention: Issues, models, and practical strategies* (pp. 191–214). Baltimore: Paul H. Brookes Publishing Co.
This chapter provides a succinct overview of coaching in relation to mentoring and supervision, gives examples of how coaching was used in early intervention, and details practitioner/coach tasks during the six steps of coaching (initial interest, planning, information gathering, analysis, conferencing, and review).

Gersten, R., Morvant, M., & Brengelman, S. (1995). Close to the classroom is close to the bone: Coaching as a means to translate research into classroom practice. *Exceptional Children, 62*(1), 52–66.
This study explores the effectiveness of using coaching to bring research-based teaching practices into general education classrooms to improve the quality of reading instruction provided to students with learning disabilities. The process of expert peer coaching was analyzed to better understand how practitioners make changes in their practice.

REFERENCES

Ackland, R. (1991). A review of the peer coaching literature. *Journal of Staff Development, 12,* 22–27.
American Nurses Association Early Intervention Consensus Committee. (1993). *National standards of nursing practice for early intervention services.* Lexington: University of Kentucky College of Nursing.

American Occupational Therapy Association. (1999). *Occupational therapy services for children and youth under the Individuals with Disabilities Education Act* (2nd ed.). Bethesda, MD: Author.

Brandt, R. (1987, February). On teachers coaching teachers: A conversation with Bruce Joyce. *Educational Leadership*, 12–17.

Desrochers, C., & Klein, S. (1990). Teacher-directed peer coaching as a follow-up to staff development. *Journal of Staff Development, 1192*, 6–10.

Donegan, M., Ostrosky, M., & Fowler, S. (2000). Peer coaching: Teachers supporting teachers. *Young Exceptional Children, 3*(2), 9–16.

Edelman, L. (2001). *Just being kids.* Denver, CO: JFK Partners, University of Colorado Health Sciences Center and Early Childhood Connections, Colorado Department of Health.

Gallacher, K. (1997). Supervision, mentoring and coaching. In P.J. Winton, J.A. McCollum, & C. Catlett (Eds.), *Reforming personnel preparation in early intervention: Issues, models, and practical strategies* (pp. 191–214). Baltimore: Paul H. Brookes Publishing Co.

Garmston, R. (1987). How administrators support peer coaching. *Educational Leadership, 44*(5), 18–26.

Gersten, R., Morvant, M., & Brengelman, S. (1995). Close to the classroom is close to the bone: Coaching as a means to translate research into classroom practice. *Exceptional Children, 62*(1), 52–66.

Gingiss, P. (1993). Peer coaching: Building collegial support for using innovative health programs. *Journal of School Health, 63*(2), 79–85.

Gordon, S., Nolan, J., & Forlenza, V. (1995). Peer coaching: A cross-site comparison. *Journal of Personnel Evaluation in Education, 9*, 69–91.

Hall, G., & Hord, S. (2000). *Implementing change: Patterns, principals, and potholes.* Boston: Allyn & Bacon.

Hall, G., Hord, S., Rutherford, W., & Huling-Austin, L. (1987). *Taking charge of change.* Alexandria, VA: Association for Supervision and Curriculum Development.

Hall, G., & Loucks, S. (1978). A developmental model for determining whether the treatment is actually implemented. *American Educational Research Journal, 14*(3), 263–276.

Hanft, B., & Place, P. (1996). *The consulting therapist: A guide for occupational and physical therapists in schools.* San Antonio, TX: Therapy Skill Builders.

Hasboruck, J., & Christen, M. (1997). Providing peer coaching in inclusive classrooms: A tool for consulting teachers. *Intervention in School and Clinic, 32*(3), 72–77.

Hendrickson, J., Gardner, N., Kaiser, A., & Riley, A. (1993). Evaluation of a social interaction coaching program in an integrated day care setting. *Journal of Applied Behavior Analysis, 26*, 213–225.

Individuals with Disabilities Education Act Amendments of 1997, PL 105-17, 20 U.S.C. §§ 1400 *et seq.*

Joyce, B., & Showers, B. (1982). The coaching of teaching. *Educational Leadership, 40*, 4–10.

Joyce, B., & Showers, B. (1987). Low cost arrangement for peer coaching. *Journal of Staff Development, 8*(1), 22–24.

Kohler, F., McCullough, K., & Buchan, K. (1995). Using peer coaching to enhance preschool teachers' development and refinement of classroom activities. *Early Education and Development, 6*(3), 215–239.

Kovic, S. (1996). Peer coaching to facilitate inclusion: A job embedded staff development model. *Journal of Staff Development, 17*(1), 28–31.

McREL (Mid-Continent Regional Educational Laboratory). (1983). *Coaching: A powerful strategy for improving staff development and inservice education.* Kansas City, KS: Author.

Mello, L. (1984). *Peer-centered coaching: Teachers helping teachers to improve classroom performance.* Indian Springs, CO: Associates for Human Development. (ERIC Document Reproduction Service No. ED 274648)

Miller, S. (1994). Peer coaching within an early childhood interdisciplinary setting. *Intervention in School and Clinic, 30*(2), 109–113.

Pellicer, L., & Anderson, L. (1995). *A handbook for teacher leaders.* Thousand Oaks, CA: Corwin Press.

Robbins, P. (1991). *How to plan and implement a peer coaching program.* Reston, VA: Association for Supervision and Curriculum Development.

Robbins, P. (1995). Peer coaching: Quality through collaborative work. In J. Block, S. Everson, & T. Guskey (Eds.), *School improvement programs: A handbook for educational leaders* (pp. 70–85). New York: Scholastic.

Rogers, E. (1983). *Diffusion of innovation* (3rd ed). New York: Free Press.

Rogers, S. (1987). If I can see myself, I can change. *Educational Leadership, 45*(2), 64–67.

Rush, D.D., Shelden, M.L., & Hanft, B.E. (2003). Coaching families and colleagues: A process for collaboration in natural settings. *Infants and Young Children, 16*(1), 33–47.

Sandall, S., McLean, M., & Smith, B. (2000). *DEC recommended practices in early intervention/early childhood special education.* Longmont, CO: Sopris West.

Showers, B. (1985). Teachers coaching teachers. *Educational Leadership, 42*(7), 43–48.

Showers, B., Joyce, B., & Bennett, B. (1987). Synthesis of research on staff development: A framework for future study of state-of-the-art analysis. *Educational Leadership, 45*(3), 77–87.

Sparks, G., & Bruder, S. (1987). Before and after peer coaching. *Educational Leadership, 45*(3), 54–57.

Strother, D. (1989). Peer coaching for teachers: Opening classroom doors. *Phi Delta Kappan, 70*(10), 824–827.

Swafford, J. (1998). Teachers supporting teachers through peer coaching. *Support for Learning, 13*(2), 54–58.

Vail, C., Tschantz, J., & Bevill, A. (1997). Dyads and date in peer coaching: Early childhood education in action. *Teaching Exceptional Children, 30*(2), 11–15.

Appendix

Key Components Supporting Effective Peer Coaching in Early Childhood

Identify group/program: _____

Completed by: _____   Date: _____

Components of effective peer coaching	Need to work on	Making good progress	Doing very well
1. Peer coaching is voluntarily supported by early childhood practitioners as part of life-long learning.			
2. Flexible formats (expert/reciprocal approaches) to peer coaching are used.			
3. Learners' desires for additional knowledge/skill are addressed.			
4. Peer coaches understand adult learning and interaction.			
5. Spontaneous opportunities for coaching are supported as well as planned sessions.			
6. Learner and coach are matched by desired experience and knowledge.			
7. Administration or leadership allocates resources and supports peer coaching.			

The aspect of peer coaching that works best for me is:

The one thing I would modify about peer coaching is:

Coaching Worksheet: Conference Ideas in Action

Learner: _Daniel, Sue, and LaVerne_ Coach: _Daniel, Sue, and LaVerne_ Date: _March 5_

INITIATION

Coaching opportunities observed or presented

Travel home after Daniel, Sue, and LaVerne attended a workshop on natural learning opportunities

The purpose of the coaching relationship is

To use reciprocal peer coaching to help early childhood practitioners apply information from an in-service session

Intended learner outcomes resulting from the coaching relationship

Learn how to assist families in identifying natural learning opportunities for their children.

Support and encourage one another while integrating training into daily practice.

Support families to help their children participate in home and community activity settings.

Barriers to the coaching process	Strategies to address barriers
Daniel, Sue, and LaVerne do not work for the same agency; Daniel is a part-time contractor with the early intervention program.	All three attended the workshop together, respect one another, and want to engage in peer coaching. Each practitioner agreed to audiotape interactions with a family to review with the others because schedules are limited.

Ground rules

Each practitioner will schedule time at the end of the week to observe the other two implement strategies from the conference; reflection sessions will be scheduled at the end of the day or after the next day's scheduled visits to families.

OBSERVATION

	What/where	When
Coach observes learner's actions and interactions	Each practitioner made an audiotape of interactions with one family and reviewed it with the others.	Three audio observations over 1 month
Learner observes coach model actions	Each observed the other two implement strategies from the workshop with families and took a turn being observed.	Six in-person observations over 2 months
Learner observes self	same as above	
Coach/learner observe environment		

ACTION

	What/where	When
Coach models for learner (coach present)		
Learner practices an action (coach present/absent)	Daniel, Sue, and LaVerne practice strategies regarding natural learning opportunities with families that they learned from one another and the workshop.	Between observation and reflection sessions
Learner describes experience (coach absent)		
Coach/learner observe environment		

REFLECTION

	Description		
Learner reflects on action or observation	After each in-person observation and audiotape review, Daniel, Sue, and LaVerne analyzed the effectiveness of his or her actions and what else could be tried.		
Coach gives feedback about observation or action following reflection	After each learner's reflections, Daniel, Sue, or LaVerne as coach gave input about their in-person observation or audiotape review.		
Learner uses resources (e.g., print, video, peer)	The coach and learner frequently looked over their workshop handouts and made a special effort to obtain and read recommended print sources about natural learning opportunities.		
Coach confirms learner's understanding and summarizes			
Coach/learner plan next steps	Who	What	When
Observations	The first round of observation/reflection sessions gave Daniel, Sue, and LaVerne many strategies to try.		
Practice	They agreed to implement their ideas with other families and make another round of audiotapes to review with one another in group reflection sessions.		
Resources			

EVALUATION

Coach Self-Reflection

1. Is the learner accomplishing his or her goals?

   All three practitioners felt that the support and ideas they received from one another were invaluable in implementing a new practice.

2. What changes, if any, do I need to make in the coaching process?

   More time was needed to put ideas into practice, and another round of audiotaping and reflection sessions was scheduled.

3. Should I continue as this learner's coach? (If not, who would be more effective?)

   Daniel, Sue, and LaVerne decided to continue peer coaching and also wanted to present their ideas about natural learning opportunities to other colleagues for further discussion at weekly staff meetings.

Coach Asks Learner

1. Shall we continue coaching or have your goals been accomplished (continuation)?

   Yes, continue coaching

   If continuing coaching:

   - What changes need to be made in the coaching plan?

     See plan for continuation of peer coaching in question #3 for coach self-reflection.

   - What observations and/or actions should take place between coaching sessions?

     Each early childhood practitioner will introduce the natural learning opportunities approach with another family and make an audiotape to present to the others for reflection and feedback.

   - How will we communicate in between sessions?

     E-mail and interaction at the early intervention program office

   - Do we have a plan for the next session?

     Yes, see above.

2. If goals have been reached (resolution):

   - Is the learner committed to and capable of self-assessment, self-correction, and self-generation?

   - Has a plan for reinstituting coaching been discussed?

Coaching Worksheet: Jason's Play Time

Learner: _Joanie_   Coach: _Phyllis_   Date: _October 15_

INITIATION

Coaching opportunities observed or presented

Phyllis prompted Joanie's reflection about Jason's progress during a staff review conference; several more spontaneous discussions encouraged Joanie to ask Phyllis for planned peer coaching sessions.

The purpose of the coaching relationship is

To guide Joanie to support Alma in using natural learning opportunities with Jason in their home

Intended learner outcomes resulting from the coaching relationship

Joanie will assist Jason's family and others to identify their interests and potential or current activity settings so that they can use natural learning opportunities to prompt Jason's participation in specific settings.

Jason will have more opportunities to play with his brother and neighborhood children.

Barriers to the coaching process	Strategies to address barriers
Scheduling time for reflection immediately after observation is limited.	When Joanie and Phyllis have scheduling conflicts that prevent them from reflecting together right after an observation, they will talk over lunch within 2 days of the observation.

Ground rules

Joanie and Phyllis agree to meet twice per month for 3 months and then evaluate Joanie's satisfaction with her progress in reaching her outcomes.

OBSERVATION

	What/where	When
Coach observes learner's actions and interactions		
Learner observes coach model actions	Joanie accompanies Phyllis on a home visit with another family to observe Phyllis coach a mother.	October 20
	Joanie reviews videotape of early childhood practitioners modeling strategies for family members.	October 25
Learner observes self		
Coach/learner observe environment		

ACTION	What/where	When
Coach models for learner (coach present)	Phyllis models how she begins and ends a coaching session, prompts a mother, and follows the mother's lead.	October 20
Learner practices an action (coach present/absent)		
Learner describes experience (coach absent)		
Coach/learner observe environment	Joanie raises her concern about how to talk with a family about changing her approach with them.	October 20

REFLECTION	Description		
Learner reflects on action or observation	Joanie realized importance of guiding a mother to expand successful actions and make decisions about who should try out strategies with a child during a coaching session. She also identified an activity setting for Jason (playing with brother and neighborhood "big" kids in the backyard) that she could talk with Alma about.		
Coach gives feedback about observation or action following reflection	Phyllis shared how she prompts a parent to build on successes and individualize a coaching session; she and Joanie role-played an anticipated conversation with Alma about changing an approach.		
Learner uses resources (e.g., print, video, peer)	Joanie discussed with Phyllis her observations from the videotape she reviewed.		
Coach confirms learner's understanding and summarizes	Phyllis asked Joanie for her observations first, then reinforced her points and added information as appropriate.		
Coach/learner plan next steps	Who	What	When
Observations	Joanie scheduled two more observations of Phyllis coaching a parent and one time for Phyllis to accompany her on her bi-monthly visit with Jason and Alma.		
Practice	Joanie will follow up with Alma to address her concern about including Jason in play with his brother and other neighborhood children.		
Resources			

EVALUATION

Coach Self-Reflection

1. Is the learner accomplishing his or her goals?

   Joanie asks great questions about using natural learning opportunities as the basis for her visits with Alma and Jason; her observations of my coaching facilitate a good discussion of the benefits of this approach.

2. What changes, if any, do I need to make in the coaching process?

   We should talk about how Joanie can use this approach with other families that she visits.

3. Should I continue as this learner's coach? (If not, who would be more effective?)

   Yes, we still have a lot of ground to cover.

Coach Asks Learner

1. Shall we continue coaching or have your goals been accomplished (continuation)?

   Yes, continue coaching

   If continuing coaching:

   - What changes need to be made in the coaching plan?

     Joanie agrees that she would like to start thinking about using natural learning opportunities with other families.

   - What observations and/or actions should take place between coaching sessions?

     Joanie will introduce this approach with two other families and then talk about it at our next reflection session.

   - How will we communicate in between sessions?

     Our desks are next to one another in the main office, so we can leave notes easily.

   - Do we have a plan for the next session?

     Yes, see above.

2. If goals have been reached (resolution):

   - Is the learner committed to and capable of self-assessment, self-correction, and self-generation?

   - Has a plan for reinstituting coaching been discussed?

Coaching Worksheet: Kim's Professional Development

Learner: _Kim_   Coach: _Bijul_   Date: _April 17_

INITIATION

Coaching opportunities observed or presented
Evaluation for a child's eligibility to an early intervention program

The purpose of the coaching relationship is

To refine Kim's professional skills by engaging in planned peer coaching with a colleague who has expertise in evaluating infants and toddlers

Intended learner outcomes resulting from the coaching relationship

Kim will understand the requirements for eliciting evaluations for Part C services under IDEA and will learn how to use a specific evaluation tool.

Kim will participate on the early intervention program's evaluation team in the future, as appropriate colleagues and families will benefit from Kim's expertise in observation.

Barriers to the coaching process	**Strategies to address barriers**
Arranging schedules for Bijul to observe Kim and reflect with her afterward; also, for Kim to observe Bijul and review her practice videos with her	Requesting permission from the program administrator for Bijul to use professional development release time for coaching

Ground rules

Coaching sessions will take place over a 2-month period; observations will take place during regularly scheduled evaluations. Reflection sessions will be scheduled for the end of the work day.

Note: The following notations illustrate how Bijul and Kim's coaching sessions were implemented after their initiation discussion presented in Chapter 7.

OBSERVATION

	What/where	When
Coach observes learner's actions and interactions	Bijul watches Kim's practice videos with her.	May 15
Learner observes coach model actions	Bijul observes Kim during a team evaluation.	April 20
	Kim observes another occupational therapist doing an evaluation for eligibility.	May 6
Learner observes self	Kim reviews practice videos of herself using the evaluation tool with children in her neighborhood.	May 8
Coach/learner observe environment		

ACTION	What/where	When
Coach models for learner (coach present)	*Bijul demonstrates what she does and looks for during a child's eligibility evaluation.*	*April 26*
Learner practices an action (coach present/absent)	*Kim practices using an evaluation tool with children in her neighborhood (and makes a video to review with Bijul).*	*April 29*
Learner describes experience (coach absent)		
Coach/learner observe environment		

REFLECTION	Description		
Learner reflects on action or observation	*Kim talks with Bijul about her observations of Bijul doing an eligibility evaluation.* *Kim talks with Bijul about what she learned during her practice sessions with children in her neighborhood and observing another occupational therapist.*		
Coach gives feedback about observation or action following reflection			
Learner uses resources (e.g., print, video, peer)	*Kim summarizes the key administration points in the test manual with Bijul in preparation for Kim's practice sessions.*		
Coach confirms learner's understanding and summarizes			
Coach/learner plan next steps	Who	What	When
Observations	*Bijul will observe Kim during a team evaluation May 21.*		
Practice	*Until May 21, Kim will continue to practice using the specific evaluation tool with children of different ages than she practiced with previously.*		
Resources			

EVALUATION

Coach Self-Reflection

1. Is the learner accomplishing his or her goals?

   Kim has identified a comprehensive plan for refining her evaluation skills so that she can take part in her program's multidisciplinary evaluation.

2. What changes, if any, do I need to make in the coaching process?

   None, so far. Bijul and Kim will consider this again as they begin coaching sessions.

3. Should I continue as this learner's coach? (If not, who would be more effective?)

   Bijul understands what Kim wants to learn and is confident that she has the expertise to guide her in reaching her goals. Bijul will also benefit from talking with Kim about her observations when Kim watches Bijul doing an evaluation because Kim is such a skilled observer.

Coach Asks Learner

1. Shall we continue coaching or have your goals been accomplished (continuation)?
   Yes, continue coaching

   If continuing coaching:

   - What changes need to be made in the coaching plan?
     None at this point.

   - What observations and/or actions should take place between coaching sessions?
     Plans are in place to practice using the evaluation tool and to observe Kim and another colleague.

   - How will we communicate in between sessions?
     Kim and Bijul see one another at least twice per week, when their schedules overlap, and they are both in the program office. Otherwise, they both use email.

   - Do we have a plan for the next session?
     Yes, see above.

2. If goals have been reached (resolution):

   - Is the learner committed to and capable of self-assessment, self-correction, and self-generation?

   - Has a plan for reinstituting coaching been discussed?

INDEX

Page numbers followed by *f* indicate figures; numbers followed by *t* indicate tables.